IF YOU LIKE
THE
RAMONES...

IF YOU LIKE

THE RAMONES...

HERE ARE **OVER 200** BANDS, CDS, FILMS, AND OTHER ODDITIES THAT YOU WILL LOVE

PETER AARON

Backbeat
Books

AN IMPRINT OF HAL LEONARD CORPORATION

Published in 2013 by Backbeat Books
An Imprint of Hal Leonard Corporation
7777 West Bluemound Road
Milwaukee, WI 53213

Trade Book Division Editorial Offices
33 Plymouth St., Montclair, NJ 07042

Book design by Michael Kellner

Printed in the United States of America

Library of Congress Cataloging-in-Publication Data
is available upon request.

ISBN 978-1-61713-457-9

www.backbeatbooks.com

For Dad, who always knew I could do this

CONTENTS

IF YOU LIKE
THE RAMONES...

The Ramones, circa 1978 (left to right): Johnny, Marky, Joey, and Dee Dee. (Photofest)

Introduction

2A has long been one of the most popular watering holes on the Lower East Side. But when I lived in New York during the 1990s, on most early Tuesday evenings, say about seven or eight o'clock, it was pretty slow. That's when I most liked to go. And it seemed to be the same for Joey Ramone, as the occasional Tuesday night was usually when I saw the Ramones front man there. The Dictators' Handsome Dick Manitoba, always good for conversation, would be holding court from behind the bar, and would bring in mixtapes—as in actual *cassette* tapes—he'd play on the bar stereo.

Anyway, on one of those nights I was sitting at the bar, about two or three empty stools down from Joey. Manitoba was spinning a great compilation of British Invasion stuff, classics by the Beatles, the Zombies, the Hollies, the Yardbirds. Just one gem after another. Other than the music, not much was happening. Once in a while Manitoba or I would make some little observation about one of the tunes, but that was all. Joey was just sitting there in silence, lost in thought with his drink in front of him and that famous avalanche of black hair hiding his face. He was stock still. I wondered if he'd fallen asleep on his stool. But, then, after a few more of the nuggets on Manitoba's tape had gone by, something wonderful happened.

The Who's "The Kids Are Alright" came on: a ringing D chord by Pete Townshend, then his voice in harmony with Roger Daltrey's—*I don't mi-i-i-ind*—before Keith Moon's drums bring in the next lyric—*Other guys dancing with my gir-r-r-l-l*. After those first six seconds, the whole band comes in and the song explodes. And when it did on this particular night, Joey's head shot up as if he'd been shaken from a daze, jolted with electricity. He looked around the near-empty room. "All riiiight…" he purred, barely audible, as his eyes met mine from across the rims of his trademark granny shades. He smiled for a second, slowly nodded. And that was all. He put his head back down and returned to nursing his booze, staying silent for the duration of the night.

It was a fleeting glimpse. But it was a perfect snapshot. It summed up what Joey and his bandmates—cofounders guitarist Johnny, bassist Dee Dee, and drummer/producer Tommy Ramone, and later drummers Marky and Richie and bassist C. J. Ramone—were all about: an undying love of and unshakable belief in rock 'n' roll and all of its transformative promise. A love of great songs that make you feel good from the first moment you hear them and never fail to do the trick after that. I mean, how many times must Joey have heard "The Kids Are Alright"? The Who was his favorite band. He saw the group on its first U.S. tour in 1967, opening for Herman's Hermits, a pivotal experience, he said many a time afterward. He probably bought the single of "The Kids Are Alright" when it came out, and wore out that and all the other tracks on the *Meaty Beaty Big and Bouncy* anthology. I even saw him sing the song once, complete with lasso-swinging, Daltrey-esque microphone action and the Dictators backing him up, at his 1998 birthday gig at the now-gone Coney Island High on St. Mark's Place (in an example of cosmic symmetry, Joey and Pete Townshend even have the same birthday: May 19). Yet hearing that song for the umpteenth time that night at 2A *still* clearly and greatly thrilled the vocalist. It got him tapping his hi-topped foot. Maybe made the back of his neck a little warm and tingly, gave him a few goose bumps here and there. It put that little grin on his face and got him to forget about whatever was bugging him for two minutes and forty-five seconds. Even made his night. I've treasured the moment ever since.

And therein, music lovers, seems to lie the essence of the Ramones: the desire to create great, liberating rock 'n' roll in the spirit and tradition of the same artists who inspired *them*. To celebrate the medium by being aggressive, melodic, dead simple, impossibly catchy, and really, really funny (in a darkly twisted way, of course), quite often all within the space of the same song. Yet when they stepped on stage for the first time—March 30, 1974, at Manhattan's Performance Studio, where they rehearsed—the foursome not only put forth the nuts-and-bolts *musical* concepts so many players who followed them would embrace. They also boldly demonstrated that "Hey, anyone can do this." This was key. It was a philosophical Big Bang that inspired legions of artists, in all kinds of media, to believe in themselves and their own ideas, whatever they might be, and *go for it*. And this may be the Ramones' biggest contribution, really. Something that transcends even the timeless greatness of their songs and performances. Which is saying a lot.

Today, nearly forty years after that first show, the sound, style, and spirit of "da brudders" is everywhere. Generations of artists have aped the chainsaw guitars, bubblegum-snapping melodies, cartoonish humor, and unyieldingly pounding four-four rhythms of the Ramones. The quartet's ripped jeans and black leather jackets are beyond clichéd, something septuagenarians buy off the rack at the mall and wear on whatever weekends they opt *not* to play golf. Their lowbrow, kitsch, B-movie, and trash-TV inspirations have become the stuff of scholarly dissertations and museum exhibits. And filling our eyes and ears are commercials hawking everything under the sun soundtracked by a driving, crunching pop attack ripped straight from the template laid down by those four hoppin' cretins from Forest Hills so long ago.

The Ramones made some of the most infectiously fun music that will ever be. Music that appeals to pretty much anyone with a beating heart, be they middle aged or diaper aged. It lets you get your dark aggressions out, as all human beings must, and at the same time gets you feeling happy and lost in its unstoppably propulsive forward motion. Of course you already know that, it's what led you here. But, as unique as they are, the Ramones didn't evolve in a vacuum. They had their antecedents, the key musical acts that influenced them, like Joey's faves, the Who. They had their fellow travelers, contemporary comrades in arms during the early waves of punk rock. There were the movies, TV shows, and other dubiously tasteful scraps of pop culture that informed the Ramones' aesthetic and provided subject matter for so many of their songs. And of course there were and are those who came after, acts inspired by the Ramones who've kept the band's vision alive via their own mutations of the quartet's rapid-fire ramalama. But it's a big, crazy world, this rock 'n' roll high school chaperoned by our four leather-jacketed heroes. Where do you start once you're in?

Welcome to *If You Like the Ramones*. The aim of this book is to use your, shall we say, brudderly love as the pogoing-off point for a whole universe of Ramones-related stuff. Stuff you're sure to love. So what are you waiting for? Put your faith in the backbeat, and dig in. "Hey Ho Let's Go!"

Freight-train sound: Bo Diddley's rhythmic, hard-driving guitar style presaged
Johnny Ramone's. (Photofest)

1

DO YOU REMEMBER ROCK 'N' ROLL RADIO?: THE ROOTS OF THE RAMONES

Because of all it inspired—everything from punk emulators to hyper-speed hardcore, thrash metal, sing-along teen pop, and TV commercial backing tracks—it may be tough to grasp just how revolutionary the Ramones' self-titled debut was when it hit the racks in 1976. Believe it or not, many naysayers wrote the band's music off as being simply too fast even to be *considered* rock 'n' roll. By the mid-1970s, though, what was passing for rock 'n' roll to the ears and wallets of the masses was questionable. There were a few bright spots here and there, which we'll get to later in this book, but rock, overall, had lost the plot and moved far away from the adventure and liberating fun of the 1950s and sixties. It had become a morass of precious soft rock, mewling singer-songwriters, and arena acts featuring pompous snobs with classical pretensions. Slow-moving sham music that wannabe grownups bought by the boatload, and fooled themselves into liking in order to appear sophisticated to their equally lost peers. The seventies airwaves were dominated by the likes of Styx, James Taylor, America, the Eagles, and (gag) Chicago—stuff that, to anyone who stuck a fork in its puffy marshmallow marrow, was revealed as being utterly disconnected from *real* rock 'n' roll. This prevailing brown-suede order rejected and mocked the Ramones for their extreme musical simplicity and straightforwardness, took their sick humor at face value and branded them as genuinely sick.

Yet the band and their underdog champions defiantly insisted— rightly, as time has revealed—that the music of the Ramones was rock 'n' roll at its purest. Rock stripped straight to the bone, rock that peeled away years of needlessly arpeggiated layers to free the beating rebel heart inside. Raised during the golden age of rock 'n' roll radio, the members saw themselves as continuing and contributing to that tradition, and proudly wore the concept on their black leather sleeves via hot-wired versions of forgotten, "naïve" oldies like Chris Montez's "Let's Dance," Freddy Cannon's "Palisades Park," and Bobby Freeman's "Do You Wanna Dance." The music of their antecedents, their inspiration, was now near death and desperately needed resuscitation.

EARLY ROCK 'N' ROLL

Rock 'n' roll, a synthesis of blues, rhythm and blues (R&B), and country, emerged in the mid-1950s, not long after the four original Ramones themselves emerged: Johnny was born John Cummings in 1948; Joey and Dee Dee as, respectively, Jeffry Hyman and Douglas Colvin in 1951; the surviving Tommy as Thomas Erdelyi in 1952. The members of the Ramones were first drawn to music by the major rock 'n' roll pioneers, but while their music certainly retains the wild spirit of the founding forefathers, the actual physical *sound* of those greats isn't directly evident in that of the Queens quartet. According to band members, much of this is down to technical ability; far from mastering the blues progressions and syncopated rhythms inherent to fifties-style rock 'n' roll, the Ramones were figuring out how to play their instruments when the band began. The guys' lack of chops notwithstanding, their not sonically referencing the trailblazing, blues-based rockers was also by design. Early on, they made the conscious decision to set themselves apart from the prevailing trend of the day, which saw most hard rock bands chasing the virtuosic, guitar-and-drum-solo-filled approach of bluesy late-sixties acts like Cream, Led Zeppelin, and Jimi Hendrix. Eschewing such pursuits, they reduced the music's structure until it was even *more* basic than that of its first-flush fifties form. (Johnny said repeatedly that part of the group's M.O. was to have no standard "blues" elements whatsoever.) Still, knowledge of certain bedrock artists is basic to appreciating the breadth of the music and the Ramones' psyches, so if you aren't already familiar with rock's beginnings, get your learner's permit with these quick-qualifying compilations: Elvis Presley, *The Sun Sessions* and *Top Ten Hits*; Chuck Berry, *The Great Twenty-Eight*; Bill Haley, *The Best of Bill Haley and His Comets: Millennium Collection*; Fats Domino, *Greatest Hits: Walking to New Orleans*; Jerry Lee Lewis, *18 Original Sun Greatest Hits*; Little Richard, *The Very Best of Little Richard*; the Everly Brothers, *Cadence Classics: Their 20 Greatest Hits*; Gene Vincent, *The Screaming End: The Best of Gene Vincent*; Ritchie Valens, *Ritchie Valens* and *Ritchie* (his "La Bamba" was a childhood favorite of Joey's); and Carl Perkins, *The Essential Sun Collection*. There are, however, several instances in which the sounds of select vanguard rockers *are* fairly detectable in the Ramones' music.

Bo Diddley

The case of Bo Diddley might not, at first, seem to be one of them. After all, even the primitive, shuffling "shave-and-a-haircut" beat so famously developed by the Mississippi-born singer, guitarist, and gunslinger (he made that last one up) is still more intricate than the Ramones' heads-down, four-on-the-floor power-drive. With his longtime accompanist, maracas man Jerome Green, Diddley (real name: Ellas Otha Bates, 1928–2008) worked up the rhythm he called his "freight-train sound"—the singular, irresistibly bouncy "Bo Diddley beat" that set hits like "Bo Diddley," "Pretty Thing," "Diddy Wah Diddy," "Who Do You Love?," "Mona," "Road Runner," and "You Can't Judge a Book by Its Cover" far apart from those of other R&B and rock 'n' roll trailblazers. While you won't hear that beat in the Ramones' music, the relentless drive of Diddley's trademark square and rocket-shaped guitars are a sonic granddaddy of Johnny Ramone's attack. All distorted, barely shifting barre chords and with a minimum of lead playing, Diddley's guitar locks in with the drums, rather than the bass, to ram the songs along much as Johnny's does in your average Ramones tune (an unusual approach in rock 'n' roll, when you think about it). Diddley's 1950s Chess singles are boilerplate rock 'n' roll, and can be heard on *His Best: The Chess 50th Anniversary Collection*, which cherry-picks from his early albums.

Buddy Holly

Buddy Holly boldly borrowed Bo's beat for his immortal "Not Fade Away." Though he sadly didn't live to see the decade's end—the singer/guitarist perished in the same 1959 plane crash that killed rockers Ritchie Valens and J. P. "The Big Bopper" Richardson—the Texan remains one of the greatest 1950s rock 'n' roll legends. Holly's music is linked to the Ramones' by the way it casts singsongy vocal melodies above insistent, major-chord rhythms. According to a 1982 interview with Johnny, early on the Ramones rehearsed Holly's "I'm Gonna Love You Too." Released before Holly's name was out front, 1957's *The "Chirping" Crickets* is repeatedly cited as one of the most influential debuts in all of rock 'n' roll. The disc is home to hits like "Oh Boy!," "That'll Be the Day," and "Maybe Baby." *Buddy Holly* (1958) includes the classics "Peggy Sue," "Rave On!," and the lovely "Everyday." *The Definitive Buddy Holly* or *Buddy Holly Gold* makes a great place to start.

Eddie Cochran

Another short-lived great was rockabilly king Eddie Cochran. A god to the Beatles, the Who, and legions of other sixties U.K. bands, Cochran, who was killed in a 1960 car crash, was an excellent singer and songwriter. He was also a fine guitarist whose two-note hammer-on riffs are audible in those of Johnny Ramone and other punk rock six-stringers. Cochran was only twenty-one when he died; thus his powerful discography is frustratingly slim. Occasionally producers pushed him into cutting lame ballads. There are several best-ofs that round up top rockers like "Twenty Flight Rock," "Cut Across Shorty," "Weekend," "Nervous Breakdown," and his biggest U.S. single, 1958's "Summertime Blues," songs whose themes of teenage frustration and release foreshadow those of the Ramones. *Somethin' Else: The Fine-Lookin' Hits of Eddie Cochran* is a concise tutorial.

Roy Orbison

What ties this genius to the Ramones is the two acts' shared flair for torchy, melodramatic ballads. Although in his pre-shades,

1950s days the Texas-born Roy Orbison made great rockabilly sides for Sun Records ("Ooby Dooby"), it's his early-sixties hits for the Monument label that made him a legend. Orbison's wounded tear-jerkers like "Crying," "Only the Lonely," "In Dreams," and "Running Scared" point the way to heart-baring Ramones ballads like "I Remember You," "I Want You Around," and "She Belongs to Me." And even during his peak years of pop mini-dramas, Orbison could still rock: see "Candy Man," "Pretty Woman," and "Mean Woman Blues." *16 Biggest Hits* is a fast pass to the art of this American genius.

Link Wray

Link Wray's bank account never equaled Eric Clapton's, but as far as rock guitarists go he's at least as influential. Clapton himself is an admitted fan, and Pete Townshend has said that were it not for Wray's menacing 1958 instrumental "Rumble" he'd never have picked up an electric guitar in the first place. Credited with being the inventor of the power chord, Wray kicked out an über-raw, ultra-distorted style of caveman guitar that blazed the trail for pretty much every hard-edged rock genre that came next.

Frederick Lincoln Wray began his career in his native North Carolina, playing country. With Link Wray and the Ray Men he switched to rock 'n' roll and rockabilly, concentrating on instrumentals highlighting his guitar after he'd lost a lung to tuberculosis. The overdriven, feedback-drenched "Rumble," named for its street-gang feel, became a big hit, despite—or maybe because of—its being banned by several U.S. radio stations for "inciting juvenile delinquency." In the seventies, Wray capitalized on his reputation as a punk godfather with shows at New York club Max's Kansas City and albums with singer Robert Gordon. The 1960 debut, *Link Wray and the Ray Men*, boasts the aptly named "Raw-Hide" and the chugging "Comanche." The same year's *Jack the Ripper* is a stone classic, featuring "Rumble" and the sadistic title cut. *Rumble! The Best of Link Wray* is a fine introduction.

Joey Dee and the Starliters

Joey Dee and the Starliters kicked the twist dance craze into overdrive with "The Peppermint Twist (Part 1)"—named for their residency at New York's Peppermint Lounge—a monster number one in 1962. Due to their faddish associations time has unfairly branded Dee (born Joseph DiNicola) and the Starliters as a novelty act, but they were an A-1 rock 'n' roll band capable of holding their own against most others of the day. Formed in New Jersey in the mid-1950s, the multiracial outfit at various times included a young Jimi Hendrix, future actor Joe Pesci on guitar, members of the Young Rascals, and others. Brimming with Italian-American élan, Dee and the Starliters delivered stacks of lively singles that pop like pistons and draw a line straight to the sound of a certain Forest Hills foursome: "Dance, Dance, Dance," "Hot Pastrami with Mashed Potatoes," "Hey Let's Twist," and many credible R&B covers. *Doin' the Twist at the Peppermint Lounge* or *Hey Let's Twist!: The Best of Joey Dee and the Starliters* covers the bases.

Del Shannon

Del Shannon made his mark with brooding, minor-key mini-dramas exemplified by "Runaway," his outer-space-organ-imbued 1961 number one single. Born Charles Westover in Grand Rapids, Michigan, Shannon also wrote the hits "Hats Off to Larry," "Little Town Flirt," "Keep Searchin' (We'll Follow the Sun)," and "Stranger in Town," which, like "Runaway," pair tortured lyrical content with hummable melodies. *Greatest Hits* (twenty songs) should be your first stop, although 1965's *One Thousand Six-Hundred Sixty-One Seconds of Del Shannon* echoes the Ramones' good taste in covers with its versions of Bobby Freeman's "Do You Wanna Dance" and the Searchers' "Needles and Pins."

THE BRILL BUILDING SOUND

As tough as the Ramones' music is, it's decidedly and unabashedly pop music at the same time. In their own way, chestnuts like "Blitzkrieg Bop," "I Remember You," and "Rockaway Beach" are as evocative and as flawlessly constructed as "Stardust," "Singin' in the Rain," or any other classic of the Great American Songbook, and thus deserve their place alongside such evergreens. (One could say "Now I Wanna Sniff Some Glue" even has its drug-referencing precedent from this period; see the original lyrics of Cole Porter's 1934 "I Get a Kick Out of You," which blithely mention cocaine sniffing.) Like those standards, the Ramones' songs are an indelible part of the New York–centered lineage of pop songcraft that stretches from the early twentieth-century Tin Pan Alley tunesmiths through the Broadway composers of the 1920s, thirties, and forties (Porter, Irving Berlin, George and Ira Gershwin, Harold Arlen, among other greats) to the Brill Building sound, a songwriting school that flowered from the late 1950s to the mid-1960s.

Joey Ramone seemed at least casually conscious of his band's connection to the Brill Building era, which produced a huge swath of the most timelessly popular Western music of the post–World War II period, much of it fomented by the early-sixties girl groups so beloved of the band. Not necessarily confined to the eleven-story, 175,000-square-foot songwriting office and studio facility at 1619 Broadway for which it's named—activity also took place a block up at 1650 Broadway's Aldon Music publishers—the Brill Building scene was the domain of dozens of composers whose work became, through the mouths of others, hallmark hits of the burgeoning rock 'n' roll age: "Twist and Shout," "Hang On Sloopy," "Hound Dog," "Stand by Me," "A Teenager in Love," "Save the Last Dance for Me," "This Magic Moment," and "Will You Love Me Tomorrow," to name a few. The Brill Building repertoire can be readily explored through the anthologies that cover the individual artists who recorded it and the labels that released the songs, and there are some fine overviews of the songwriters themselves to check out. The four-CD box *The Brill Building Sound* is exhaustive, while *The Songmaker's Collection: Music from the Brill Building* makes a good casual introduction.

GIRL GROUPS

Concurrent with the Brill Building days was the early-sixties rise of the girl groups, a vocal ensemble–dominated phenomenon that evolved out of the preceding, predominantly male doo-wop period. Girl groups were in effect the vessels of the songwriter-and-producer auteurs who guided the trend, and while rooted in earlier rock 'n' roll and R&B were generally more epic and polished than either; Phil Spector described his Wagnerian "Wall of Sound" production style as "little symphonies for the kids." The super-catchy songs often have driving backbeats, their themes of teenage crushes and heartbreak yearningly innocent and sweet, even melodramatic (but what seems quaint today sure worked well in the charts at the time). Girl groups had a profound influence on the pop and rock acts that followed, such as the Beatles and the Hollies, and subsequently the Ramones and many of their CBGB compatriots, especially Blondie and the Dictators. You can hear the melodies and themes of the girl group tunes they'd absorbed even in some of the hardest, punkest Ramones recordings—in a much more electrified form, of course.

Spin the foursome's "Oh, Oh, I Love Her So," from *Leave Home*, their sophomore LP, back to back with, say, the Crystals' galloping 1963 hit "Da Doo Ron Ron." In both songs, tales of giddy young love are set to loud, joyously clattering, hook-heavy backdrops. The lineage is, shall we say, crystal clear. Although it swaps grinding guitars for the Crystals' churning piano and massed brass, the Ramones' "Oh, Oh, I Love Her So" is an obvious girl group and Brill Building–to-Bowery update, with its lines about "[falling] in love by the soda machine."

Because the girl group scene was mainly about singles, the few albums by these acts tend to be comprised of those tracks surrounded by filler material; thus, the one-artist anthologies and multi-act compilations are the preferred way to explore this estrogen-spiked field. *Girls! Girls! Girls!: 25 All-Time Classics of the Girl Group Sound* features hits by the Angels ("My Boyfriend's Back"), the Chiffons ("He's So Fine," "Sweet Talkin' Guy"), the Dixie Cups ("Chapel of Love"), the Essex ("Easier Said Than Done"), and the Murmaids ("Popsicles and Icicles"), as well as the bigger names we'll examine below. The mother lode is the four-disc *One Kiss Can Lead to Another: Girl Group Sounds, Lost and Found*.

The Chantels

Girl groups as such really begin with the Chantels, who came together in 1956 as one of the few all-female doo-wop acts and bridged the space between doo-wop and girl groups proper. These girls were *young* pioneers, too: at the time of their first recordings, the ages of the Bronx fivesome's members, Arlene Smith, Lois Harris, Sonia Goring, Jackie Landry, and Rene Minus, ranged from fourteen to seventeen. Nineteen fifty-eight's pleading ballad "Maybe" was a huge smash, hitting number two on the pop charts and living on today as an archetypal performance of the age. *The Best of the Chantels* has everything you'd want by these trailblazers.

The Shirelles

The first truly major girl group was the Shirelles. Shirley Alston, Doris Coley, Addie "Micki" Harris, and Beverly Lee recorded their charging, infectious original "I Met Him on a Sunday" in Passaic, New Jersey, in 1958, on a label run by a high school friend's mother. The song shot into the Top Fifty a few months after the group was picked up by Decca Records. (The Shirelles later re-recorded the song in a harder version with fuzz guitar mixed in, bringing the sound even closer to the Ramones' hubris.) After some follow-up singles flopped, the outfit signed with Scepter Records, where from 1959 to 1963 the hits were large and many: the sweet "Dedicated to the One I Love" (reprised as a 1967 hit by the Mamas and the Papas); the bouncy "Tonight's the Night"; the majestic number ones "Will You Love Me Tomorrow" and "Soldier Boy"; and two final pop/R&B Top Ten triumphs, "Baby It's You" and the sublime "Foolish Little Girl." *The Best of the Shirelles* lives up to its title, packing all the hits and then some.

The Crystals

Producer Phil Spector discovered the Crystals—lead singer LaLa Brooks, plus Barbara Alston, Dee Dee Kennibrew, Mary Thomas, and Patricia Wright—while working at the Brill Building, where the Brooklyn teenagers were making song-publishing demos for the company Hill and Range. He signed the quintet to his new

Philles Records label, moved Alston into the lead spot, and with the group's early recordings laid the foundation for his legendary Wall of Sound. The original Crystals' early singles "There's No Other Like My Baby," "Oh, Yeah, Maybe, Baby," "Uptown," and the creepily twisted "He Hit Me (It Felt Like a Kiss)," are widescreen pop dramas filled with adolescent angst and epic use of strings, horns, handclaps, and layered percussion. The act's biggest hit, however, the 1962 number one "He's a Rebel," and its follow-up, "He's Sure the Boy I Love," were Crystals records in name only; Spector had taken ownership of the group's moniker and cut the tunes with outside singer Darlene Love. By the following year, though, the real group, with Brooks back out front, had waxed its remaining signature hits, "Then He Kissed Me" and "Da Doo Ron Ron." All of the essentials are rounded up on *Da Doo Ron Ron: The Very Best of the Crystals.*

PHIL SPECTOR

It's safe to say there's no modern record producer more famous—and in some ways more infamous—than Phil Spector. The creator behind the larger-than-life "Wall of Sound" production technique that colored stacks of early 1960s smash records by, primarily, archetypal girl groups like the Ronettes and the Crystals, this troubled auteur was also an accomplished session musician, a visionary label executive, and a brilliant songwriter who penned or co-penned many of the worldwide hits he produced. Over the course of his epic career, he worked with the Beatles for 1970's *Let It Be* and with both John Lennon and George Harrison as solo artists, as well as with Ike and Tina Turner, the Righteous Brothers, and, yes, the Ramones.

"Phil Spector's music was always kinda like early punk rock," says Joey, a Spector devotee since childhood, in the 2005 documentary *End of the Century: The Story of the Ramones.* "[It was] very cutting edge." Indeed, it was. Taking a symphonic approach to what had previously been largely considered disposable children's music, Spector's studio style elevated the sound of pop rock to sweeping new heights. With the cream of the Brill Building writers supplying the tunes and the peerless group of studio musicians known as the Wrecking Crew at the core of the sound, Spector pioneered the use of strings, massed horns, booming and ornamental percussion, unison playing by dozens of instruments, and innovative miking methods in rock 'n' roll. A giant influence on producers like the Beach Boys' Brian Wilson, the Rolling Stones' Andrew Loog Oldham, and legions of others, Spector would ultimately see his talents eclipsed in the public mind by his cruel treatment of his onetime wife, Ronnie Spector of the Ronettes, and his 2009 conviction for the murder of actress Lana Clarkson.

In a move designed to give the Ramones a much-needed breakthrough hit, Spector was paired with the band for 1980's *End of the Century* album. Unfortunately, during the sessions at the producer's legendary Gold Star Studios in Los Angeles, his notoriously erratic behavior, alcoholism, and controlling personality all came to the fore; according to several accounts, he more than once pulled a gun on band members in attempts to get his way. That way may have been difficult for those who were along for the ride during Spector's problem-plagued career, but there's no denying it resulted in some glorious music.

For a sampling of that music, there are several recommended routes. The 1991 four-CD box set *Back to Mono* is the most all-encompassing option, covering Spector's golden period of 1958 to 1969 (Ben E. King's "Spanish Harlem," 1963's *A Christmas Gift to You from Philles Records*). *The Essential Phil Spector* boils things down to two CDs and, true to its title, has the producer's most vital masterpieces. As a bite-sized, single-disc summation of the Spector magic, try either *Wall of Sound: The Very Best of Phil Spector* or *Phil Spector's Wall of Sound Retrospective*.

The Ronettes

Joey was perhaps the Ramones' biggest girl group fan, and the Phil Spector–produced Ronettes topped his list of favorite femme-fronted acts. On the Ramones' ballads especially, it's plain how much Joey's quavering baritone was shaped by Ronettes lead singer Ronnie Spector's. "Here Today, Gone Tomorrow," from 1977's *Rocket to Russia*, and "Bye Bye Baby" from 1987's *Halfway to Sanity*, are just two fine illustrations. The Ronettes—Ronnie (née Veronica Bennett) and her sister Estelle Bennett and cousin Nedra Talley—were formed in New York's Spanish Harlem–Washington Heights area in 1959 and influenced by doo-woppers like Frankie Lymon and the Teenagers and Little Anthony and the Imperials. The three girls worked as stage dancers and backup singers for Joey Dee and the Starliters (see earlier) and other acts before coming to the attention of Phil Spector, who remade the trio's image into that of gum-snapping New York "bad girls," complete with tight skirts, heavy eyeliner, and beehive hairdos. The very first single made with Spector, 1963's "Be My Baby," was a worldwide smash and remains one of the most uplifting and transcendentally perfect pop singles. Other magical hits followed, like "Walking in the Rain," "I Can Hear Music," and "Baby, I Love You," a cover of which would be the lead single from *End of the Century*. *Be My Baby: The Very Best of the Ronettes* is the perfect primer. (No doubt Joey was in high heaven when he later coproduced Ronnie's 1999 *She Talks to Rainbows*.)

The Shangri-Las

There must be some serious attitude juice in the Queens water supply. Because besides our boys, the borough also gave us the Shangri-Las, who, even more than the Ronettes, embody the "tough chick" side of girl-groupdom. Along with the occasional requisite swooning tune about young love, the Shangri-Las sang unusually dark songs about bikers, loves gone bad, and runaway kids, many filled with the emotional spoken passages that made their records feel more like stage dramas than pop singles. Made up of two pairs of teenage sisters, Mary and Betty Weiss and identical twins Marge and Mary Ann Ganser (although the group sometimes appeared in photos and on TV as a trio), the Shangri-Las began in 1963 and were tapped soon after by producer/songwriter George "Shadow" Morton to cut a demo of his newly penned song "Remember (Walking in the Sand)." The epic lament of loneliness—complete with mournful strings, haunting harmonies, and dubbed-in seagull sounds—was one of 1964's biggest hits. The next release, the same year's "Leader of the Pack," was even bigger, a U.S. number one that became the Shangri-Las' signature tune. Replete with revving motorcycles and breaking glass, the mini-saga of a doomed romance with a bad-boy biker is perhaps the ultimate girl group recording, and it certainly fit the girls' boots-and-black-leather image. Other winning tracks followed: the ebullient "Give Him a Great Big Kiss," the murky "Out in the Streets," and the moody "He Cried" and "Dressed in Black." (Ramones heroes the New York Dolls and the solo Johnny Thunders each covered "Give Him a Great Big Kiss." The Dolls even swiped its spoken intro for their own "Looking for a Kiss.") The Shangri-Las split in the late sixties but were welcomed for a 1977 reunion show at CBGB. *Leader of the Pack*, the quartet's 1965 Red Bird debut, is one of the few uniformly superb girl group albums, with jumpin' R&B covers ("Shout," "You Can't Sit Down") amid the trademark orchestrated gloom 'n' doom. The double CD has the complete Red Bird recordings plus curios.

The Marvelettes

Detroit's famed Motown label had its own stable of 1960s girl groups, who were more soul-oriented than their counterparts on other labels. The Marvelettes, who were signed to the subsidiary Tamla Records, lead the charge. First comprised of lead vocalists Gladys Horton and Wanda Young and harmony singers Katherine Anderson, Juanita Cowart, and Georgeanna Tillman, the Marvelettes formed in 1960 as the Casinyets (a self-deprecating play on the phrase "can't sing yet," for their still developing talents). Motown chief Berry Gordy changed their name to the Marvelettes upon their signing in 1961, and a few months later released their first single, the chipper "Please Mr. Postman"—an instant worldwide hit. The smashes continued throughout the decade: "Playboy," "Beechwood 4-5789," and "Don't Mess with Bill," among others. Ironically, the Marvelettes and their Motown and girl group peers helped usher in their own passing by inspiring the British acts who'd soon supplant them (see the Beatles' raw version of "Please Mr. Postman"). Nineteen sixty-one's *Please Mr. Postman* is a fine though somewhat uneven debut, while '67's *The Marvelettes* (a.k.a. *The Pink Album*) is the group's most consistent long-player. *The Ultimate Collection* is the best overview.

Martha and the Vandellas

Martha and the Vandellas (later Martha Reeves and the Vandellas) were the next all-girl hit makers at Motown. The core of the group, which changed much during its lifetime, dates from 1960 and first hit with the ballad "I Guess I'll Have to Let Him Go," which was only intended to be a demo; the label had rechristened the group Martha and the Vandellas and issued the track as a single that reached the Top Forty. Suffering from road fatigue, founding member Gloria Williams left and the act continued as the trio of ex-Motown secretary Reeves, Annette Beard, and Rosalind Ashford, which from 1962 to 1967 had massive hits with "(Love Is Like a) Heat Wave," "Jimmy Mack," "Quicksand," "Nowhere to Run," and "Dancing in the Street." The 1965 LP *Dance Party* is everything its title promises, with the latter two evergreens and the pounding biker ode "Wild One." The double-disc *Gold* has the major hits and overlooked B sides.

The Supremes

The biggest-selling of all the girl groups—in fact, one of the biggest-selling acts of the 1960s—was the Supremes. Formed in 1959 in Detroit's Brewster-Douglass Housing Projects, the original group signed to Motown in 1961 and pared down to the trio of Diana Ross, Florence Ballard, and Mary Wilson. More slick and mannered than many of their female competitors, the Supremes enjoyed colossal crossover popularity that at one point rivaled that of the Beatles. The threesome made some of the most exquisite and enduring pop records of the day, enjoying a 1964–1965 run of five consecutive number one singles, mostly written by in-house team Brian and Eddie Holland and Lamont Dozier: "Where Did Our Love Go?," "Baby Love," "Stop! In the Name of Love," "Come See About Me," and "Back in My Arms Again," all led by Ross's cooing voice. Although the doomed Ballard (she died in poverty in 1976) was replaced by the brilliantly named Cindy Birdsong, for the next few years the hits just kept on coming: "I Hear a Symphony," "My World Is Empty Without You," "Love Is Like an Itching in My Heart," "You Can't Hurry Love," "Someday We'll Be Together," "You Keep Me Hanging On," and the psychedelia-tinged "The Happening," "Reflections," and "Love Child." The act was re-billed as Diana Ross and the Supremes, before Ross left to pursue the solo career that eventually made her a disco queen; in 1970 her place was taken by Jean Terrell, and the outfit continued into the late seventies, never again hitting the highs of its years with Ross. The original Motown albums *Meet the Supremes* (1962), *Where Did Our Love Go?* (1964), and *More Hits by the Supremes* (1965) are all tight girl group fare, but the rocking covers party *The Supremes A' Go-Go* (1966) is the most essential. The two-CD *Gold* has all the hits in their remastered splendor.

SURF

The prevailing story is that, in the years between Elvis Presley's early RCA recordings and the British Invasion, the pop landscape was a musical no-man's-land—a soulless, saccharine hell ruled by teen-idol mannequins like Pat Boone, Fabian, and Frankie Avalon and thus completely devoid of redeeming rock 'n' roll. Not entirely true. Besides the sublime sounds of the girl groups and the Brill Building song-spinners covered above, there was the phenomenon known as surf rock, or, simply, surf. Born on the West Coast, surf was designed to evoke the crashing Pacific Ocean swells and California's perceived breezy, carefree vibe. The music came in two waves: instrumental and vocal. The instrumental variety, which evolved first, is dominated by wordless, guitar-driven singles acts whose twangy, echo-soaked music can be fiery or moody. The surf vocal style uses tightly arranged pop harmonies to transmit lyrics about surfing, girls, beaches, surfing, girls, cars, surfing, girls, bikinis, sun, surfing, girls, waves, and, well, surfing and girls. But, hey, let's not waste any more time: Cowabunga! Surf's up!

Surf Instrumentals

Surf instrumentals sprang from earlier rock 'n' roll instrumentals like the Champs' "Tequila" from 1958, or Johnny and the Hurricanes' 1959 "Red River Rock," records that share surf's reverb-heavy guitars but are more R&B-based and heavier on wailing saxophones and spacey organs. Early sixties instrumental surf acts were the forerunners of the garage bands that came in the wake of the British Invasion just a few years later, when many of these very same groups began emulating their new heroes by adding vocals and growing their hair out (more on that in a bit). But before America's young players fell under the spell of the Beatles, the Stones, et al., many of them got their musical feet wet via the Ventures and Dick Dale, whose records begat countless young groups clad in matching sharkskin suits and picking out echo-laden tunes with surfing-related titles. Most of these acts only released local singles. If they were lucky enough to land a regional hit, they might get scooped up by a major label that re-released the single and perhaps an album; the Surfaris genre-defining "Wipe Out" reached number two in 1963, and the Chantays hit the same year with the spooky standard "Pipeline." It's the minimal, uncluttered sound, gripping melodies (crucial for instrumental pop), and honest, unfussy spirit of this stuff that we later hear in the Ramones' music. As surf gained in popularity it was seized upon by L.A. studio moguls, who, with the aid of crack session musicians, made dozens of excellent genre records under fictitious names. The surf sound, though, wasn't confined to the West Coast. The wave reached as far inland as Colorado, home to the excellent Astronauts ("Baja"), and parts of the Midwest.

The lines are blurred when it comes to instrumental surf's twin, rubber-burning cousin, hot rod music. Hot rod evolved out of surf and the two are largely interchangeable, save for the former's automotive themes and added sounds of squealing tires and revving engines. There are some superb compilations out there, many stretching into multiple volumes. *The Birth of Surf*, in two volumes, has most of the necessaries, while the *Lost Legends of Surf Guitar* and wild *Strummin' Mental* series dive into murkier depths.

Dick Dale

Hailed as the "King of the Surf Guitar," Dick Dale not only
lives up to the title with his incendiary, pick-melting chops, he's
also credited with single-handedly inventing the instrumental surf
genre. (One early fan was Jimi Hendrix, who was as blown away
by Dale's flashy, left-handed showmanship as by his musicianship.)
Dale got hooked on surfing in his twenties after his family had
moved from Boston to Southern California, and began trying to
musically capture the splashy sounds and physical rush he got on his
surfboard. He put together a backing band called the Del-Tones,
which began performing at the Balboa, California, Rendezvous
Ballroom, a former big band venue that is to surf what CBGB is
to punk. Released in 1961, the debut single "Let's Go Trippin'"
is the first surf instrumental record and was a giant regional and
nationally placing hit. Dale's red-hot, single-string staccato-picking
style is worlds away from Johnny Ramone's mighty downstroke,
but the two players are kindred souls thanks to their shared love of
high energy and deafening volume. No wonder Johnny cited Dale
as one of his top ten guitar players. Dale's best-known tune is his
frantic 1962 reworking of the traditional Greek song "Misirlou,"
which in 1994 revived his career (and instrumental surf music as
a genre) when it was featured in the film *Pulp Fiction*. Dale's 1962
debut *Surfer's Choice* is a rock 'n' roll landmark highlighting the
leader's scorching skills and pioneering use of guitar reverb and
other effects via wild workouts like "Surf Beat," "Surfing Drums,"
"Shake and Stomp," and "Peppermint Man." When hot rod music
hit, Dale roared off the line with 1963's *Checkered Flag* and 1964's
high-octane *Mr. Eliminator.* The definitive anthology is *King of the
Surf Guitar: The Best of Dick Dale and His Del-Tones*.

The Ventures

As far as instrumental rock acts go—surf or otherwise—the Ventures are the biggest-selling of all, geniuses of tone and technique
known as "the band that launched a thousand bands." Since the
Tacoma, Washington, quartet's pre-surf 1958 formation as the Im-
pacts, it's released literally hundreds of albums of winningly sparse

music, the records often based around a titular theme. Thanks to a run of *Play Guitar / Electric Bass Along with the Ventures* instructional LPs, over the years the band has motivated legions of young musicians to start out themselves. Johnny Ramone was a longtime fan, choosing his trademark Mosrite guitar because such "good references" as the Ventures played them. (Interestingly, before they were musicians, founding Ventures guitarists Bob Bogle and Don Wilson were construction workers, like Johnny and Dee Dee were when they bought their instruments and decided to start the Ramones.) After debuting with a self-released single, Bogle and Wilson stabilized the lineup with the additions of bassist Nokie Edwards and drummer Skip Moore (Bogle and Edwards swapped instruments around 1962).

Of the boatloads of recordings the Ventures have released over five decades, surprisingly few are dogs. In fact, a good many of the band's Dolton and Liberty label discs are classics worthy of any rock 'n' roll library. These include 1960's *Walk Don't Run*, 1961's *Twist with the Ventures* and *Twist Party 2*, 1962's *Mashed Potatoes and Gravy*, 1963's *Surfing* and *Play Telstar and the Lonely Bull*, 1964's *The Fabulous Ventures* and *The Ventures in Space*, and 1969's smash *Hawaii Five-O*. One could easily go blind flipping through all the Ventures best-ofs clogging the bins. Make it easy on yourself with *Walk Don't Run: The Best of the Ventures*.

International Instrumentalists

Europe, of course, isn't known for its surfing or hot rodding. But while the U.S. was reveling in sounds that celebrated those activities, the U.K. and the continent had a parallel scene of cool instrumental rock 'n' rollers. At the top were England's the Shadows, who first found fame as the backing band for Cliff Richard and were wildly popular in other parts of the world, but never hit in America. Their lead guitarist, Hank Marvin, influenced the Beatles and future guitar heroes like Jeff Beck and Jimmy Page, while their drummer, Tony Meehan, was likewise idolized by aspiring players and their bassist, Jet Harris, popularized the electric bass in British rock. The group ruled the early sixties U.K. airwaves with twangy tunes like "Man of

Mystery," "F.B.I.," "Jet Black," and their biggie, 1960's "Apache." *The Shadows' Greatest Hits* has 'em all in mono and stereo. Also from Britain were the Tornados, who, as the protégés of legendarily innovative and eccentric producer Joe Meek, hit the international stratosphere with 1963's spaced-out, organ-fueled "Telstar." *Ridin' the Wind* has everything the band recorded. The spacesuit-wearing Spotnicks, from Sweden, were one of the mainland's first major rock 'n' roll bands, and are similar in sound to their U.S. and U.K. counterparts. Blast off with the compilation *Spotnicks in the '60s*.

Surf Vocals

Surf began as instrumental music, but it really broke big when it was adapted to a vocal form. The field included a healthy number of one-hitters like Ronny and the Daytonas ("G.T.O."), the Rip Chords ("Hey Little Cobra"), Bruce and Terry ("Summer Means Fun"), the Fantastic Baggys ("Tell 'Em I'm Surfin'"), and the Hondells ("Go Little Honda," "Hot Rod High"). The best-known surf vocal arbiters were those giants of American music, the Beach Boys, who at first played both instrumental and vocal numbers. Their only real competition was Jan and Dean, who evolved slightly before them, influencing their sound and sharing many of the same session players on recording dates.

The Beach Boys

The Beach Boys are the most quintessentially American band of all—seconded by the Ramones, of course—and their importance, both to modern popular music *and* to the Ramones, can't be overstated. The Beach Boys' consummately melodic pop sensibility is a bedrock element of the Ramones' sound, which marries that pop to guitar-driven hard rock. Another Ramones-related aspect of the Beach Boys' early records is their air of innocent, down-to-earth teen fun, an elemental rock 'n' roll quality the Ramones felt had been left for dead by the excesses of the mid-seventies arena acts. Indeed, such Ramones landmarks as "Sheena Is a Punk Rocker" and "Rockaway Beach" are about as glaringly Beach Boys-influenced as you can get.

Initially called the Pendletones, the Hawthorne, California, group—brothers Brian Wilson (vocals, bass, keyboards), Carl Wilson (Chuck Berry–style guitar, vocals), and Dennis Wilson (drums, vocals), plus cousin Mike Love (vocals) and Brian's college chum Al Jardine (guitar)—debuted with the catchy but simple 1961 single "Surfin'" and by the mid-1960s would rival the Beatles for commercial success. Influenced by doo-wop, R&B, and jazz vocal groups like the Four Freshmen, Brian Wilson blossomed to become the man many credit as America's greatest living pop composer.

The Beach Boys' high-water mark is the 1966 masterpiece *Pet Sounds*, which contains the yearning hit "Wouldn't It Be Nice" and redefined pop music with its emotionally complex and sonically rich compositions. But the peppy records leading up to it, those made between 1962 and 1965, impacted our heroes even more. These include *Surfin' Safari*, the band's 1962 debut, with the hit title track plus "Surfin'" and "409"; 1963's *Surfin' USA*, with the sun-and-sand-celebrating title cut and drag-racing smash "Shut Down," and *Surfer Girl*, with the namesake slow-dance favorite, the wistfully magnificent "In My Room," and the rollicking "Catch a Wave" and "Little Deuce Coupe"; 1964's *All Summer Long*, with the freewheeling "I Get Around" and the "Little Honda"; 1965's *Today!*, with its jubilant blast through Bobby Freeman's "Do You Wanna Dance" (perhaps our boys referenced this version for the one on *Ramones*), "Dance, Dance, Dance," and "Help Me Rhonda," and *Summer Days (And Summer Nights!!!)*, which is best known for the feel-good perennial "California Girls" and sees Brian Wilson pay homage to his hero Phil Spector via a cover of the Crystals' "Then He Kissed Me" (as "Then She Kissed Me"); and *Beach Boys' Party!*, a 1965 set of R&B, Beatles, and Bob Dylan (!) covers with a hit remake of the Regents' "Barbara Ann."

From there, it was on to the glorious heights of *Pet Sounds*, the fabled *SMiLE* sessions, *Smiley Smile* (with the 1967 smash "Good Vibrations"), and further brilliance. For greatest hits compendiums, 1974's double album *Endless Summer* retains its perfection.

Jan and Dean

The other titans of surf vocals are Jan and Dean, who across their formidable string of Top Ten chirpy chestnuts embodied the suntanned innocence of the early 1960s. Known to their moms as Jan Berry and Dean Torrence, Jan and Dean got their start in the Barons, a high school doo-wop group that did some recording in Berry's garage with future Beach Boys guitarist Bruce Johnston and drummer Sandy Nelson (the 1959 hit instrumental "Teen Beat"). The two singers befriended the Beach Boys, who began backing them up at gigs, and Berry and Brian Wilson cowrote "Surf City," which became Jan and Dean's first number one (the Ramones did the song on their 1994 covers album, *Acid Eaters*). The pair rode the hit-making wave for three years, until the injuries Berry sustained in a 1966 car crash slowed the momentum; the vocalist was thought to have been killed before he was pulled from the wreck, making the duo's "Dead Man's Curve" eerily prescient.

That song shares top billing with another giant hit on 1964's *Dead Man's Curve / The New Girl in School*, one of the great car-themed albums. *Drag City*, also from 1964, continues the car concept with the engine-roaring title tune and the kooky "Surfin' Hearse." The hit title track of that year's *The Little Old Lady from Pasadena*, about a mysterious, drag-racing granny, is winningly kooky as well (the album also has some fun skateboarding tunes, like the hit "Sidewalk Surfin'"). And for recommended Jan and Dean albums, that's where the sidewalk ends. To get the killer and not the filler, pick up *Surf City: The Best of Jan and Dean*.

The Trashmen

"A-well-a everybody's heard about the bird / Bird, bird, bird, b-bird's the word!"

Lumped in with the surf vocal lot are landlocked junk mavens the Trashmen, whose immortally unhinged 1964 "Surfin' Bird"—a mash-up of West Coast doo-woppers the Rivingtons' "The Bird's the Word" and "Papa Ooh Mow Mow"—probably fits in better with surf's immediately overlapping descendents, frat rock and garage rock. Led by drummer/vocalist Steve Wahrer's demented, stuttering voice, the Minnesota quartet's divinely shambolic mess of a single was a key proto-proto-punk touchstone not only for the Ramones, who recorded it for 1977's *Rocket to Russia*, but for their forbears the Stooges, who cited it as influential, and their peers the Cramps, who made it the epic closer of many a set.

The Trashmen—Wahrer, lead guitarist Tony Andreason, guitarist Dan Winslow, and bassist Bob Reed—got together in 1962, having evolved out of rockabilly combo Jim Thaxter and the Travelers. The single of "Surfin' Bird" reportedly sold thirty thousand copies in its first week of release, and the Trashmen next taped their only official album, 1964's *Surfin' Bird*, which doesn't disappoint. Besides several tumultuous instrumentals, the essential title blaster and its follow-up singles, "Bird Dance Beat" and "Bird Bath," the CD version boasts rocking vocal tunes like "King of the Surf," "Kuk," and "Break-Up." In 2010, a Facebook campaign attempting to get the track to number one in the U.K. was launched. Almost fifty years later, the bird is still the word.

FRAT ROCK

Frat rock constitutes the first thrashings of what would later be termed garage rock or garage punk. Just before the Beatles hit, grassroots American rock was rich with local bands that banged out trashy covers of R&B and early rock 'n' roll hits (the Isley Brothers' "Shout," Ray Charles's "Hit the Road, Jack," etc.) for good-paying, drunken keg parties at college fraternity houses—hence the style's name. Raw, wild, simple, catchy, and crazy-fun, this stuff represents the last gasp of Kennedy-era musical innocence.

The Kingsmen

The kings of frat rock were, well, the Kingsmen, whose royal perch in the rock 'n' roll pantheon stems from one of the most perfectly inept recordings of all time: their 1963 smash version of Richard Berry's "Louie Louie" (which uses, hmm, the same three-chord progression as "Blitzkrieg Bop"). Cut with original singer/guitarist Jack Ely for fifty dollars in the band's hometown of Portland, Oregon, the tune hit regionally before rocketing to number two nationally. A reconfigured lineup with drummer Lynn Easton as lead vocalist (early keyboardist Don Galluci would leave to form Don and the Goodtimes and later produce Ramones idols the Stooges) toured and did TV spots to push the single, whose slurred lyrics were at one point investigated by the FBI for possible subversiveness (your tax dollars at work, folks). The Kingsmen's best albums are 1963's *The Kingsmen in Person Featuring Louie Louie*, 1964's *The Kingsmen, Volume II*, and 1965's *The Kingsmen, Volume 3*, all stuffed with slopped-out renditions of tunes by Barrett Strong, James Brown, and other R&B/soul greats. *Louie Louie: The Best of the Kingsmen* collects the signature hit and similarly boisterous nuggets like "Jolly Green Giant," "Long Green," and "Death of an Angel."

The Rivieras

With its intro of pounding drums and bouncy organ/guitar call-and-response riff, the Rivieras' "California Sun" is summer fun writ large. Named for the desirable early-sixties Buick automobile model, the Rivieras were from South Bend, Indiana, and mere teenagers in 1964 when they had a number five U.S. hit with the song (it had been a prior hit for R&B singer Joe Jones and was written by legendary producer Henry Glover). The Rivieras—who shouldn't be confused with the doo-wop crew of the same name—placed three more singles in 1964's Billboard Hot 100 and released three LPs of mainly R&B and rock 'n' roll covers before imploding in 1966. According to legend, it was the Dictators' cover of "California Sun," on their 1975 debut, *Go Girl Crazy!* (see Chapter Four), that planted the seed for the Ramones' version on 1977's *Leave Home*. *The Best of the Rivieras* has the goods on these hopped-up Hoosiers.

The Swingin' Medallions

Frat rock was all over by 1966. But apparently no one told South Carolina's Swingin' Medallions—or the many record buyers who made their cover of Dick Holler and the Holidays' "Double Shot

(Of My Baby's Love)" a number seventeen hit that year. Starting in the late 1950s, the group made its name on the soul covers–dominated "beach music" circuit of the Carolinas before releasing the drunken, Farfisa-wheezing slur-along "Double Shot" on the local 4 Sale imprint (it was soon picked up by major label Smash Records). "She Drives Me Out of My Mind," "Hey, Hey Baby," and other beer-blasters followed but didn't hit. *Anthology: Double Shot (Of My Baby's Love)* has the high points, as well as (beware) later tracks by dubious editions of the band.

The Wailers

No, not Bob Marley's outfit. Considered by many to be America's very first garage band, the Wailers began in Tacoma, Washington, in 1958, playing sax-driven instrumentals and frat rock. Initially called the Fabulous Wailers, the group was made up of high schoolers Kent Morrill (organ), Mark Marush (saxophone), Mike Burk (drums, later replaced by drummer/singer Ron Gardner), and John Greek and Richard Dangel (guitars). In 1961 the Wailers released the first rock 'n' roll (pre-Kingsmen!) version of "Louie Louie," sung by sometime vocalist "Rockin' Robin" Roberts, and soon became hugely popular in the Pacific Northwest. The hit instrumental "Tall Cool One" leads off their 1959 debut, *The Fabulous Wailers*, which, like 1962's *The Fabulous Wailers at the Castle* and 1964's *The Wailers and Company*, is rousing party rock of the first order. By mid-decade the Wailers had switched personnel and transitioned from frat-bashers into British Invasion-stoked garage rockers. Amid its R&B and contemporary covers, 1966's *Out of Our Tree* includes two savage fuzz-bombers: the title cut and the venomous "Hang Up." That year's *Outburst*, with the fiery "Bad Trip," "Hold," and "You Won't Lead Me On," gives the early Kinks a run for their pound notes. *The Boys from Tacoma: Anthology 1961–1969* encompasses the vanguard years.

Street-fighting men: Without the Rolling Stones, there would be no Ramones and no punk rock. (Photofest)

2

TEENAGE LOBOTOMY: THE RAMONES VS. RAGING HORMONES

The teenage years are when we really start to define ourselves as individuals. Whatever we encounter and absorb then tends to profoundly shape our view of the world around us and how we relate to it. During that phase of our lives, when we find something that clicks as an outlet of expression and helps us better understand ourselves and our peers—be it art, sports, literature, knitting, or, hey, music—it tends to stick with us through the rest of our days. And during the great music renaissance of the 1960s, Joey, Johnny, Dee Dee, Tommy, and Marky were all disenfranchised teens trying to figure out who they were—prime material for soaking up the sweeping new changes in rock 'n' roll that came from across the Atlantic to take hold of and reshape America's—and, thus, the world's—musical landscape. It was during these heady mid-to-late sixties that each of the Ramones connected with music enough to want to play it for themselves (although Joey and Dee Dee wouldn't seriously start until the following decade).

THE BRITISH INVASION

Much like punk when it hit later, in the musically spotty mid-seventies, the British Invasion came ashore at just the right time. Outside of the bright points we covered in Chapter One, much of what was on the radio wasn't so hot. Many of the original rockers had slowed in their careers (Elvis even joined the Army) or gone the supper-club route, and there were way too many easy-listening smoothies, fake folkies, and prefab idols in the charts. Not much to meet the needs of your typical angsty, hormonal teenager. Music needed a big change. So it's easy to see why when the Beatles landed in 1964 there was a furor akin to the Second Coming among U.S. teens. Here were four slightly older, swell-looking, highly intelligent, and entertaining guys who not only had a completely new way of dressing, talking, and wearing their hair, but were songwriting geniuses whose records sounded like little else before. And right behind them, with what seemed like daily regularity from 1964 to early 1967, came one similarly great English act after another.

The British Invasion sound began in the early sixties with Merseybeat. A driving, melodic hybrid of British skiffle and American R&B and rock 'n' roll, Merseybeat was named for Liverpool's Mersey River and was pioneered by the Beatles and unsung trio the Big Three. Next came similar "beat" bands from other parts of the U.K., and a slightly later wave of acts, headed by the Rolling Stones, that were rawer and more strongly blues- and R&B-based. The irony of these acts' success in America is twofold: in their desire to imitate the American blues artists *they* worshipped, they in turn inspired many a teenager over here to pick up an instrument to imitate *them*—and get an education in their own country's marginalized black music in the process. Such teens formed the local U.S. "garage" bands whose music would later be rediscovered by and directly influence the punks of the seventies. But we're getting a bit ahead of ourselves. First, to the landing craft...

The Beatles

Call this writer crazy, but he's guessing that just *maybe* you've heard of these guys. There's certainly enough already on the shelves about this little Liverpudlian quartet, so don't worry; I won't throw yet another Beatles encyclopedia at you. Just the Fab Four facts, and some talk about how the group commonly cited as the biggest-selling and most influential popular music band of all time—guitarists John Lennon and George Harrison, bassist Paul McCartney, and drummer Ringo Starr, all of whom sang and composed—rolled out the pavement for our four Ramones.

The very concept of a self-contained, four-man rock 'n' roll band that generates its own original music can be traced to the Beatles, and, although the idea of band members wearing identical outfits goes back at least to John Philip Sousa's time, with their image the Ramones were plainly playing off the Beatles' early shags-and-matching-duds look and giving it, like the music itself, a street-tough update. And then there's the name. It was Dee Dee who learned that Paul McCartney had used "Paul Ramon" as an alias; after adding an "e" at the end, the former Douglas "Dee Dee" Colvin adopted it as his own surname, inspired the others to do the same, and, as they say, the rest is history. When *Ramones* came out in 1976 it was seen by the band, and by many who appreciated and understood it, as a modern, urban take on the early Beatles records. Despite Johnny's moments of budding contrarianism (he brought a bag of rocks to throw at the Beatles during their 1965 Shea Stadium concert), the Ramones loved and repeatedly cited the Beatles' music as pivotal.

The Beatles formed in Liverpool, England, out of folk-blues skiffle band the Quarrymen, and in 1960 became the Silver Beatles, then simply the Beatles. Lennon, McCartney, Harrison, and drummer Pete Best honed their skills in Hamburg, Germany's notoriously rough red-light district clubs before returning to Liverpool, where they became the popular house band at the Cavern Club. They signed up with manager Brian Epstein, who persuaded them to swap their leather jackets for tailored suits and got them signed to EMI subsidiary Parlophone. Ringo Starr replaced Pete Best in 1962, and the four started making records that changed the world.

Although one gets the sense the Ramones enjoyed much of the Beatles' output, it's the early records, the tight, pre-psychedelic LPs released from 1963 to 1965, that most figure into da bruddas' concept of minimalist rock 'n' roll. But before we get to those there's the archival *1962 Live at the Star Club in Hamburg*, whose sound is sub-sub-lo-fi but dense with the kind of raw, youthful energy heard on bootlegs of early Ramones gigs at CBGB. The Beatles' official debut, 1963's *Please Please Me* (EMI; released in the U.S. as *Introducing... The Beatles*), is one of music's greatest opening statements. The incredible songcraft and amazing harmonies are already in place, and the group's roots in early rock 'n' roll, R&B, girl groups, and Brill Building sounds are clear on exuberant chart-smashers like "I Saw Her Standing There," the title track, and Lennon's raw-throated tour de force on "Twist and Shout." The same year's U.K. follow-up, *With the Beatles*, is perhaps even stronger, with Lennon-McCartney's totally plowing "I Wanna Be Your Man" and rocking R&B covers like the Marvelettes' "Please Mr. Postman" and Barrett Strong's "Money (That's What I Want)." (The set was given a truncated American release as *Meet the Beatles!*) *The Beatles' Second Album*, from 1964, is misleadingly titled; it really should've been called *The Second Beatles Album Released by Capitol in the U.S., Which Is Basically a Hodgepodge of Various Single, EP, and U.K.-Only Tracks*—but that wouldn't have been very shrewd marketing, now, would it? Whatever you want to call it, *The Beatles' Second Album* is one of the band's best flat-out rock 'n' roll albums, with the kicking Chuck Berry and Little Richard covers and Lennon-McCartney greats like "You Can't Do That" and "She Loves You." Next in 1964 came *A Hard Day's Night*. The de facto soundtrack to the film of the same name, it's split between swooning ballads and slamming rockers like the propulsive title song—which the Ramones reportedly attempted in early soundchecks. (Most of *A Hard Day's Night*'s material reappeared, only weeks later, as *Something New*.)

Beatles '65 (a retooled-for-the-U.S. edition of late 1964's British *Beatles for Sale*) includes a deliciously dark trilogy of Lennon-sung gems, "No Reply," "I'm a Loser," and "Baby's in Black," plus the upbeat "She's a Woman" and the feedback-laced "I Feel Fine." *Beatles IV* (1965) pairs a few newer songs with British import LP cuts and stray singles. One of the latter is the stupidly catchy "Eight Days a Week," a giant hit from earlier that year; other highlights include a raucous medley of Wilbert Harrison's "Kansas City" and Little Richard's "Hey-Hey-Hey-Hey!" The storming title theme that opens the soundtrack to 1965's *Help!* is one of the Beatles' crowning accomplishments, an amphetamine-fueled nervous breakdown (and transparent treatise on fame) set to two minutes and eighteen seconds of desperate rocking. Outside of that blaster and the lively "The Night Before," *Help!* is mainly given to the group's more melodic side; songs like "Ticket to Ride" and "You're Going to Lose That Girl" left their marks on sweeter Ramones tunes like "Questioningly." Starting with 1966's *Rubber Soul* the Beatles entered a bold new phase of sonic and compositional experimentation that took them into more cerebral realms—which were indisputably genius, but far afield from the compact style of the Ramones. The classic anthology *1962–1966* (a.k.a. *The Red Album*) is a peerless early overview.

The Dave Clark Five

In the brief window of time before the arrival of the Rolling Stones, it was the Dave Clark Five that most challenged the Beatles for American chart supremacy. Led by thundering drummer Dave Clark and featuring the leather-lunged Mike Smith on lead vocals and keyboards, the outfit racked up nearly twenty U.S. Top Forty hits between 1964 and 1967 and appeared on "The Ed Sullivan Show" more than any other British Invasion group. Although the self-producing quintet was very adept at ballads (1964's "Because"), it's mostly identified with loud stompers like "Bits and Pieces," "Over and Over," and "Glad All Over." And given the group's hard-pounding sound, it's no surprise the Ramones were fans. In fact, a blasting version of the DC5's "Anyway You Want It" was the last song the Ramones ever played together, at their farewell show at the Hollywood Palace on August 6, 1996. Perhaps the band's pre–Swinging London tenure (it began in 1957) brought with it an attachment to old-school-showbiz "Don't fix it if it ain't broke" values, because, even as their peers were experimenting with sounds and songwriting ideas that took rock 'n' roll in new directions, Clark and company stuck to the straight-and-narrow approach that had brought them their initial success. This ended up being to their detriment, as by the late sixties they were largely seen as stiff and stuck in the past. There's certainly something of the later Ramones in this, although as out of date and obstinate as the Ramones may have appeared to their detractors during their artistically lean 1980s and nineties, they were still more consistent songwriters and record-makers than the Dave Clark Five, whose overwhelmingly spotty LPs make them the very definition of a "singles band."

Nevertheless, for three years the Five was on—*really* on— when it came to cutting awesome sixties rock singles. And even though albums were not its forte, the band made a few thoroughly winning long-players for U.S. label Epic Records; 1964's domestic debut *Glad All Over* and *American Tour*, 1965's *Coast to Coast* and film soundtrack *Having a Wild Weekend*, and 1966's *I Like It Like That* are the best. The double set *The History of the Dave Clark Five* has the above-mentioned tunes plus the roaring "Can't You See That She's Mine," "At the Scene," and "All Night Long"; the jubilant youth anthem "Catch Us If You Can"; the sweet "(Everybody Knows) I Still Love You"; and the R&B covers "I Like It Like That" and "You Got What it Takes."

The Rolling Stones

As with the Beatles, it's a good bet you've heard of these guys. The Rolling Stones were founded in London in 1962 by a gang of young blues fanatics: vocalist Mick Jagger, guitarists Keith Richards and Brian Jones, and ancillary pianist Ian Stewart (the unseen "sixth Stone"); drummer Charlie Watts replaced Tony Chapman and bassist Bill Wyman took over for Dick Taylor. The Stones were the sneering, unkempt alternative to the sweeter, snappier-looking Beatles, and are thus in many ways more of an influence on the Ramones' mindset. Make no mistake: without the socially defiant, libidinous sounds and stance of the Rolling Stones, there would be no Ramones and no punk rock. The Stones inspired a whole generation of raw, aggressive U.S. sixties garage bands, along with the edgier Stooges, MC5, and New York Dolls, all of whom were profound influences on the Ramones and their first-wave-punk peers. There's the odd lazy clunker along the way, but, generally speaking, the albums the Rolling Stones made from the mid-sixties through the late seventies are indispensable components of any rock 'n' roll library. Because of their more concise, hard-hitting tracks, it's the group's earliest efforts that will most appeal to Ramones fans.

Their debut, *England's Newest Hitmakers*, was released in May of 1964 and is ground zero for much of the divinely dirty rock 'n' roll that came after. The U.S. version opens with a hit romp through Buddy Holly's "Not Fade Away" and proceeds to hammer away mainly with the tough blues and R&B standards that formed the group's early repertoire (Chuck Berry's "Carol," Muddy Waters's "I Just Want to Make Love to You," Slim Harpo's "I'm a King Bee") but also establishes the songwriting prowess of Jagger and Richards (the single "Tell Me"). *12x5*, which came out in the U.S. six months later, kicks off with "Around and Around," another ace Chuck Berry rocker, and is home to more barnstorming R&B covers like Bobby Womack's "It's All Over Now" and two originals that would become staples for many a garage punk band, "Empty Heart" and "Grown Up Wrong." Nineteen sixty-five brought *The Rolling Stones, Now!*, another slab of rough, reimagined blues/R&B ("Little Red Rooster," "Everybody Needs Somebody to Love," the sex-oozing "Down Home Girl") that's complemented by genius Jagger-Richards compositions like the stomping "Off the Hook" and the forlorn "Heart of Stone."

It was that year's landmark *Out of Our Heads*, however, that saw the Rolling Stones truly come into their own as songwriters. While it does contain a couple of the by-now expected raving R&B chestnuts, for the first time it's the band's *own* works that steal the show: hits like the driving "The Last Time," the haunting "Play with Fire," and the song that made the Stones the superstars they are and crystallized their sound, "(I Can't Get No) Satisfaction." *December's Children (and Everybody's)* was released in, you guessed it, December of 1965, and is the first Stones LP not to be dominated by cover material—although the rowdy live takes of Larry Williams's "She Said Yeah" and Bobby Troup's "Route 66" are definite high points. As far as standout originals go, there's the sublime ballad "As Tears Go By," and the pounding hit single "Get Off of My Cloud" and its stirring B-side, "I'm Free." The group at last delivered its first album comprised entirely of originals with 1966's

Aftermath, which houses the propulsive "Paint It, Black," the moody and vibraphone-laced "Under My Thumb," and the wonderfully nasty "Stupid Girl." Even though it has a pair of hits, the sweet "Ruby Tuesday" and the lusty "Let's Spend the Night Together," 1967's *Between the Buttons* is one of the Stones' more underrated albums from this era and finds them moving farther away from their blues roots and into inventive pop territory. Its quality deep cuts ("All Sold Out," "My Obsession," and "Miss Amanda Jones") rank alongside the best of the band's canon.

When the Beatles threw down the psychedelic gauntlet with *Sgt. Pepper's Lonely Hearts Club Band*, the Stones made their own genre statement with 1967's *Their Satanic Majesty's Request*. Maligned by many followers for its eschewing of the band's blues foundation, the album has since taken on the aura of a classic of the form, thanks to the lilting DayGlo pop of "She's a Rainbow," the darkly swirling "2000 Light Years from Home," and the hard-riffing "Citadel." In 1968 the group made a glorious return to its roots with *Beggars Banquet*. Easily one of the top rock albums of the 1960s (and thereafter), the ten-song set unfolds with the sprawling, epic "Sympathy for the Devil," a conga-driven confessional apparently from Old Scratch himself, and is rounded out by beautifully lonesome country folk ("No Expectations," "Salt of the Earth") and bluesy filth ("Dear Doctor," "Stray Cat Blues"). Ramones fans will recognize the revolution-charged "Street Fighting Man," which the Queens rockers covered to great effect (it appears on 1984's British *Howling at the Moon* EP and expanded reissues of *Too Tough to Die*). *Let It Bleed* (1969) is another back-to-the-blues landmark that stands as one of the Stones' best—despite the fact that they were in the transitional spot of phasing out doomed guitarist Brian Jones (he died just before the album's release) and working in new guy Mick Taylor. Like *Beggars Banquet*, the set opens dramatically, with the mysteriously mounting, apocalyptic "Gimme Shelter"; the program segues into ribald country cuts and touching evergreens like the title track and "You Can't Always Get What You Want." "Live with Me," a charging, four-four ode to decadence, is the pick that most ties into the Ramones' "One-two-three-four!" rumpus.

Get Yer Ya-Ya's Out! (1970) captures the Stones at their best during the *Let It Bleed* tour. The show kicks off with a roaring version of "Jumping Jack Flash" and just keeps on kicking with blistering performances of mainly 1968/1969-era songs. Another Stones cornerstone is 1971's *Sticky Fingers*. Sleeved in a provocative, Andy Warhol-designed LP cover with a fully operational jeans zipper, its harrowing "Sister Morphine," lovely ballads "Wild Horses" and "Moonlight Mile," and rockers "Sway," "Bitch," "Dead Flowers," "Can't You Hear Me Knocking," and "Brown Sugar" show the band's energy fully on tap.

The album that came next, though, is arguably the Rolling Stones' greatest achievement and a towering masterpiece of the rock genre: the 1972 double album *Exile on Main Street*, a sweeping, alchemical assemblage of raw rock 'n' roll. The only thing as extreme as the murky and primitive production on this biblical beast of a record is the towering greatness of the songwriting itself. The bump 'n' grinder "Tumbling Dice" was the set's sole hit single and serves as the teaser for clattering classics like the opener "Rocks Off," "Rip This Joint," "All Down the Line," "Ventilator Blues," and the Keith-sung "Happy," and bleary-eyed weepers like "Sweet Virginia" and "Torn and Frayed." With a pervasively grimy luster, *Exile* is a trip through the full scope of human emotions that reveals new sonic surprises with every spin. In its divinely trashy rock 'n' roll lies the sound of the New York Dolls, who were sauntering just around the corner and about to directly impress Joey, Tommy, Johnny, Dee Dee, and Marky. *Exile on Main Street* is simply an album you must own if you consider yourself a fan of the stuff we call good music.

Nineteen seventy-three's *Goat's Head Soup* and 1974's *It's Only Rock 'n' Roll* have their moments, but the band's next great album is 1978's *Some Girls*. Although best known for the disco smash "Miss You," this return to form shows that the Stones—now with Mick Taylor's replacement, Ron Wood, on guitar—had their ears to the underground, as it boasts some fine punk-payback moves in the form of "Shattered," "Respectable," and "When the Whip Comes Down." Nineteen eighty-one's *Tattoo You*, with the raunchy-riffed

"Start Me Up," the punchy "Neighbors," and Richards's sleazy "Little T and A," is another winner. After that? Most Stones albums have an okay song or two, and but none are essential. For just-the-hits collections, the double albums *Hot Rocks* and *More Hot Rocks (Big Hits and Fazed Cookies)* are unbeatable.

The Who

Joey Ramone must've really loved that T-shirt—the one imprinted with the classic "Maximum R&B" poster for the Who's fabled Tuesday night residency at the Marquee club. After all, he's proudly wearing it in so many offstage photos. Boy, that shirt must've smelled something fierce (okay, we'll assume he had more than one). Seriously, though, it makes perfect sense that Joey and the guys would be fans of the Who: with their thrashed-out chords, rebellious lyrics, and caustic performances, the British's band's initial singles are elemental punk touchstones.

The Who began in the early sixties as the Detours and were briefly known as the High Numbers: guitarist and main songwriter Pete Townshend, vocalist Roger Daltrey, bassist John Entwistle; the monstrous musical gifts of Keith Moon, the group's second drummer, would eventually be eclipsed by his similarly Olympian talent for self-destruction. The group's energized covers of American soul hits, and the frequent spectacle of Townshend and Moon's onstage trashing of their instruments, made the Who a sensation with London's burgeoning mod scene (the defiant mods set themselves apart visually from the mainstream via sharp, Italian-cut suits, and their outsider stance made them clear punk ancestors). With producer Shel Talmy at the helm, the Who was soon in the upper reaches of the U.K. charts with a trifecta of masterfully rambunctious, feedback-ridden youth anthems: "I Can't Explain," "Anyway, Anyhow, Anywhere," and "My Generation."

Released in 1965, *The Who Sings My Generation* is one of the most commanding entrances in rock, a neck-snapping treatise in crashing drums, thundering bass, squalling guitar noise, and flawless pop songwriting that's rich in catchy hooks and melodies.

The declamatory title song is the Who's defining moment. Built around a fast back-and-forth two-chord riff, it plainly foretells the Ramones, although the album's other punky crunchers ("The Kids Are Alright," "Out in the Street," "Much Too Much," "The Good's Gone," "La-La-La Lies") point the same way. *A Quick One (Happy Jack)* (1966) is less consistent overall, but still mighty fine. Townshend's "So Sad About Us," a poignant tale of doomed love backed by his ringing Rickenbacker, charging "Run Run Run," and nine-minute operetta "A Quick One While He's Away" stand out, as does Entwistle's spooky "Boris the Spider." *The Who Sell Out* (1967) finds the band embracing psychedelia, a move that theoretically might put off more grounded Ramones fans. But the powerful, horizon-filling "I Can See for Miles," the group's first and biggest U.S. hit, is far from hippy-dippy fluff, and there's definitely a lot of Joey in sweeter, romantically wounded tunes like "I Can't Reach You" and "Mary Anne with the Shaky Hand" (the latter about masturbation, supposedly). *Magic Bus* (1968) reprises tracks from *A Quick One* and *Sell Out* and various U.K. singles for the U.S. market, including the amphetamined "Call Me Lightening" and "Pictures of Lily," a winningly warped Townshend ditty about the narrator's perverted obsession with a woman in an antique photograph (Pete, seriously—what's up?).

The two-record *Tommy*, from 1969, has been long cited as the first commercially successful rock opera. But to Ramoniacs, we say skip it. Outside of the ghostly "I'm Free" and triumphant "We're Not Gonna Take It," it's a headache-inducing harbinger of the very musical excesses that punk would rail against. (Nineteen seventy-three's conceptual double set *Quadrophenia* is far more focused, has superior songs, and is infinitely more recommended.) Besides, *Tommy*'s music is represented well enough by the "Sparks" / "Amazing Journey" medley on 1970's *Live at Leeds*, which documents the powerhouse band at its bone-crunching heaviest. One of rock's finest live albums, it finds the foursome blowing up Leeds University's concert hall with visceral abandon on extended band faves and destructive versions of Eddie Cochran's "Summertime Blues" and Mose Allison's "Young Man Blues." If you want to know why older fans foam at the mouth when talk turns to seeing the Who back in the day, step right this way.

Next? That'd be 1970's *Who's Next*, which is widely considered to be the group's studio masterpiece. Some listeners may, understandably, prefer the garagey simplicity of *The Who Sings My Generation* to the more emotionally and sonically varied *Who's Next*, which is colored by Townshend's pioneering use of synthesizers. Still, there's no denying the sheer power and life-affirming loudness of this record. They're omnipresent classic rock staples these days, but for a young Ramone in 1971, encountering the massive, mountain-moving heroics of "Baba O'Riley" and "Won't Get Fooled Again" must have been a formidable experience. The opus's bracing hard rock is tempered with moody, brilliant ballads ("Behind Blue Eyes," "The Song is Over") and humor (Entwistle's henpecked-husband lament "My Wife"). But in terms of solid records, there would be no "next" for the Who. The best Who compilation is still 1971's *Meaty Beaty Big and Bouncy*, which collects the foremost sixties singles, many of them non-LP at the time of the LP's release. A high spot is 1966's magnificent "Substitute," whose convention-questioning lyrics are offset by a captivating chiming guitar riff and stop-start arrangement. The tune was covered by the Ramones on *Acid Eaters*—with Townshend himself on guest vocals.

The Kinks

The early records by this English foursome are undoubtedly among the clearest influences on the Ramones' sound. How so? Two words: Dave Davies. Granted, his brother, singer/guitarist Ray Davies, is one of the greatest pop songwriters of the modern age. But it's younger guitarist Dave, a mere seventeen at the time the Kinks first hit worldwide, who should be credited with forging the hard, blunt, heavily distorted barre-chord backbone of the Ramones' music and the punk sounds it inspired, plus that of heavy metal, hardcore, and grunge. The Kinks' career has been one of balancing—not always successfully, it must be said—their initial primal hard rock side with their frilly, flowery, and quite often brilliant, "English" side. Beginning in London's Muswell Hill section in 1963 as the Ravens, the Kinks (the Davies brothers, bassist Peter Quaife, and drummer Mick Avory), as with most of their Brit Invasion contemporaries, started out playing American blues, R&B, and rock 'n' roll. Under the ears of future Who producer Shel Talmy, the band found success with 1964's savagely noisy "You Really Got Me." The next single, "All Day and All of the Night," continued the tough-edged formula and scored high as well. During the mid-sixties the band continued to do well in the charts, albeit with hits that lean more toward the group's winningly whimsical side: "Set Me Free," "Tired of Waiting for You," "Sunny Afternoon" and "A Well Respected Man."

The 1964 debut *Kinks* contains "You Really Got Me" and the wistful "Stop Your Sobbing" and is pretty rocking overall, though weighted toward of-the-times Merseybeat tracks and customary R&B covers (it was released in the States as *You Really Got Me*). The next year's *Kinda Kinks*, however, is mostly Kinks originals and sees Ray Davies coming into his own as a songwriting genius with the churning mover "Come On Now" and the redemptive "Something Better Beginning." *The Kink Kontroversy* (1965) is considered a key transitional album with its seamless blending of the Kinks' blues influences, crude guitar sound, and Ray Davies's ever-maturing compositions: the lustful "Till the End of the Day" (which re-channels the slamming riffs of "You Really Got Me") and "Where Have All the Good Times Gone," a thumping, mid-tempo lament to lost youth.

With 1966's *Face to Face* the band began an earnest turn toward tunefully nostalgic ruminations on Britain's vanishing Victorian past, but "I'm Not Like Everybody Else," a stellar B side from this period (included on the CD reissue), is, thematically speaking, strongly reminiscent of "I Don't Care" and similar Ramones outsider anthems. *Something Else by the Kinks* (1967) has the pinnacle of Ray Davies's acoustic-dominated music hall / Noel Coward style, the pastoral, bittersweet "Waterloo Sunset," and shows Dave Davies's arrival as a formidable songwriter with the beautifully sad "Death of a Clown" and shuffling "Love Me 'til the Sun Shines."

These three tunes echo wistfully through reflective Ramones songs like "It's a Long Way Back to Germany" and "Something to Believe In," while the disc's punkest cut, "David Watts," anticipates da brudders' forward-driving assault.

Next came stylistically deeper albums like 1968's *The Village Green Preservation Society* and 1970's *Lola vs. Powerman and the Money-Go-Round, Part One*, which are classics but musically removed from the Ramones. In the late seventies and early eighties, however, the Kinks sensed the influence of their early sixties singles on the new wave and reclaimed their punk-pioneer status with new songs that recalled the crunchers of yore. Besides the sneering title track, 1979's *Low Budget* has the adrenalized triple threat of "Attitude," "Pressure," and "Misery," and 1981's sardonically named *Give the People What They Want* is even more consistent, with the seriously kicking "Around the Dial" and "Destroyer" (a retooled "All Day and All of the Night"), and the beguiling "Better Things," one of the band's best ballads. The rowdy 1980 live *One for the Road* is ample evidence of a band that could rock just as hard as most acts its junior. There are many Kinks anthologies to be had, but *The Singles Collection* is the best one-disc summation.

The Troggs

These blokes are the other British Invasion act whose sound most loudly resonates in that of the Ramones. Even less blues-reliant than the Kinks, the Troggs (short for Troglodytes, their original name, which means "cavemen") will be forever known for their pummeling chart-topper, "Wild Thing." And with good reason: the 1966 tune is a primordial punk landmark. But despite history's tendency to write the Troggs off as mere three-chord wonders, a little bit of spelunking reveals that the rock-crushing hubris of "Wild Thing" was no one-off. Successive tunes like "Night of the Long Grass," "66-5-4-3-2-1," "Gonna Make You," "I Want You," and "I Can't Control Myself" (the latter among the covers on our champs' *Acid Eaters*) are the ultimate in tough, stripped-down simian grunt, and even the comparatively sunny "With a Girl Like You" clangs with force. At the same time, the Troggs were also capable of some of the sweetest, most tender balladry this side of Lord Byron (see 1968's "Love Is All Around").

The Troggs' lineup has varied greatly over the years, but the original configuration of sneering singer Reg Presley, guitarist Chris Britton, drummer Ronny Bond, and bassist David Wright came together in 1964. The band enjoyed massive success in Europe and didn't visit the U.S. until 1968 but was lionized by proto-punks and punks alike. Ramones reference points the MC5, the Stooges, and David Bowie, and fellow punks like the Buzzcocks have all cited the Troggs as influential. The U.S. version of the band's essential 1966 debut, *Wild Thing*, has a song list that's superior to its British counterpart, *From Nowhere*—the edition that remains in print today. But even that version's a blaster, with grinders like "Lost Girl" and "From Home" and the cascading "Our Love Will Still Be There."

Moving forward, the Troggs' late sixties / early seventies discography shows them to be more of a singles band than an album act. But when punk was looming, the Troggs were tuned in, making an aggressive return to form with 1976's *The Troggs Tapes* (not to be confused with an identically titled outtake of hilarious studio banter released without the band's authorization) and taping 1981's raunchy *Live at Max's Kansas City* at the namesake punk venue. *Archeology (1967–1977)* works well as an introduction to these savages, and deserves special mention for the lecherous, crushing "Come Now."

The Animals

When it comes to raw mid-sixties British R&B, the Animals are second only to the Rolling Stones. To many, front man Eric Burdon's full-throated, gravelly wail—gloriously displayed on the band's haunting hit, "House of the Rising Sun"—makes him the leading vocalist of the era. The band, which reportedly got its handle from its wild stage antics, was born in industrial Newcastle-on-Tyne in 1963. The Animals' name-making lineup of Burdon, keyboardist Alan Price, guitarist Hilton Valentine, bassist Chas Chandler, and drummer John Steel hit in early 1964 with the boisterous "Baby Let Me Take You Home," following it soon after with "House of the

Rising Sun." The band worked like crazy during the peak British Invasion years, cutting LPs dominated by gritty, garagey R&B reinterpretations (Chuck Berry, Ray Charles, Fats Domino, etc.) and enjoying immense hits with winners like "I'm Crying," "Don't Let Me Be Misunderstood," "It's My Life," and "Don't Bring Me Down." By 1967 the act had been reincarnated as the decidedly psychedelic—and thus less Ramones-related—Eric Burdon and the Animals.

For reasons that are utterly confounding, most of the Animals' highly influential early albums—both versions of their U.K. and U.S. 1964 self-titled debut; 1965's U.S.-only *The Animals on Tour*; second U.K. album *Animal Tracks*; third U.S. album, also called *Animal Tracks*; and 1966's superb U.S. *Animalization* and its U.K. counterpart, *Animalisms*—are out of print at the time of this writing. Still available, however, is their best, 1966's *Animalism* (which shouldn't be confused with the above *Animalisms*). Its howlingly hoarse "All Night Long" and workouts on "Rock Me Baby," "Hit the Road Jack," "Lucille," and Sam Cooke's "Shake," make it a pre-punk frontrunner. Cub listeners can try *Absolute Animals 1964–1968*, which tracks the early and later highs.

The Yardbirds

To most members of the classic rock generation, the Yardbirds are just that little band that gave us Eric Clapton, Jeff Beck, and Jimmy Page. Which is so unfair it has steam coming out of this writer's ears. No mere guitar-hero finishing school, the Yardbirds were one of the greatest bands of the British Invasion. With their pioneering, experimental use of feedback, distortion, and extreme live volume, they broke the ground for hard rock, psychedelia, and progressive rock, while their crashing, accelerated guitar-and-harmonica-driven instrumental passages—dubbed "rave-ups" by the band—were crucial to the development of punk rock. (Johnny Ramone, who named Page and Beck as his two favorite guitarists, caught the band's fabled concert at the Lower East Side's Anderson Theatre on its last tour.) And the Yardbirds' songs were excellent, too: "For Your Love," "Shapes of Things," "Over Under Sideways Down,"

"Heart Full of Soul," to name a few. Taking flight in 1963, the line-up of singer/harmonica player Keith Relf, guitarists Eric Clapton (who'd replaced Anthony "Top" Topham) and Chris Dreja, bassist Paul Samwell-Smith, and drummer Jim McCarty became the rage at London's Crawdaddy Club. Clapton left and was replaced by Jeff Beck; Samwell-Smith next bowed out and Jimmy Page came in on bass, but soon swapped roles with Dreja. Beck left in late 1966 and the Yardbirds soldiered on as a four-piece until their final landing in 1968. Page next started Led Zeppelin, which was originally called the New Yardbirds and recycled Yardbirds repertoire (i.e., "I'm Confused" became "Dazed and Confused").

The Yardbirds' official debut, 1964's *Five Live Yardbirds*, is a brazen set of hotwired R&B fueled by blues-wailing harp and scratchy, stinging guitars. Part of 1965's U.S.-released *Having a Rave Up* includes the newly added Beck, whose bold innovations took the music into challenging new realms. Generally considered the Yardbirds' finest album, *Rave Up* repeats some Clapton-era *Five Live* tracks next to its fuzz guitar–licked singles "Heart Full of Soul" and "Shapes of Things" and the off-the-rails rock-roots covers "Train Kept A-Rollin'" and "I'm a Man." *For Your Love* (1966) is a collection of mainly U.S.-only tracks that repeats, yet again, several of the *Five Live* sides with Clapton and has the crazed "I'm Not Talking" and "I Ain't Done Wrong," as well as the moody title single. *Roger the Engineer* was released in 1966 in abridged form as *Over Under Sideways Down*. Its title track is another fuzz-fueled field day for Beck, the explosive "Lost Woman" is one of the band's wildest songs, and the breathtaking, nascent hard rock of "Happenings Ten Years Time Ago" stars Beck and Page on dueling lead guitars. By the time Beck left, the group had come to be seen as more of a "musician's band" in the U.S., whose market made or broke the fortunes of touring British acts. Nineteen sixty-seven's pop-aiming, U.S.-only *Little Games* is disappointingly dopey overall but nevertheless has some great moments, like the proto-acid rock "Smile on Me," the hard-blowing harp workout "Drinking Muddy Water," and the stutter-riffed "Little Games." But the game was soon up for the Yardbirds, as the album proved a commercial flop.

There are tons of weird Yardbirds compilations out there. *Happenings Ten Years Time Ago 1964–1968* is the best way to go, with twenty-seven cuts spanning the Clapton, Beck, and Page eras.

Other Invaders

As stated earlier, the above acts weren't alone in their American assault. There were other Liverpool-based Merseybeat bands, like the Searchers (whose 1964 hit "Needles and Pins" inspired the Ramones' version), Gerry and the Pacemakers, and the Swinging Blue Jeans. Harder, R&B-based sounds came from the Steve Winwood–fronted Spencer Davis Group, Manfred Mann, the Nashville Teens, the Van Morrison–led Them, and the Pretty Things, whose wild-and-woolly R&B rivals the early Rolling Stones and has made them legends seemingly everywhere but the U.S. (the Pretties' founding lead guitarist is original Stones member Dick Taylor). Respectable middleweight hit makers include the Hollies, Wayne Fontana and the Mindbenders, and the cool Zombies. There were also lightweights like Freddie and the Dreamers, the Tremeloes, the Honeycombs, and Herman's Hermits, whose "I'm Henry VIII, I Am" is the source of the line "Second verse, same as the first" in the Ramones' "Judy Is a Punk." Then there were the Who's mod peers, who were very popular in their native land, such as the Creation ("Making Time"), the Move, and the Small Faces, whose power-piped front man Steve Marriott's bowl haircut was cited by Dee Dee as the inspiration for his own. While there are innumerable artist-specific CDs available by all of these bands, the most recommended initial avenues of English exploration are the compilations. *Merseybeat: The Story of the 60s Liverpool Sound* is a superb two-disc survey of that city's vanguard scene. Rhino's nine-CD series *The British Invasion: The History of British Rock* casts a wider net, covering poppier solo acts alongside proper bands. But most resoundingly recommended is the four-CD *Nuggets II: Original Artyfacts from the British Empire and Beyond 1964–1969*, which samples mod, beat, and psychedelic treasures.

NUGGETS

Released on Elektra Records in 1972, *Nuggets: Original Artyfacts from the First Psychedelic Era 1965–1968* (commonly referred to as, simply, *Nuggets*) was compiled by Elektra founder Jack Holzman and future Patti Smith Group guitarist Lenny Kaye. In an era when rock had, for the most part, clearly forgotten its roots, *Nuggets* was a revelatory reminder of what the music was *supposed* to be: wild, fun, and unpretentious noise made by and for the people, rather than by the stadium-gracing "golden gods" of the day. The two-LP set, which was issued again in 1976, was a call to arms for the punk generation and made its way into the collections of many of the eventual key players on the New York and London scenes (*England's Dreaming*, Jon Savage's essential book on the U.K. punk explosion, names *Nuggets* as a major influence on British bands). In fact, Kaye's original liner notes for the release feature one of the first usages of the term "punk rock," which, until it was co-opted for the very wave it inspired, was the name collectors affixed to this peculiarly American breed of basic, mid-to-late-sixties, Anglo-inspired rock 'n' roll.

Presumably Holzman and Kaye decided on the "psychedelic" descriptor as a contemporaneous catch-all, since "punk rock" would have been less familiar, and perhaps even off-putting, to potential buyers at the time. But most of the original compilation's twenty-seven tracks are decidedly Beatles/Stones/Kinks-derived rock, and there are only a few that truly have psychedelic elements. And even the ones that do—the Electric Prunes' "I Had Too Much to Dream Last Night," the Magic Mushrooms' "It's-A-Happening"—are marked by a grounded aggression that belies the psych tag. The other *Nuggets* incongruity is that some of its acts were studio-only units and not "real" bands: the Strangeloves, with future Richard Hell and the Voidoids producer Richard Gottehrer ("Night Time"), Sagittarius (the production-heavy "My World Fell Down"), the admittedly hokey Third Rail ("Run, Run, Run"). But in this case the variety makes the overall listening experience more fun, and doesn't detract from the abundance of smart pop and gloriously snotty rock 'n' roll.

And what excellent rock 'n' roll it is: "Dirty Water" by the Standells,

"Pushin' Too Hard" by the Seeds, "You're Gonna Miss Me" by the 13th Floor Elevators, "Psychotic Reaction" by Count V, to name four *Nuggets* tracks covered by dozens of seventies punks. Also here are songs by bands whose members went on to further notoriety: "Open My Eyes" by the Nazz, featuring a young Todd Rundgren; "Baby Please Don't Go" by the Amboy Dukes, with a pre-beard Ted Nugent on guitar (the Ramones' version of the Dukes' "Journey to the Center of the Mind" opens *Acid Eaters*); and "Respect" by the Vagrants, a Long Island quintet beloved of Johnny Ramone that included one of his guitar heroes, future Mountain man Leslie West.

In 1998 Rhino turned on a whole new generation of garage heads with the expanded, four-CD *Nuggets* box set, which adds 91 tracks to the original 27 for a total of 118 winners, and is mandatory for anyone who loves moving music of any variety (check the Music Explosion's "Little Bit O' Soul," which our leather-clad idols covered). In 2001 the label released the internationally focused *Nuggets II: Original Artyfacts from the British Empire and Beyond, 1964–1969*, which was followed by *Love Is the Song We Sing: San Francisco Nuggets 1965–1970* and *Where the Action Is! Los Angeles Nuggets 1965–1968*, all of which feature pop and psych as well as garage. Two thousand five's *Children of Nuggets: Original Artyfacts from the Second Psychedelic Era, 1976–1995* presents later sounds rooted in the *Nuggets* tradition.

GARAGE ROCK

The term "garage rock" didn't actually come into use until after the era of its original practitioners had passed. Theoretically, this music, also called garage punk, was developed by amateurish, middle-class teens who rehearsed in the garages of their families' suburban American homes in the mid-1960s. That's only partially accurate; many of the musicians who played it were slightly older professionals who hailed from urban areas. But whatever their ages or hometowns happened to be, garage bands were united via their simple, crude rock 'n' roll inspired by British Invasion acts like the Beatles, the Rolling Stones, and the Kinks. And when it comes to garage rock, the simpler and cruder the better. Imagine a gang of pimply suburban kids doing their best to master "Satisfaction" in the garage or rec room. The sound tended to be wildly rudimentary when compared to that of their heroes. But it's precisely that primitive quality that makes it so electrifying, just like it did with the Ramones when they burst on the late-1970s scene. Some of these regional garage bands were able to save enough money from playing teen clubs and school dances to cut a single. Though ineptly produced by the local polka or country studio, the record might get played on the town radio station, making the Humble Servants, or whatever they called themselves, into the local Rolling Stones for five minutes. (Here come the girls!) And if they were really lucky their record might get picked up by a major label and even become a national hit. The best examples of such records are elementary originals smeared with nasty fuzz guitar and spite-spewing lyrics of the my-woman-done-me-wrong ilk. In high school, Johnny and Tommy Ramone were in one such group, the Tangerine Puppets (Johnny played bass and Tommy played guitar; the band made a two-song demo that remains unreleased). Joey played drums in the Intruders, who never made it out of the basement, and the short-lived Hudson Tube. These little bands are like cockroaches, but in a good way: for every big-hitting garager like the Standells or Paul Revere and the Raiders, lurking beneath the surface are literally hundreds of lesser-known but similarly great groups waiting to be discovered.

And the best way to discover them is through the innumerable—at last count well over a thousand—various-artist garage compilations packing the racks. Some garage bands did release albums, and we'll get to a few that did, but, as with most early rock 'n' roll, garage is more of a singles-oriented genus. So rather than stumble blindly through LPs that have one or two good songs amid weak cover tunes (leave those to the fanatics), you're encouraged to first get your hands nice and dirty by exploring the era's surprising sonic variety and breadth via the comps. Without doubt *Nuggets* (see sidebar) is the one to start with. But thumping close behind are *Uptight Tonight: The Ultimate 60s Garage Collection* and, delving into the most primitive and obscure spider holes of garagedom, the multi-volume

Pebbles and *Back from the Grave* series. Right here, though, we'll hit on a few of the higher-profile garage bands that lodged themselves in the Ramones' DNA (or at least sound like they could have).

The Sonics

Raised in the rainy climes of Tacoma, Washington, the Sonics were perhaps the loudest, rawest, and most maniacal of all sixties U.S. garage bands. Assembled as an R&B/instrumental outfit in 1960 by guitarist Larry Parypa and the insanely screaming Gerry Roslie on lead vocals and keyboards, the group was a fixture on the same area teen club circuit that featured fellow locals the Wailers (see Chapter One) and the early Paul Revere and the Raiders. The band's first album, 1965's *Here Are the Sonics!!!*, is an unchallenged garage punk milestone, with the sinister "The Witch," "Psycho," "Strychnine," "Boss Hoss," "Have Love, Will Travel," and other face-blasters. *Boom!*, the '66 sophomore set, is no less scorching, encompassing savage pounders like "Cinderella" and "Shot Down" and the menacing "He's Waiting." (*Psycho-Sonic* pairs these first two LPs with outtakes and live tracks.) Nineteen sixty-six also brought album number three, which, owing to a label change, is confusingly titled *Introducing the Sonics*. It reprises "The Witch" and "Psycho" and boasts more classics in the form of "High Time," "You Got Your Head on Backwards," and "Maintaining My Cool." If your idea of sixties rock is all peace and love and flowers in your hair, the Sonics have quite a nasty surprise for you.

Paul Revere and the Raiders

Don't let the cutesy Revolutionary War costumes fool you: during their peak years, Paul Revere and the Raiders made some of the hardest rock around. From 1966 to 1969 they dominated the charts with crunching cuts like "Hungry," "Just Like Me," "Kicks," "Let Me," and "Him or Me—What's It Gonna Be?," giving the Beatles and the Rolling Stones some serious competition. The band was founded in Boise, Idaho, in 1958, by keyboardist Revere (unfortunate real name: Paul Revere Dick) and singer/saxophonist Mark Lindsay. Like the Sonics, the group was originally an R&B/

instrumental club band; the name change to Paul Revere and the Raiders came with the release of the band's initial singles, one of which, 1960's instrumental "Like, Long Hair" edged into the Top Forty. The Raiders relocated to Oregon, becoming a top regional act and attracting the attention of Columbia Records, which signed them on the strength of their 1963 single of "Louie, Louie" (like Chapter One's the Kingsmen, who had the bigger hit with the Richard Berry song, the Raiders supposedly learned it from local pals the Wailers). Producer Terry Melcher, who helped the quintet—by now Revere, Lindsay, drummer Mike "Smitty" Smith, guitarist Drake Levin, and bassist Phil "Fang" Volk—develop a harder vocals/guitar/organ-oriented sound. Nineteen sixty-five's live, high-energy, covers-heavy *Here They Come!* dovetailed perfectly with the debut of the TV variety show "Where the Action Is," on which the Raiders served as house band (see Chapter Five; "Happening '68" and "Happening," hosted by Revere and Lindsay, came next). Nineteen sixty-six's *Just Like Us!* features tough R&B and Brit-band covers (Stones, Animals) and the grinding punkers "Just Like Me" and "Steppin' Out," but even better is that year's *Midnight Ride*, which includes the anti-drug classic "Kicks," the group's best-known hit, along with the clobbering "Louie, Go Home" and "I'm Not Your Stepping Stone" (the Monkees' better-known version was a cover). *The Spirit of '67* (which actually came out in '66) is the band's best LP, with the snarling "Good Thing" and "Louise," the lust-filled "Hungry," and the fuzz-stinging "The Great Airplane Strike." While poppier and not quite as consistent, 1967's *Revolution!* is highlighted with the infectious "Him or Me—What's It Gonna Be?" and the pounders "Gone—Movin' On" and "Reno," and is still darn good. (Sundazed Music's reissue adds the driving single "Ups and Downs" and more). Subsequent albums, however, are less interesting. The best single-disc Raiders overview is 1967's *Greatest Hits*.

The Seeds

Fronted by weirdo supreme Sky Saxon, whose voice recalls the squeaky yelp of the doomed scientist in the 1958 film *The Fly* ("Help meeeee!"), the Seeds were genius makers of minimal, repetitive, and dead-simple riffs that blatantly foreshadowed those of the Ramones. The L.A. group took root in 1965, when Saxon (born Richard Marsh) joined up with guitarist Dan Savage, drummer Rick Andridge, and the band's secret weapon, keyboardist Daryl Hooper, whose spectral lines give the group a unique sound (and noticeably impacted the Doors' Ray Manzarek). The Seeds were so cavalierly punk that they simply reused the music for 1966's "Pushin' Too Hard," their biggest hit, for many of their other tunes—and somehow made it work. Their first single, 1965's pleading hit "Can't Seem to Make You Mine" (covered by the Ramones on 1993's *Acid Eaters*) opens their 1966 debut, *The Seeds*. In addition to "Pushin' Too Hard," this mandatory disc is home to equally rebellious fuzz-punkers like "Evil Hoodoo," "Girl I Want You," and "No Escape." *A Web of Sound* appeared a few months later, and with its edgy and surreal tracks—"Mr. Farmer," "Tripmaker," "Pictures and Designs"—the disc is no sophomore slump. *Future* (1967) sees the Seeds lyrically reclaiming their flower-power (they're credited with coining the term) roots, but don't get the idea it's featherweight stuff: see the bashing, paranoid "Two Fingers Pointing at You," the snide "Out of the Question," and the creepy "Flower Lady and Her Assistant." *Raw and Alive in Concert at Merlin's Music Box*, from 1968, is one of those typically fake sixties "live" albums with dubbed-in applause, but is great, nevertheless. Besides the hits, it features some growling, fuzzy songs not previously available: "Gypsy Plays His Drums," "Satisfy You," "Night Time Girl." As a starter, *Pushin' Too Hard: The Best of the Seeds* has the Seeds you need.

The Standells

Because of the declaration "Boston, you're my home" in their 1966 hit "Dirty Water," it's often assumed the Standells were Beantown boys. Wrong-o, kids. Like the Seeds, the Standells were from Los Angeles, and they had the showbiz connections to show for it: organist Larry Tamblyn is the brother of actor Russ Tamblyn and the uncle of actress Amber Tamblyn; drummer / lead vocalist Dick

Dodd is a former Mouseketeer who'd also previously played with surf legends the Bel-Airs; and the band, which also included bassist Gary Lane and guitarist Tony Valentino, appeared in movies and on TV's "The Munsters" (see Chapter Five). The Standells formed in 1962, with Dodd replacing Gary Leeds (later of pop-vocal trio the Walker Brothers) in time for their 1965 debut, *The Standells in Person at P.J.'s*, a rowdy frat rock set. But it was when the foursome linked up with producer/songwriter Ed Cobb that things took off. Swapping their shorter hair and matching suits for shags and mod duds, the band adopted the harder, Stonesy sound that permeates 1966's *Dirty Water*. The same year saw the release of the covers LP *The Hot Ones!*, a misstep you should miss yourself; it was followed, however, by the much improved *Why Pick on Me*, whose winning title cut is joined by similarly punky gems like "Mr. Nobody" and "Sometimes Good Guys Don't Wear White." The leering titular tune of 1967's *Try It!*, the band's last studio album, was banned from airplay for supposedly promoting free love and drug use. That record's other highlights include the belligerent "Barracuda" and "Riot on Sunset Strip," the frantic theme to the exploitation film starring the band and fellow garage unit the Chocolate Watchband. *Hot Hits and Hot Ones: Is This the Way That You Get Your High?* collects twenty-one of the Standells' best.

? and the Mysterians

Odds are people who've never even heard the term "garage punk" are already familiar with the idiom via ? and the Mysterians' million-selling 1966 hit, "96 Tears." Fronted by the inimitable ? (a.k.a. Question Mark and Rudy Martinez), the Vox organ–pumping fivesome formed in 1962 in Michigan as an instrumental combo and snagged their name from a Japanese sci-fi flick. "96 Tears" became a regional hit before being picked up by the major Cameo-Parkway imprint and topping the U.S. charts. The follow-up single from 1966's excellent *96 Tears* album, "I Need Somebody," was another Top Forty hit. *Action*, the band's 1966 sophomore album, sold poorly, although its 1967 single "Can't Get Enough of You Baby" did chart (the song would be a much bigger hit for pop band Smash Mouth in 1998). Unable to regain the rights to its Cameo-Parkway releases, the group later re-recorded many songs, including all of the *96 Tears* LP tracks in the same running order. These sessions are woefully inferior and best avoided. But don't cry those tears just yet: *The Best of ? and the Mysterians: Cameo Parkway 1966–1967* fills the "mysterious" void with the above and other rockers like "Smokes," "'8' Teen" and the lecherous "Girl (You Captivate Me)," which the band often performed live as "Girl (You Masturbate Me)." No wonder critic Dave Marsh called these guys "punk rock" years before the Ramones existed.

The Shadows of Knight

Bred in the bustling blues town of Chicago, the Shadows of Knight were another shining light of the magical garage rock year of 1966. Led by howling singer Jim Sohn, the Shadows began in 1964 and worked up their Stones / Pretty Things / Yardbirds–modeled sound in Windy City teen clubs before signing with local label Dunwhich, which released a single of the group's smoldering version of Irish band Them's "Gloria," a number one hit in several U.S. markets. An essential garage band album, 1966's *Gloria* rattles the walls with raging romps through blues staples and snot-blowing originals like "Light Bulb Blues" and "It Always Happens This Way." The 1966 second album, *Back Door Men*, is even better, tearing out of the gate with another Irish beat band cover, the Wheels' "Bad Little Woman," and crashing through more ravers like "I'll Make You Sorry," "Gospel Zone," and "I'm Gonna Make You Mine." In 1969 Sohns took a new Shadows grouping to the Team label for one last hit, the tough bubblegum mover "Shake."

Sam the Sham and the Pharaohs

Sam the Sham and the Pharaohs are another example of an act whose sole number one hit, "Wooly Bully," is so ubiquitous that it's known by listeners far removed from the garage scene. Unfairly branded a novelty outfit due to their fratty sound and goofy themes, the Pharaohs were early innovators of Tex-Mex rock 'n' roll. Beturbaned singer/organist Sam the Sham (a.k.a. Domingo

Samudio; his stage moniker was an in-joke about his professed vocal shortcomings) began the Pharaohs in his native Dallas, Texas, in 1961; the group's name and nutty Middle Eastern costumes were inspired by Yul Brynner's character in *The Ten Commandments*. An independent single, "Haunted House," helped the band land a deal with MGM Records, which released "Wooly Bully," a song Sam wrote for his cat that topped the charts for eighteen weeks. Besides its titular Farfisa-squeezing party classic, the band's 1965 debut, *Wooly Bully*, jumps with garage R&B thumpers ("Go-Go Girls," "Gangster of Love") and numbers that lay out the group's *caliente* Tex-Mex side. The plainly titled *Their Second Album* came later that year, and includes the hit "Wooly Bully" rewrite "Ju-Ju Hand" among its uniformly voodoo/magic-themed tunes. Nineteen sixty-five also saw the release of *On Tour*, which is heavier on the R&B / rock 'n' roll end with wild versions of Billy Lee Riley's "Red Hot" and Little Junior Parker's "Mystery Train." The band's fourth album, *Little Red Riding Hood* (1966), bears the wily, wolf-howling title track, the band's second-biggest hit, and the evil, organ-dominated "The Phantom." The same year's *Sam the Shame Revue*, the Pharaohs' last album, has the quintet joined by girl backup singers the Shamettes. For best-of CDs, *Pharaohization!* is the first choice.

The Count Five

The vampire-caped members of the Count Five were barely out of high school when they created one of garage rock's most crazed contributions, 1966's "Psychotic Reaction." The San Jose, California, quintet of singer/guitarist Sean Byrne, lead guitarist John "Mouse" Michalski, bassist Roy Chaney, drummer Butch Atkinson, and harmonica player / vocalist Ken Ellner existed barely long enough to enjoy the ride, forming just over a year before it made its lone Top Five hit and disintegrating a couple of years later. According to legend, it was the Irish-born Byrne who wrote the demented, Yardbirds-derived "Psychotic Reaction" in a health education class (cruel irony has him dying of diabetes and cirrhosis of the liver in 2008), which went to number one in L.A. before beginning its national ascension. The band quickly banged out an album, called (what else?) *Psychotic Reaction*, whose eleven uniformly raw punkers include "Pretty Big Mouth," "Double Decker Bus," and "They're Gonna Get You," and show the five had more fuzz in the tank than their "one-hit wonders" tag suggests. While the Ramones never got around to covering "Psychotic Reaction," it was a staple in the set lists of many 1970s punks, including Television, the Cramps, the Vibrators, and the Radiators from Space. *Psychotic Revelation: The Ultimate Count Five* collects everything the teens recorded.

Love

Also from the Los Angeles area was the groundbreaking Love, whose brilliant music spanned tough garage punk, folk rock, hard rock, and baroque psychedelia. Led by the eccentric genius singer-songwriter Arthur Lee, the group formed in 1965 and swiftly rose to become one of the Sunset Strip's biggest attractions, greatly influencing the Doors (the story goes it was Lee who hipped Love's label, Elektra Records, to his pal Jim Morrison's group). Influenced by neighbors the Byrds and the usual British Invasion greats, Love was originally called the Grass Roots, but changed its moniker in deference to the identically named "Let's Live for Today" hit makers. Love's classic early lineup also featured another songwriting mastermind in guitarist Bryan MacLean, and was rounded out by guitarist Johnny Echols, bassist Ken Forssi, and drummer Alban "Snoopy" Pfisterer.

The group's 1966 debut, *Love*, is a stunner, with the punked-up regional hit version of the Burt Bacharach / Hal David tune "My Little Red Book" and the raving "My Flash on You," "Can't Explain" and "No Matter What You Do." *Da Capo* (1967) is crucial to the Ramones' legacy, due to its breakneck, bomb-blasting single "7 and 7 Is" (another *Acid Eaters* cover). Love's third album, the ambitious, haunting *Forever Changes*, is one of rock's greatest, on par with the Beatles' *Sgt. Pepper* and the Beach Boys' *Pet Sounds*, but less relevant here. *Love Story (1966–1972)* is the preferred way to start your Love affair.

The Blues Magoos

Local heroes during our boys' pliable years, the Bronx-based Blues Magoos were formed in 1964. They featured singer/guitarist "Peppy" Castro, guitarist Mike Esposito, organist Ralph Scala, bassist Ron Gilbert, and drummer Geoff Daking, all of whom for a time adopted Magoo as a common surname—kinda like another, later band we all love. The five made their name on the Greenwich Village scene before releasing 1966's *Psychedelic Lollipop*, home to the band's biggest hit, the acid punker "(We Ain't Got) Nothin' Yet," and a manic, extended version of folkie J. D. Loudermilk's "Tobacco Road" that later appeared on the vital *Nuggets* garage compilation. As the opening act for the 1967 American tour by Herman's Hermits and the Who, the Magoos turned heads with their custom-made, light-up electric stage suits. The same year, they released *Electric Comic Book*, which is on the whole more trippy than its predecessor but still boasts several punky tunes like the single tracks "Pipe Dream" and "There's a Chance We Can Make It." Nineteen sixty-eight's *Basic Blues Magoos* is even more lysergic but delivers moments of aggressive, garagey goodness (especially the fine reading of the Move's "I Can Hear the Grass Grow"). "(We Ain't Got) Nothin' Yet" was covered later by Ramones buddies the Dictators, and hardcore punks the Dead Kennedys stole its bass line for 1980's "Let's Lynch the Landlord." *Kaleidesopic Compendium: The Best of the Blues Magoos* culls tracks from the first three albums.

The 13th Floor Elevators

Beginning their ascent in Austin, Texas, in 1965, the 13th Floor Elevators—howling madman Roky Erickson on vocals and guitar, Stacy Sutherland on lead guitar, John Ike Walton on drums, Benny Thurman on bass, and Tommy Hall on amplified electric jug (!)—were the head honchos of a Lone Star psych/garage scene that included fellow weirdoes like the Moving Sidewalks, the Bubble Puppy, and the Red Krayola. Although the band's sound was heavily based on the Kinks and other British acts, its members' pioneering personal experiments with LSD (still legal in the mid-sixties) were audibly manifested in the music. Many name the Elevators as the first-ever psychedelic band, but rest assured, punker: this psychedelia is wrapped in raw, crunching guitars and bashing drums, not airy pastel rainbows. The group signed up with local label International Artists for the 1966 debut *The Psychedelic Sounds of the 13th Floor Elevators*. Kicking off with the band's only national hit, the feral "You're Gonna Miss Me," this essential beast unfurls with too many spooky and howling rockers: "Rollercoaster," "Fire Engine," "Monkey Island," "Tried to Hide," and so on. Nineteen sixty-seven brought a revamped rhythm section and *Easter Everywhere*, which burns with the face-frying garage cuts "Slip Inside This House," "I've Got Levitation," and the tellingly named "Earthquake." By 1968's *Bull of the Woods* the Elevators were beginning their descent, largely due to the incapacitating drug intake that sidelined Erickson and Hall for most of the recordings. A final album that's understated and cool, it's one you should work your way up to by way of its two precursors. Beware '68's *13th Floor Elevators Live*, a laughably phony live album of studio outtakes covered in canned crowd noise. There are enough Elevators anthologies in print to bust your brain. The finest currently is *Absolutely the Best*, which offers remastered tracks from the first three albums. Backed by various bands, the troubled Erickson resurfaced in Austin punk clubs during the seventies. Much of his post-Elevators output is well worth investigation. For that, try the career overview *I Have Always Been Here Before: The Roky Erickson Anthology*.

The Music Machine

Even without hearing "Talk Talk," the Los Angeles band's neck-snapping 1967 garage punk hit, it's clear from the group's photos that the Music Machine helped pave the way for the Ramones. Clad head to toe in black, their bowl haircuts dyed to match, the five members seethe with the same menace that would ooze from the CBGB stage a decade later. Gravel-voiced singer/guitarist Sean Bonniwell assembled the Music Machine in 1965 from parts left over from folk rock unit the Ragamuffins, plus bassist Keith Olsen, drummer Ron Edgar, keyboardist Doug Rhodes, and guitarist Mark Landon. "Talk Talk" is the band's first single and the pride of 1966's *(Turn On) The Music Machine*. Bonniwell was known as a taskmaster, which likely contributed to the band's breaking up while taping its second album in 1967, mere months after "Talk Talk" had charted (titled *Close*, the sophomore sessions were issued in 1969 under the name T. S. Bonniwell but are light pop and nothing like the grinding punk of the Music Machine). The anthology *The Ultimate Turn On* has fifty selections highlighted by "The Eagle Never Hunts the Fly," "Double Yellow Line," and "Masculine Intuition," songs that'll have you shaking your head in disbelief at the under-recognized power of the Music Machine.

The Remains

Boston's Remains (sometimes billed as Barry and the Remains) never broke nationally, but remain local legends that elicit solemn nods and joyful tears from those lucky enough to have seen them at the fabled Rathskeller back in the day. Barry Tashian formed the group in 1964 after experiencing the British beat boom on a trip to London. With Tashian on lead vocals and guitar, Chip Damiani on drums, Bill Briggs on keyboards, and Vern Miller on bass, the band debuted in 1965 with the rambunctious "Why Do I Cry." The follow-up single, a cover of Bo Diddley's "Diddy Wah Diddy," battled it out in the charts with Captain Beefheart and the Magic Band's version. The Remains' unique approach lies mainly in their dynamics; while there is the occasional garage-fuzz solo by Tashian, his comparatively clean sound leaves the rhythm section to drive the tunes, and, instead of the de rigueur Vox organ, Briggs played an electric piano. *The Remains* (1966), the band's sole official LP, is one of the American garage era's most solid, filled with strong R&B performances and resoundingly great originals, like the driving and moody "Heart," the Kinksy "You Got a Hard Time Coming," and the group's pièce de résistance, the epic "Don't Look Back." The group moved to New York and replaced Damiani with N. D. Smart in time to open for the Beatles on their final tour, but broke up soon after (reforming in the late 1990s). The Remains' biggest Boston competitors were the Barbarians and the Rockin' Ramrods. The Barbarians, featuring hook-handed drummer Victor "Moulty" Moulton (his theme song, "Moulty," is another *Nuggets* classic), appeared in the 1964 concert film *The T.A.M.I. Show* and released one album, 1965's *Are You a Boy or Are You a Girl?*, whose acerbic title cut is a pre-punk hoot. The Rockin' Ramrods toured with the Rolling Stones and are best remembered for 1964's primitive pounder "She Lied," which can be found on *Rockin' Ramrods Best*.

The Chocolate Watchband

Another West Coast crew, Stones clones the Chocolate Watchband started out near San Francisco in 1965 and were fronted by the Jagger-swaggering David Aguilar, whose snarls were the envy of any eighties and nineties retro-garage band singer worth his bowl haircut (although it wasn't always Aguilar the acolytes were imitating; one of the Watchband's most iconic tracks, the slamming "Let's Talk About Girls," was performed by session vocalist Don Bennett). The Watchband was founded by guitarist Mark Loomis in 1965 and eventually fleshed out with Aguilar, bassist Bill Flores, drummer Gary Andrijasevich, and Brian Jones lookalike Sean Tolby on guitar. By 1966 the five were tearing up Bay Area stages with their matching Vox equipment and working with producer Ed Cobb, whose other charges, the Standells, would be cast alongside the Watchband in the teen exploitation flick *Riot on Sunset Strip*. The early singles "Sweet Young Thing" and "Misty Lane" brim with foreboding angst, but it's 1967's dark "Are You Gonna Be There (at the Love-In)"—which appeared on the soundtrack of *The Love-Ins*, another exploito-job—that shows the Chocolate Watchband at its best. With a loping bass, stinging guitar, and gnarled vocals over a simmering backbeat, it's just mean as hell. The title tune and other cuts on the debut *No Way Out* are first-rate psychedelic-punk fusion, and the album is a period classic despite Cobb's using a studio band for almost all of it (prompting everyone in the band save for Loomis and Flores to quit). Aguilar returned for 1968's *The Inner Mystique*, which is highlighted by covers of the Kinks' "I'm Not Like Everybody Else" and Bob Dylan's "It's All Over, Baby Blue." *One Step Beyond* (1969) is laid-back psych-folk and features pre-Aguilar vocalist Bill Phay. *Melts in Your Brain Not on Your Wrist: The Complete Recordings 1965 to 1967* has one CD of "real" Watchband sides and another by the "faux" Watchband.

The Monks

The Monks were another fantastic American band, albeit one that spent its brief 1960s existence in Germany. They're also one of the craziest acts in rock history: five ex-G.I.'s playing weird, aggressive music on an odd combination of instruments while sporting black cassocks and traditional Christian monastic tonsures. Consisting of lead vocalist and guitarist Gary Burger, organist Larry Clark, electric banjoist Dave Day, bassist Eddie Shaw, and drummer Roger Johnston, the group began in 1964 as a rather innocent surf/beat combo, the Five Torquays. A year later the members reinvented themselves as "anti-Beatles" by reshaping their sound into something mockingly nihilistic, noisy, and totally infectious and adopting a provocative new image and name. After working the Hamburg clubs, the Monks released their only studio album, 1965's *Black Monk Time*. Perhaps *the* great lost ür-punk album, this dark, Dadaist opus is much like the Ramones' music: an inexplicable, sonically minimal balance of absurd humor and hard belligerence. Titles like "I Hate You," "Shut Up," and "Complication" show where the band's lyrical heads were at, and the pumping, polka-like rhythms of some of the songs, while not along the lines of our Bowery boys' four-four M.O., are just as addictive. The group's insane mélange of chanted vocals, roller-rink organ, scraping banjo, and wild fuzz bass is like nothing else. Miss it and ye shall surely do penance.

Davie Allan and the Arrows

If you dig the wild fuzz—which you should, being a Ramones fan—Los Angeles outfit Davie Allan and the Arrows should be near the top of your "Bands to Check Out" list. Headed by lead guitarist Allan, the group played only instrumentals and bridged the gap—*loudly*—between the surf and post-British Invasion eras. After debuting with 1965's Ventures / Dick Dale–styled *Apache*

'65 as, simply, the Arrows (Paul Johnson, rhythm guitar; Steve Pugh, bass; Larry Brown, drums), the band began working with producer and future California Lieutenant Governor Mike Curb on soundtrack music for a series of low-budget biker movies (of which the Ramones were ardent fans) that were released on Curb's Sidewalk label. The first, 1966's *The Wild Angels*, finds Allan discovering the mercilessly overdriven distorted guitar sound that made his legend, and features the Arrows' signature "Blues' Theme," a scorching ear-blaster that weaves the sounds of revving motorcycles through its insistent, descending riffs. The tune was reworked brilliantly as "Blues Trip" for 1968's *Cycle Delic Sounds*, an orgy of smoking fuzz and wordless, bike-themed workouts like "Grog's Hog" and "13th Harley." The double-disc *Devil's Rumble: Anthology '64–'68* assembles forty of Allan's sizzling singles, album cuts, and rarities.

Outside the Garage

There are a few examples of contemporaneous acts who weren't garage bands per se, but whose pop sensibilities and occasional raw edges seem to have left their marks on the budding Ramones. New York's Young Rascals (later the Rascals) were hometown heroes more known for their blue-eyed soul hits, but their early LP's are also rife with rocking, garagey tracks. The chart-topping "Good Lovin'" (1966), a wired, energetic remake of an earlier R&B hit for vocal group the Olympics, as well as tough covers of Larry Williams ("Slow Down") and Wilson Pickett ("Mustang Sally," "In the Midnight Hour") and the kicking original "Do You Feel It," all appear on their 1966 debut, *The Young Rascals. Collections*, released the same year, has more gritty, Hammond organ–powered Motown and R&B tracks and the kicking "Come On Up." Besides the sunny title tune, 1967's *Groovin'* packs the abrasive "You Better Run," which sports Gene Cornish's punked-up guitar. Also on the garage soul tip were Michigan's Mitch Ryder and the Detroit Wheels, whose wailing white R&B for a time made them one of America's top bands. *Rev Up!!: The Best of Mitch Ryder and the Detroit Wheels* takes in the hits "Jenny Take a Ride," "Sock It to Me Baby,"

"Devil with the Blue Dress On / Good Golly Miss Molly," "Little Latin Lupe Lu," and other screamers. Los Angeles had the Turtles, revered for artful pop singles like "Happy Together" and "Elenore." But bypass the hits collections and head for their first two albums, 1965's *It Ain't Me Babe*, with the title Dylan cover and the similarly sneering "Your Maw Said You Cried," and 1966's *You Baby / Let Me Be*, with the propulsive "Almost There" and the defiant "Let Me Be." L.A. also gave us the Byrds, the leading exponents of folk rock and pioneers of psychedelic and country rock. But how, you ask, do Roger McGuinn and company, with their jangling guitars and soaring vocal harmonies, relate to the heated blasts of the Ramones? The melodies. Both acts knew the value of a good major-chord hook and never lost sight of that, and it's clear the Ramones appreciated this quality about the Byrds. It's the Byrds' more streamlined albums, their first four, that will most appeal to Ramones lovers. *Mr. Tambourine Man* (1964) has the beguiling Dylan title tune, the Bo Diddley–beating Jackie DeShannon song "Don't Doubt Yourself, Babe," and "Feel a Whole Lot Better," a pounding kiss-off to an ex-lover. *Turn! Turn! Turn!* (1965) includes more innovative covers, of Dylan and Pete Seeger (the latter with the smash title cut), and the Beatles-ish "It Won't Be Wrong" and "Wait and See." While the groundbreaking "Eight Miles High" is the Ramones-removed centerpiece of 1966's *Fifth Dimension*, the set also has linear cuts that include the garage warhorse "Hey Joe." *Younger Than Yesterday* (1967) includes another Dylan cover, "My Back Pages," which our leather-jacketed geniuses adapted for *Acid Eaters*, and the sarcastic hit "So You Want to Be a Rock and Roll Star." Nineteen sixty-seven's *Greatest Hits* samples the high flights of the early Byrds.

BUBBLEGUM

Although the name would be revived and applied to more recent kiddie pop, bubblegum was originally the term for a wave of manufactured pop aimed at teens and preteens that stretched from, roughly, 1967 to 1972. The phrase was coined by New York producers Jerry Kasenetz and Jeffrey Katz, whose Super

K production team cranked out lightweight, annoyingly catchy singles by fictitious groups, many composed by songwriters Joey Levine and Artie Resnick and released on Buddha Records. Aimed at kids who were in the throes of puberty, these giddy tunes tapped into their hormone-hatching sexual tension with double-entendre lyrics that (heh, heh) went right over the heads of both their intended audience and its parents, such as "Yummy Yummy Yummy" by the Ohio Express (chorus: "Yummy, yummy, yummy / I've got love in my tummy") and the non-Buddha "Come On Down to My Boat" by Every Mother's Son. Heavily marketed with tie-ins to Saturday morning kids' shows (songs sometimes appeared as cardboard cutout records on boxes of sugary cereals), some bubblegum productions were presented as the work of costumed (the Banana Splits, the Bugaloos), cartoon (the Archies, Josie and the Pussycats), and live-action (the Partridge Family) acts. By the mid-1970s bubblegum had become the most uncool music around—goofy "kids' music"—as post-Beatles rock was increasingly taking itself far too seriously. But despite, or perhaps because of, its kitsch phoniness and innocent fun, to some bubblegum's addictive melodies and simple song structures were closer to the true essence of rock 'n' roll than whatever the hack classical wannabees in the stadiums were up to. Thus, the Ramones were huge bubblegum fans, its lighthearted themes and driving rhythms dovetailing perfectly with their own approach. Johnny Ramone even described his band's music as "twisted bubblegum."

1910 Fruitgum Company / Ohio Express / Super K Productions

Considered the first true bubblegum act, the 1910 Fruitgum Company began as Jeckell and the Hydes, a New Jersey garage band signed by Buddha in 1967 and quickly remade in the studio by Kasenetz and Katz. Between 1968 and 1969 the group hit the Billboard Hot 100 seven times, its perky, peppy singles "Simon Says," "1, 2, 3, Red Light," and "Indian Giver" (the latter performed by the Ramones on *Subterranean Jungle*) selling millions.

The band cranked out several albums, most of them pushing the current hit single and padded with filler. Sitting through all of them will make you diabetic, so instead chew on *The Best of the 1910 Fruitgum Company*, whose twenty-eight cuts include the hits and better album selections.

Legend has it the Ohio Express was another real garage band that was retooled by the Super K team, the Rare Breed, whose 1966 single "Beg, Borrow and Steal" became a bigger hit after it was re-released on Buddha under the group's new name. Most of the Ohio Express's members never played on their records; producer-songwriter Joey Levine sang on "Yummy Yummy Yummy" and the hits that followed, "Chewy Chewy," "Down at Lulu's," and "Mercy." The group released four albums but, again, unless you're a sucrose glutton, go with *Best of the Ohio Express*. By mixing and matching their studio singers and players (tracks were often released more than once under different band names) the Buddha / Super K team gave the illusion of having more acts in its sticky, sticky stable. Buddha's *Bubblegum Music Is the Naked Truth* (1969) is a classic compilation starring the 1910 Fruitgum Company, the Ohio Express, the Lemon Pipers ("Green Tambourine"), and others.

The Monkees

Detractors dismissed them as the "Prefab Four" because they were assembled as the cast of a television series and didn't, at first, write or play on their own records. But the fact is that the Monkees made some of the best pop music of the 1960s. The group—bassist-keyboardist Peter Tork, singer/guitarist Michael Nesmith, singer / tambourine player Davy Jones, and singer/drummer Mickey Dolenz—auditioned for and landed their respective roles as members of the titular band in NBC's comedy *The Monkees*, which premiered in 1966 (Tork and Nesmith were already real musicians, while Jones and Dolenz came from theatrical backgrounds and would later learn to play "on the job," as it were). The show clicked with teenyboppers immediately and every week found the foursome getting into slapstick adventures and lip-synching to songs sourced by music coordinator Don Kirshner. Many of those songs, chiefly written by the team of Tommy Boyce and Bobby Hart, became huge hits. Although few then besides the Monkees' prepubescent fans and bean-counting overseers took these records seriously, time has shown them to be first-class rock 'n' roll creations with the same hard-hitting edges, sublime melodies, and sky-reaching heights as their hipper contemporaries. By 1967 the Monkees had proven themselves sufficiently to be granted creative control over their own music, and recorded a series of superb albums that showed their innate talents. Tork left in 1968 and was followed by Nesmith in 1969; with only Dolenz and Jones remaining, the Monkees released their ninth album in 1970 before splitting.

Opening with the exuberant TV show theme, 1966's *The Monkees* includes the jangling number one single "Last Train to Clarksville" and similarly garagey pop wonders like "Tomorrow's Gonna Be Another Day." *More of the Monkees* (1967) is even greater, with the fuzzed-up rockers "She," "Mary, Mary," "Your Auntie Grizelda," and, arguably, the definitive version of "(I'm Not Your) Stepping Stone," as well as the Neil Diamond–penned hits "Look Out (Here Comes Tomorrow)" and "I'm a Believer." The sessions for the same year's *Headquarters* (which this Monkees maniac considers their best album) were the first that saw the members mostly on their own in the studio, and the results are both commercially *and* artistically redeeming: Nesmith's uplifting "You Told Me" and "You Just May Be the One"; the movers "No Time," "Randy Scouse Git," and "For Pete's Sake"; and the tender Barry Mann–Cynthia Weil tune "Shades of Grey." Nineteen sixty-seven also brought *Pisces, Aquarius, Capricorn and Jones Ltd.*, which is best known for the sly suburban protest hit "Pleasant Valley Sunday" and bears the Beatles-esque "Salesman" and "Star Collector." The band overreached somewhat on 1968's ambitious *The Birds, the Bees and the Monkees*, but it's worthwhile for the sunny "Daydream Believer" and fuzz-flavored "Valleri." The Monkees went bananas in 1968's whacked-out film *Head*, which takes the surrealism of their NBC series to even weirder worlds. The soundtrack has Nesmith's Byrdsy "Circle Sky" and Tork's charging "Long Title: Do I Have to Do This All Over Again" but may challenge more in-the-pocket Ramones lovers with its overall psychedelic peculiarity. *The Best of the Monkees* has their top numbers and even comes with a five-song karaoke CD.

The Archies

Having learned his lesson, courtesy of the Monkees, about dealing with artistically rebellious human protégés, in 1967 Don Kirshner created the Archies, a band comprised of the characters on "The Archie Show," a Saturday morning animated series—secure in the knowledge that cartoon characters couldn't challenge their overlord. The show, based on the popular *Archie* comic books, ran from 1968 to 1972 and each week featured lead character Archie Andrews's garage band playing a new song. Released on Kirshner's own label, several of these ditties were composed by the magnate's old Brill Building pals, Jeff Barry and Ellie Greenwich (the latter even sang on a few), and were huge hits; the bubbly "Sugar, Sugar" was the biggest-selling pop single of 1969. The lead vocalist of the five-piece "band"—Archie himself—was studio singer Ron Dante, who also hit as the singer of another bubblegum act, the Cuff Links (1969's "Tracy"). As is the rule with bubblegum, a little of this stuff goes a long way. There were actually four albums released under the Archies name, but *Absolutely the Best of the Archies* should be good 'n' plenty, its effervescent cuts including "Sugar, Sugar," "Bang-Shang-A-Lang," "Jingle, Jangle," and "Sugar and Spice."

Tommy James and the Shondells

The Ramones must've been stoked to work with producer and songwriter Ritchie Cordell for 1983's *Subterranean Jungle*: in addition to being a former Kasenetz-Katz team member, Cordell had once called the shots for one of the foursome's fave sixties acts, Tommy James and the Shondells. Formed in Niles, Michigan, in 1960, when lead singer James was a mere thirteen, the Shondells broke up after their second indie single, a raw, clattering version of the Barry-Greenwich song "Hanky Panky," went nowhere. Three years later, James got a call from a promoter in Pittsburgh, where the song had become a local hit, and put together a new Shondells lineup, which snared a contract with the national Roulette Records and soon had a number one smash with the re-released "Hanky Panky." The chugging 1967 singles "I Think We're Alone Now" and "Mirage" saw the Shondells take their place as one of the decade's biggest hit machines, and the group made the Top Forty seven more times before James went solo in 1970.

Hanky Panky (1966) is a surprisingly decent frat/garage rock album that features several well-done R&B covers. The 1967 sophomore disc *It's Only Love* is disposable, but LP number three, *I Think We're Alone Now*, is the Shondells' most consistent album. Made up almost entirely of happy-bouncy Cordell compositions—save for the Isley Brothers' "Shout" and the Rivieras' (and you know who else's) "California Sun"—it's highlighted by "Mirage" and the namesake tune. Amid their pop-hit title tracks, the outfit's three fine 1968 albums, *Crimson and Clover*, *Gettin' Together*, and *Mony, Mony*, find James and company making assured moves into light psychedelia. For anthologies, tread lightly: Amazon is a minefield of dubious, quasi-legal Shondells comps. For the treetops, try *The Essentials*, which ends with James's first solo hit, 1971's "Draggin' the Line."

More Sweet Treats

Still can't get enough of those saccharine sounds? The above aren't the only rounds in the bubblegum bazooka. Also worthy of mention is Southern-born Tommy Roe, who emerged in the early 1960s as an adept Buddy Holly imitator with "Sheila" and "Everybody" before hitting the sugary stratosphere later in the decade with "Sweet Pea," "Hooray for Hazel," "Jam Up and Jelly Tight," and the contagious "Dizzy." His *Greatest Hits* has all of those and more. Wonderfully inane tracks by the Banana Splits and Josie and the Pussycats, the make-believe bands that starred on the so-named kids' shows, appear on the anthology *25 All-Time Greatest Bubblegum Hits*, which works well as a broad intro, combining familiar confections with obscurities by the likes of (yes!) Captain Groovy and His Bubblegum Army.

Raw power: It was the Ramones' shared admiration of the Stooges that first united them as friends. (Photofest)

3

ROAD TO RUIN:
THE RAMONES GET READY TO ROCK

We've talked about how vapid life in the early 1970s was becoming for real rock 'n' roll lovers—those who longed for the aggressive release of the music's founders, the fun sounds of the girl groups and bubblegum acts, and the raw buzz of the British Invasion and garage rock. By then all of that had largely gone the way of bouffants and Beatle boots. The Ramones would form in 1974 with the desire to make music that recaptured the feeling of rock's early years—and, almost on their own, they would create punk rock as we know it. Until they got the ball rolling, though, rock 'n' roll was drowning in a sea of boring, watery, middle-of-the road dreck. But that doesn't mean there weren't a few islands of salvation in those stale times. In fact, there was some utterly incredible music that, to varying degrees, markedly influenced the Ramones.

You had the head-banging hubris of early hard rock, which saw the tough rock 'n' roll of the mid-1960s develop into something even bigger and louder. There were also the acts today classified as proto-punk: rule-breaking pioneers who were *way* ahead of their time, making music on their own terms that flew in the face of most everything else and directly birthed the sounds and attitudes that later became synonymous with punk rock proper. Then there was the glitzy strut and big beat of glam rock, whose flashy style made musicians, and even their fans, feel like stars. And dotting the charts were a handful of guitar-oriented pop acts that kept alive the melodic motifs the Beatles had imparted. All of these undercurrents overlap and intersect on the timeline that leads up to the very first "One-two-three-four!" that launched the Ramones. So welcome to the dawn of the Me Decade, man. Have a nice day.

EARLY HARD ROCK

In the late sixties and early seventies, hard rock took the vigorous British Invasion and garage rock sounds that had come before and beefed them up with added volume and guitar distortion, heavier beats, and more expressive vocals. Hard rock's status as a precursor to heavy metal is obvious, and the two strains share many key elements, but the terms are not always interchangeable. What differentiates them is hard rock's strong blues base, which would largely evaporate as it evolved into heavy metal. Hard rock's main pioneers were Cream, Jimi Hendrix, and the Jeff Beck Group, and the teenage Ramones dug all three (in *Lobotomy* Dee Dee Ramone recalls Johnny Ramone's vivid remembrances of seeing Hendrix at Greenwich Village's Café Wha in 1966). But those bands were more about solos than the riffs our guys craved. The leader of the riff-centric generation that came next was Led Zeppelin, which over time turned away from its blues chord progressions and swing in favor of blockier rhythms and more exotic textures. Following Zep into the stadia were the likes of Deep Purple, Black Sabbath, Grand Funk Railroad, and Blue Öyster Cult, each of whom helped set the scene for the Ramones' sound—though transitional acts like these didn't wholly relinquish the lengthy jams and guitar solos that the Ramones' generation would jettison. Marky Ramone, as Marc Bell, got his start in high school with a hard rock band, Dust (see sidebar), and Tommy Ramone and Ramones road manager Monte Melnick once played in a similar group, Butch. Testosterone-heavy hard rock inspired punk sonically, and early on, like punk, was largely viewed as "loser" outsider music. In coming up with their sound, the Ramones took what they liked from hard rock: the crunching, distorted guitars, the vigorous rhythms, the dark vibe, and the intense loudness.

DUST

Today, Dust is all but lost to the sands of time. The hard-rocking New York proto-metal trio only released two LPs during its brief lifespan. Both of those rare albums were out of print for decades, precious artifacts long prized by collectors of early heavy metal, who still speak of the twin releases in reverent tones, thanks to their ear-bashing combination of post-garage raunch and British-style progressive rock. The discs are sought after by Ramones completists as well, since Dust featured a very young Marc Bell—the future Marky Ramone—on drums. The band also had connections to another well-known New York act, Kiss, whose first two albums would be co-produced by Dust singer and guitarist Richie Wise.

Dust, which also featured future session guru Kenny Aaronson (who later played with Bob Dylan, the reunited New York Dolls, and many others) on bass and occasional slide guitar, was formed in Brooklyn in the late sixties and basically existed during Marky's high school years. The group signed with Kama Sutra, a label best known as the home of Top 40 pop-folk act the Lovin' Spoonful, which unveiled its self-titled debut in 1971. Housed in an arresting cover with a grim black-and-white photo of mummified corpses on the front and a back panel shot of the band sporting jeans, long hair, and black leather motorcycle jackets—six years before the first Ramones album—Dust clearly wasn't a disc that was going to be snapped up by Spoonful fans. Noticeably influenced by another local hard rock trio, Mountain, the album has a couple of dated duds; "Goin' Easy" is dull country blues, and the mystic-hippie "Often Shadows Felt" is a lukewarm Ten Years After pastiche. But such flaccid lows are outweighed by tough winners like the Mountain-esque "Chasin' Ladies," the twisting epic "From a Dry Camel," and Aaronson's frenzied "Loose Goose," which sounds suspiciously like a heavy metal update of the Rock-A-Teens' 1959 rockabilly hit, "Woo-Hoo." While it does have some moments of de rigueur hippy-dippyness, 1972's *Hard Attack* mostly finds the threesome reworking their sound in line with the album's title and Viking-depicting Frank Frazetta artwork. It's vicious stuff, from the tumultuous opener "Pull

Away / So Many Times" to the punishing "Suicide" (with a mind-blowing Aaronson bass solo) and Mr. Bell/Ramone's unstoppable pounding on the instrumental "Ivory."

Vanilla Fudge

Among the local heroes during the Ramones' upbringing was Vanilla Fudge, which bridged psychedelia and hard rock. The Long Island quartet of organist Mark Stein, bassist Tim Bogert, guitarist Vinny Martell, and drummer Carmine Appice, all of whom contributed vocals, began in 1966 as the Electric Pigeons. After signing to Atco, the group changed its name to Vanilla Fudge (it's arguable if the new name was really an improvement) and began hammering out albums that stuck largely to its method of taking soul and pop tunes and doing them louder, harder, longer, and much, much slower. It's a formula that grows tiresome quickly, but for a brief window of time it was radical—and of course it's not the Fudge's lumbering tempos that play into the Ramones' art; it's the band's sheer volume. In addition to the brontosaurus-like, Top Forty hit interpretation of the Supremes' "You Keep Me Hangin' On," 1967's covers-only *Vanilla Fudge* features groaning versions of the Beatles' "Eleanor Rigby" and "Ticket to Ride." *Renaissance* (1968) has more originals, but its high point is the spooked-out adaptation of Donovan's "Season of the Witch." The same year's *The Beat Goes On* is for the bold, a half-baked concept album designed to chronicle Western history. *Near the Beginning* (1969) rocks much harder, centering on the twenty-four-minute (!) noise-fest "Break Song." While it's hard to recommend the leaden Vanilla Fudge to Ramones fans, the band had its magisterial moments and was a staple of the New York scene during a pivotal time. See how *Psychedelic Sundae: The Best of Vanilla Fudge* tastes.

Blue Cheer

To some, San Francisco power trio Blue Cheer was not only America's first true hard rock band, but also a harbinger of punk and grunge. Touted at the time as the world's loudest group, the original lineup—bassist/screamer Dickie Peterson, guitarist Leigh Stephens, and drummer Paul Whaley—hammered out two albums of earsplitting acid/biker toughness that'll put hair on your chest. Inspired by Cream and Jimi Hendrix, the threesome took its name from a strain of LSD developed by Owsley Stanley. Stanley penned the liner notes for Blue Cheer's 1968 debut, *Vincebus Eruptum*, home to the band's only hit, a crushing cover of Eddie Cochran's "Summertime Blues." The rest of the album is no less brutal, with bludgeoning, feedback-fueled stompers ("Out of Focus," "Doctor Please") and wailing biker-blues workouts ("Rock Me Baby," "Parchman Farm"). If you like loud—and I know you do—this one's mandatory. Only months later in '68 the band returned with *Outsideinside*, among whose hard 'n' heavy cuts is a destructive rendition of the Rolling Stones' "Satisfaction" (take that, Devo!). After that, lineups changed, things got folky, and 1980s rote-metal reunions happened.

Steppenwolf

Another band with a well-documented biker following, Steppenwolf began in Toronto in 1963 as Jack London and the Sparrow. In 1965, with new additions like singer John Kay, the group became, simply, the Sparrow and moved to California to work the San Francisco–Los Angeles psychedelic circuit. Once there, it became Steppenwolf after adopting a harder, heavier style. "Born to Be Wild," from *Steppenwolf*, the group's 1968 debut, has been cited as giving the heavy metal genre its name (see the line "heavy metal thunder"), and its blazing E-chord riff presages the Ramones' catalog. With its punky production, the album is very much a garage record, although the songwriting and Kay's boozy rasp keep it firmly in the blues rock camp. Nineteen sixty-eight's *The Second* is another roaring excursion, with the clattering hit "Magic Carpet Ride," the growling pot-protest piece "Don't Step on the Grass, Sam," and the soul-mashing "Tighten Up Your Wig." *At Your Birthday Party*, from 1969, is thinner overall but does have some gritty psych-soul gems ("Rock Me") and gut-bucket grinders ("Jupiter's Child"). And that's pretty much the highway Steppenwolf traveled from there on out, cutting more LPs that have, at best, a couple of okay tunes. For the high points, *16 Greatest Hits* leads the pack.

Mountain

Mountain had a home-hitting connection for the impressionable young bruddas: the band's lead singer and guitarist extraordinaire, Leslie West, was raised in Forest Hills. Early on, he became one of Johnny's favorite guitar players as a member of the excellent local garage band the Vagrants (see *I Can't Make a Friend 1965–1968*). Mountain itself had a strong link to West's own guitar idol, Eric Clapton; the group's bassist, Felix Pappalardi, had produced Clapton's band, Cream. Today, a lot of Mountain's recorded music sounds very much of its time: choogling, Cream-dipping, heavy blues rock with the rambling improvs the Ramones railed against. But, in keeping with the above observations, da brudders left behind what was lame about Mountain and retained what was good. And what was good was mostly West's guitar—hard, searing, and *loud*.

The genesis of Mountain is potentially confusing. In 1969, West recorded a solo album titled *Mountain*. Pappalardi produced and performed with drummer N. D. Smart (ex-Remains; see Chapter Two) on the LP, which is technically the first release by the band Mountain, which named itself after West's album. Got that? Anyway, *Mountain* is a heap of head-nodding stoner rock topped by West's whiskey-throated roar, and generally heavier than the proper Mountain albums that followed. As a live unit, Mountain made its debut at the Woodstock festival, soon after replacing Smart with Corky Laing for 1970's *Climbing!* That disc includes the band's wailing signature single, "Mississippi Queen," and its fellow cowbell-driven rockers "Never in My Life" and "Sittin' on a Rainbow." *Nantucket Sleighride* (1971) has a few worthy bangers, but with the title track and more similarly maudlin Pappalardi tunes, Mountain's creative crumbling was beginning. The studio-slanted *Best of Mountain* is the accepted career survey, but as Mountain was at its peak live, *Setlist: The Very Best of Mountain Live* stands tallest.

Led Zeppelin

Led Zeppelin is considered the first real heavy metal band, a godlike force to Iron Maiden, Metallica, and most other modern metal acts. But how does the often virtuosic music of Led Zeppelin, a band seen by naysayers as the very preening paragon of bloated seventies excess, connect to the dead-simple style of the Ramones? It's not such a stretch, really. When they got together as a band the Ramones wanted to rock, hard, and at that time Led Zeppelin was the world's defining hard rock band. So it's natural that the British foursome would be a reference point for our young blitzkriegers. Zep's reputation as one of rock's top bands is justified; sure, singer Robert Plant's high-register wailing can grate, but Jimmy Page (Johnny Ramone's favorite guitarist) is an absolute *monster* of riffs, and the brutally hard, impossibly tight team of drummer John Bonham and bassist John Paul Jones is arguably rock's greatest-ever rhythm section. Glints of Led Zeppelin's sound are perceptible in what the Queens quartet did; just compare Zep's rip-snorting 1969 "Communication Breakdown" with most any fast Ramones song. While all eight of Zep's studio LPs have their aggressive interludes, it's the first two, 1969's *Led Zeppelin* and 1970's *Led Zeppelin II*, that have the most. The first, a favorite of Marky Ramone, has pummelers like "How Many More Times" and the ominous "Dazed and Confused." *Led Zeppelin II* was an even more influential template for later hard rock acts, the hypnotic, powerful riffs of tracks like the chugging "Whole Lotta Love" and the downer-droning "Heartbreaker" knocking their way into the brains of our bruddas and millions of other headbangers. *Led Zeppelin III* (1970) commences with the charging "Immigrant Song" and goes on to explore the English folk influences that would likewise permeate 1971's *Led Zeppelin IV*, an album that is nevertheless also home to the muscular "Black Dog," "Rock and Roll," and "Misty Mountain Hop." *Houses of the Holy* (1973) also has both rocking and subtle passages, but points more toward later albums, where Page, as the producer, embraces the studio itself, adding more colors and complexities than many Ramones fans may want to hear. *Coda*, an outtakes collection released in 1982, is notable for the runaway-locomotive "Wearing and Tearing," touted as the group's response to punk. The two-CD *Mothership* is the best Led Zeppelin career synopsis on offer.

Black Sabbath

Early Black Sabbath is the very embodiment of boulder-hurling caveman *rawk*—and a foundational element of the Ramones' music. The Ramones' innovation of crossing Sabbath's thickly distorted guitars and linear, riff-driven sound with the sunny, good-time surf melodies of the Beach Boys was an act of forehead-slapping genius. (The Ramones even toured as the opening act for Black Sabbath in 1978, although the hostile reception from the headliner's Neanderthal audiences forced them off the tour.) Black Sabbath was formed in Birmingham, England, by guitarist Tony Iommi, singer Ozzy Osbourne, drummer Bill Ward, and bassist Geezer Butler in 1968, and its first four albums are hard rock imperatives. Nineteen seventy's *Black Sabbath* raised the bar for both volume and heaviness in post-psychedelic hard rock, and is the mother of all the stoner sludge-rock and grunge bands that followed. Its gravel-grinders, "The Wizard," "N.I.B.," and the slow-as-molasses title track, eviscerate the blues and reflect the band's bleak origins in industrial England. *Paranoid*, released later that year, stands as one of the genre's all-time most important albums. Like Led Zeppelin's "Communication Breakdown," the influence of its title tune is readily apparent in much of the Ramones' work. Also fine is 1971's *Masters of Reality*, which opens with the choking cough that kicks off "Sweat Leaf," the rock-crushing, pot-smoking ode that's one of Sabbath's signature jams. The short but seismic *Masters* packs still more highs, like the battering "Children of the Grave." *Vol. 4* (1972) sees the encroachment of out-of-character ballads ("Changes"), but is, by and large, another monolithic winner thanks to destructive tracks like the über-heavy "Supernaut" and the galloping "Tomorrow's Dream." Nineteen seventy-three brought *Sabbath Bloody Sabbath*, whose pulverizing namesake cut is one of the band's most crucial performances. *Sabotage (1975)* is the last record of Sab's glory years, marked by the maulers "Hole in the Sky" and "Symptom of the Universe," the latter clearly forecasting late-eighties thrash metal. After two subsequent, disastrous LPs, Ozzy was out and the band eased into a protracted decline matched only by its slowest, sludgiest riffs. *Symptom of the Universe: The Original Black Sabbath 1970–1973* summarizes the paramount Ozzy years.

Deep Purple

After Led Zeppelin and Black Sabbath, the final jewel in the triumvirate of classic British hard rock is Deep Purple. Deep Purple was founded by guitarist Ritchie Blackmore in 1968, the band's original lineup also including keyboardist Jon Lord, drummer Ian Paice, and vocalist Rod Evans. After three very listenable hard-psych albums and U.S.-hit versions of Joe South's "Hush" and Neil Diamond's "Kentucky Woman," Evans was replaced by Ian Gillan. It's this lineup, the so-called Mark II edition of the band, that's responsible for some of hard rock's most edificial riffs, and its three-studio album run for Warner Bros. (from 1970 to 1972) is just the spot to bang your head on. Gillan's ear-piercing voice is, of course, universes away from Joey Ramone's Ronettes-schooled tenor, and Lord's classical touches sometimes get in the way of the rock action. But the Mark II Purps' collective energy is fist-pumpingly addictive and tends to outweigh any extraneous ballast. Exhibit A: 1970's *In Rock*, which roars off the line with "Speed King," "Flight of the Rat," and "Black Night." *Fireball* (1971) is rockin', too. Its fast-shooting title track burns like the five-headed meteor on the cover, and is followed by the Hendrixian "No No No" and Gillan's amusing treatise on the travails of band life, "No One Came." It's 1972's *Machine Head*, though, that stands as the group's granite pillar. Yeah, we've all heard the lurching classic rocker "Smoke on the Water" way too many times (perhaps one day that loitering guitar store jerk will surprise us with a Ramones song instead), but, with or without that hoary chestnut, *Machine Head* is a righteous hunk of heaviosity that shakes the ground with the accelerated screamers "Highway Star" and "Space Truckin.'" Lord's overdriven Hammond organ never sounded this great again. Unfortunately, neither did Deep Purple. The band's purple patch is well served by *The Very Best of Deep Purple*.

Grand Funk Railroad

This squad was one of the biggest-selling bands of the 1970s. A byproduct of the same fertile Michigan rock scene that gave us proto-punkers the MC5 and the Stooges, Grand Funk Railroad—singer/guitarist Mark Farner, bassist Mel Schacher, and drummer Don Brewer—coalesced in 1968. Schacher was a veteran of ? and the Mysterians (see Chapter Two), while Farner and Brewer came from another garage band, Terry Knight and the Pack. The group reached its commercial zenith with the mid-seventies monster hits "We're an American Band" and "The Locomotion," but before all that, the hairy, frequently shirtless group dealt in the kind of brutish, gloriously stoopid simian rock so adored by the nascent Ramones. In *Commando*, Johnny names a 1970 GFR concert at Stony Brook University as "probably the loudest show I ever saw." High praise, indeed.

Other than the wired "Are You Ready," the Yardbirds-referencing "Into the Sun," and the crashing "High on a Horse," *On Time*, the trio's 1969 debut, is a patchy document of a group figuring out its sound. The band's best studio effort is 1970's *Grand Funk*, an overload of tough grunters propelled by Schacher's walking bass lines; see "Got This Thing on the Move," the version of the Animals' "Inside Looking Out," and "In Need." The big-production *Closer to Home* (1970) should be passed over in favor of the same year's fantastic *Live Album*. This bravura heap of fuzzed-out bass, ham-fisted guitar, and trashy tub thumping is an oil-smeared mess that beats everything else the Funk ever did. *Heavy Hitters!* has representative raw, early cuts.

Hawkwind

In Everett True's Ramones history *Hey Ho Let's Go*, Craig Leon, who produced the band's 1976 debut, cites acid-prog outfit Hawkwind as a massive influence on the Ramones' unyieldingly droney guitar sound. The formula of *Ramones*, Leon says, can be distilled down to the Beatles' "A Hard Day's Night" and Hawkwind's "Silver

Machine" (echoes of our earlier "Beach Boys meet Black Sabbath" analogy). And early Hawkwind's whirring, heavily distorted guitars and relentless rhythms were clearly on the Ramones' radar. Few others in early 1970s America were hip to Hawkwind. But that wasn't so much the case in the British band's homeland, where it was one of the leading attractions on the underground and college circuits and a motivator of British punks.

Formed in 1969 by singer/guitarist Dave Brock and singer/saxophonist/flutist Nik Turner, Hawkwind has one of the longest and most convoluted lineup histories in rock. The band's science fiction themes (sci-fi novelist Michael Moorcock contributed lyrics) and druggy aesthetic, and member Dikmik Davies's squealing, blipping electronics, made it an avatar of what came to be called space rock. But lest ye think this was nothing but a band of tripping hippies making free-floating music—although at times that's exactly what it was—consider this: Hawkwind's 1971–1975 label lineup featured future Motörhead singer/bassist Lemmy Kilmister (the song "Motorhead," for which his band is named, was originally a Hawkwind tune).

Hawkwind's psychedelic, eponymously titled 1970 debut is influenced by early Pink Floyd, and likely a bit "out there" for Ramones nuts. The following year's *In Search of Space*, though, is something else. It includes the recently recruited poet-vocalist Robert Calvert, blasts off with the rocket-fueled "You Shouldn't Do That," and features the grunge-meets-synths haze of "Master of the Universe" (the CD reissue tacks on the above-mentioned single "Silver Machine"). Lemmy joined in time for 1972's *Doremi Fasol Latido*, which has more meandering psychedelia but also packs a harder punch, as exemplified by the roaring "Brainstorm" and "Time We Left This World Today." It's 1973's double-live *Space Ritual*, however, that best represents the classic Hawkwind lineup. Recorded in Leeds and London, it shows, by way of unstoppable stompers like "Orgone Accumulator" and Calvert's surrealistic showpiece—wait for it—"Space is Deep," just how loud and musically searching Hawkwind concerts could be (if only one could see Stacia, the band's six-foot-two, iridescent-painted nude dancer).

Hall of the Mountain Grill, from 1974, is regarded by most as the band's best studio album. Fortified with extra crunch from Brock, it's a record that's not hard to imagine being spun at glue-sniffing sessions in certain Queens basements back in the day. Besides being Hawkwind's last great studio release, 1975's *Warrior on the Edge of Time*, with the blazing "Assault and Battery," "Magnu," and "Kings of Speed," is the band's final record with Lemmy, who was kicked out after its release and soon started Motörhead. Myriad personnel changes have brought less interesting records since then, despite Hawkwind's remaining a beloved live unit. *Psychedelic Warlords* gives the best glimpse of the group's brain-damaged 1970–1975 highs.

Blue Öyster Cult

Hawkwind wasn't the only band Michael Moorcock graced with his futuristic lyrics. He also penned words for Blue Öyster Cult—as did rock critic Richard Meltzer, fantasy writer Eric Van Lustbader, and poet/punk priestess Patti Smith. The band's classic configuration, the one responsible for its heavier early material as well as subdued radio hits like "(Don't Fear) The Reaper," consisted of singer/guitarist Eric Bloom, lead guitarist Donald "Buck Dharma" Roeser, keyboardist Allen Lanier, and brothers Albert and Joe Bouchard on, respectively, drums and bass. Formed in 1967 as Soft White Underbelly, after several name changes the band signed to Columbia as Blue Öyster Cult, the new moniker after cryptic characters in the sci-fi poetry of manager/lyricist Sandy Pearlman. The Cult's members were habitués of New York's early punk scene (for a time Lanier and Patti Smith were an item), and even tapped the Ramones as the opener for some of their big-venue shows— but our boys were about as well-received as they were when they warmed up for Black Sabbath (read: with open hostility). Although BÖC's vanguard stuff is more complex and multilayered than the Ramones', it rocks plenty hard. And some of it's even funny (e.g., "She's as Beautiful as a Foot"). Nineteen seventy-two's semi-psychedelic *Blue Öyster Cult* was produced by Pearlman, who went on to work with the Dictators and the Clash, and shows the band was still finding its (beautiful?) feet. But the presence of monsters like the live favorite "Cities on Flame with Rock and Roll" hints at the further heaviness on the horizon—which began in earnest with 1973's *Tyranny and Mutation*. That disc kicks open with the hyper-speed "The Red and the Black" and keeps the energy burning with "Hot Rails to Hell" and "Baby Ice Dog" (the latter with lyrics by Patti Smith). It's 1974's *Secret Treaties*, though, that's the Cult's crucial classic. Smith contributes lyrics to this one, too, which blazes with the merciless "Dominance and Submission" and the speed-freak boogie of "ME 262." *Secret Treaties* is a known proto-metal masterpiece, but as a proto-punk milestone to early punkers from Seattle to London to Melbourne it continues to fly under the radar. Nineteen seventy-five's live *On Your Feet or On Your Knees* features smoldering tunes from the first three LPs alongside fiery renditions of Steppenwolf and the Yardbirds. Thanks to "(Don't Fear) The Reaper," the big breakthrough was 1976's *Agents of Fortune*, which also includes the band's scorching retooling of L.A. proto-punkers the Imperial Dogs' "This Ain't the Summer of Love," the wicked "Tattoo Vampire," and more Patti cowrites. *Spectres* (1977) is overly slick, but of interest are the hulking, hilarious "Godzilla" and songwriting collaborations with Mott the Hoople's Ian Hunter and New York punk Helen Wheels. *Some Enchanted Evening*, another volatile live set, came out in 1978 and offers storming versions of the MC5's "Kick Out the Jams" and the Animals' "We Gotta Get Outta This Place." The live-leaning *Career of Evil: The Metal Years* is the foremost BÖC intro.

AC/DC

Australia's AC/DC is, beyond argument, one of the greatest hard rock groups the Earth has produced. And in many ways the band could be seen as the Ramones' rowdy cousins from down under. Think about it. Those simple, granite-hard, and irresistibly catchy riffs. That minimal, unwaveringly solid backbeat. That tough, unpretentious, juvenile delinquent image and sick, schoolboy humor. Although long branded a metal act, because of timing and the above assets AC/DC was initially considered a punk band. (In 1977, after rocking New York's Palladium, the antipodean outfit was even welcomed for an impromptu set at CBGB.) It's no shock that the Ramones were ardent fans. With his fifteen-year-old, school uniform–sporting younger brother Angus, Sydney guitarist Malcolm Young formed AC/DC in 1973 after the demise of his earlier band, which was called the Velvet Underground (no relation to the legendary New York band covered below). After recruiting its third singer, the charismatic Bon Scott, and conquering its homeland, the band headed to England, where it found a receptive audience in the nascent punk scene. *High Voltage* (1976) is the first of a string of six of hard rock's most essential albums. Opening with the chop-shop boogie of "It's a Long Way to the Top (If You Wanna Rock 'n' Roll)," it sets the template for prime early AC/DC: thick, unyielding, pile-driver riffs offset by Angus Young's bluesy, gut-tearing leads and Scott's lewd, throat-scraping vocals. The same year's *Dirty Deeds Done Dirt Cheap*, not released in America until 1981, is another killer chunk of brutish rock, with the badass, gangster-themed title tune and the slamming, middle-finger-flipping "Problem Child." The following year's *Let There Be Rock* is one of the band's most bracing studio efforts and perhaps the best of the whole Bon Scott era, home to the raging, raucous title ode to rock 'n' roll itself and the sleazy signature "Whole Lotta Rosie." *Powerage* (1978) is yet another bottomless notch in the band's impeccable early canon, with the thumping "Rock 'n' Roll Damnation," the thundering "Sin City," and the skull-crushing "Kicked in the Teeth." The same year's live *If You Want Blood You've Got It* is a balls-to-the-wall throwdown that sends most other "heavy rock" acts of the day scampering back to their moms. Scott died from alcoholic overindulgence just a few months after the release of 1979's *Highway to Hell*, another band landmark and, in a way, the perfect epitaph for the late singer. Besides its storming namesake track, it boasts the punk-esque punch-outs "Touch Too Much" and "Shot Down in Flames." After some soul searching by the band, new vocalist Brian Johnson was brought in for *Back in Black*, one of the most massive—in every sense of the word—rock albums ever made. You know the hits—"Hell's Bells," "Back in Black," "You Shook Me All Night Long"—but the deep cuts are just as strong: the manic "Shoot to Thrill," the ribald "Have a Drink on Me," the righteous "Rock and Roll Ain't Noise Pollution." Once you've built the mountain and stand atop it, though, it's difficult to remain up there forever, and AC/DC's later discography is mostly a downhill trudge. (Exceptions: 1981's *For Those About to Rock We Salute You*, 1983's *Flick of the Switch*, and 2001's *Stiff Upper Lip*.)

A Handful of Heavy Friends

There are some other early hard rock acts that Ramones fans may want to investigate, if only to get a feel for the context of the members' comeuppance. Iron Butterfly is remembered (or loathed, depending on where you stand) for "In-A-Gadda-Da-Vida," a moaning stoner epic that hit the U.S. Top Thirty. Led by singer and organist Doug Ingle, these California acid heads chiseled out two albums that warrant a spin: 1968's well-named debut *Heavy* and the same year's *In-A-Gadda-Da-Vida*, which shoulders the entire unedited, seventeen-minute title opus. Detroit's Frijid Pink sprang from the tough late-sixties Detroit landscape. The overlooked, Cream-inspired quartet released five LPs before packing it in in 1975. The first two are well worth tracking down. *Frijid Pink* (1970) is a monster, laden with fuzz-overloaded burners like the Pink's biggest hit, a sizzling version of "House of the Rising Sun." Also from 1970 is *Defrosted*, which offers more of Gary Ray Thompson's tumbling fuzz guitar and singer Kelly Green's gruff growl. From the streets of Brooklyn came Sir Lord Baltimore, whose 1970 debut, *Kingdom Come*, is an exercise in distorted, shuddering noise and savage tempos that forecasts punk, hardcore, thrash metal, and later grungy stoner/sludge sounds. Like its fellow Aussie act AC/DC, Rose Tattoo blurs the line between punk and blue-collar hard rock and originated at roughly the same time as the Ramones. Fronted by sawed-off, bald-headed screamer Gary "Angry" Anderson and cofounded by Oz punk stalwart bassist Ian Rilen, Rose Tat played its first gig in 1976. The quintet's 1978 debut, *Rose Tattoo*, is filled with pissed-off, perfectly subhuman songs about fistfights, whiskey, bad women, and more fistfights. With the anthemic "Rock 'n' Roll

Is King" and other nose-breakers, 1981's *Assault and Battery* doesn't let up, either. *Scarred for Life* (1982) is okay, but some listeners may find the scales tipping a tad too far into caricature. Begin with the first two or the double-disc anthology *Never Too Loud*.

PROTO-PUNK

Proto-punk is an even more nebulous term than hard rock is. Some trace its beginnings to the British Invasion and garage rock periods we covered in the last chapter (or even earlier in music history), but for our purposes proto-punk is an after-the-fact name for a loose grouping of pioneering, highly idiosyncratic bands that existed between the late 1960s and the beginnings of punk itself in 1975 and 1976. Proto-punk bands vary greatly in their musical methodology, taking in such diverse sounds as the pinched-nose folk obscenity of the Fugs; the dark, urban reality of the Velvet Underground; the primal pounding and deafening guitars of the MC5 and the Stooges; the avant squall of Captain Beefheart; glam crossover acts like the New York Dolls and Alice Cooper; and the back-to-basics rock 'n' roll of the Flamin' Groovies. Whatever their approach, what links these bastard iconoclasts together is their collective desire to challenge the dull, manufactured, post-hippie musical zeitgeist that dominated their day, and their decisive influence on the punk rebellion that followed it. The two-volume series *Dirty Water: The Birth of Punk Attitude* stretches the punk-roots concept from wild 1950s rockabilly and R&B acts through sixties garagers, the in-between period covered in this section, and straight up to punk proper's initial rumblings.

The Fugs

America's original underground rock band, the Fugs were formed by the Beat poets Ed Sanders, Tuli Kupferberg, and Ken Weaver in 1964. Backed by a changeable gaggle of mostly very amateurish local folk and jug band musicians, the three wordsmiths kicked up a shambolic acoustic din capped by hilarious, irreverent lyrics that pushed the limits of the day's moral decency and screamed with satirical sociopolitical commentary (the band's name came from a publisher's euphemism for the word "fuck" as used in Norman Mailer's novel *The Naked and the Dead*) and frequently referenced classic literature. The Fugs' rebellious, middle-finger stance led to their being monitored and harassed by the government and made them a regular presence at anti–Vietnam War rallies and other protest events. Next to the Ramones and their peers, the Fugs may sound like a gang of tone-deaf, scatologically obsessed lit majors–cum–folk players. But that's what makes them kindred spirits: they had something to say and didn't let their mere lack of musicianship keep them from saying it.

Released in 1965 as *The Village Fugs Sing Ballads of Contemporary Protest, Point of Views [sic], and General Dissatisfaction* and repackaged in 1966 as *The Fugs First Album*, the band's debut is a ramshackle riot with such baying crudities as "C.I.A. Man," "I Couldn't Get High," and "Boobs a Lot." The following year's *The Fugs*, which eventually reappeared as *The Fugs Second Album*, carries the insanely stomping "Frenzy," the lecherous "Dirty Old Man," and the anti-war "Kill for Peace." *Virgin Fugs* (1967) is a wealth of more clattering, ribald romps ("New Amphetamine Shriek," "Coca Cola Douche"), and 1968's *Tenderness Junction*, pairs the vocalists with musicians of more professional proficiency yet still retains some raw edges. *Don't Stop! Don't Stop!* compiles the first two albums plus rarities.

The Velvet Underground

Haunting the same mid-sixties Lower East Side neighborhood as the Fugs was the Velvet Underground, the group most today view as the first true proto-punk band. The Velvets—singer/guitarist Lou Reed, singer/bassist/violist/organist John Cale, guitarist Sterling Morrison, drummer Maureen Tucker, and erstwhile singer Nico—combined repetitive, primitive riffs with intense volume, feedback, and distortion; dark, taboo-shattering lyrics; and a keen sense of pop melody. While the decidedly avant band was at best dismissed or ignored by the few who heard it at the time, the VU's influence became the inverse of its lack of commercial success.

Reed and Cale met in 1964 and became interested in forming a group that crossed rock 'n' roll with the avant-garde. Taking the project's name from an S&M novel, they added Morrison and Tucker, the latter helping crystallize the sound with her rigidly metronomic beats. The band's dissonant, unconventional songs about drugs, sex, and urban fringe lifestyles attracted pop art icon Andy Warhol, who became its manager, added the eye-catching German chanteuse Nico to the lineup, and produced its arresting 1967 debut, *The Velvet Underground and Nico*. On the album's misty, drugged-out "Venus in Furs," Reed explores the forbidden world of S&M; Nico's icy voice hovers like the ghost of Marlene Dietrich over the dreamy, singsong pop of "Femme Fatale" and "Sunday Morning"; and Reed's and Morrison's tough downstrokes on "I'm Waiting for the Man" foretell the punk guitar style. *White Light / White Heat* (1968) dispenses with Nico and amps up the drugs, the sex, and, especially, the noise; the strangulated "I Heard Her Call My Name" and the nearly eighteen-minute depravity tale "Sister Ray" are speaker-shredding. Cale was out and Doug Yule was in for 1969's *The Velvet Underground*, which is largely quieter, as exemplified by the tender "Pale Blue Eyes" and the Yule-sung "Candy Says." Still, it's not without aggression; check "What Goes On" and "Beginning to See the Light." *Loaded* (1970) is the Velvets' most radio-friendly album—albeit one that shakes hands on the group's own terms, with two of Reed's most enduring songs, the chunky-riffed proto–power popper "Sweet Jane" and the liberating "Rock and Roll." The box set *Peel Slowly and See* has the essential first three LPs and more revealing riches and is vehemently recommended.

Joey Ramone was especially enamored of Reed's early solo albums, the chief ones of interest being 1972's David Bowie-produced *Transformer*, known for the gender-bending hit "Walk on the Wild Side" and the rough rocker "Vicious," and 1974's live *Rock 'n' Roll Animal*. Nineteen seventy-eight's stripped-back *Street Hassle*, which sees Reed claiming his place as a punk progenitor, is also worthy.

The Doors

The Doors? Punks? Hell, yes. Okay, you can't turn on the FM

without hearing their hits among the classic rock pabulum, and when taken on their own Jim Morrison's lyrics and theatrical style approach the overwrought. But, nevertheless, the Doors were defiant, darkly driven provocateurs whose hard, adventurous, and haunting sound and performances flew in the face of polite pop and laid the stage for Ramones idols the Stooges (see later). The infamously selective Johnny Ramone even named them as his favorite American band. The Doors—Morrison, keyboardist Ray Manzarek, guitarist Robbie Krieger, and drummer John Densmore—got their start in Los Angeles in 1965. *The Doors* (1967) is best known for the Baroque bossa nova of "Light My Fire," a tune that's been neutered by hack versions by everyone from José Feliciano to Woody Herman. But don't let that put you off. It's one of rock's foremost debuts, an id-baring classic that takes flight with the propulsive "Break On Through" and descends into a murky, swirling maelstrom encompassing more hard-hitting garage rockers ("Take It as It Comes—covered on the Ramones' *Mondo Bizarro*—and "Twentieth Century Fox") and mystery-shrouded psych-outs ("End of the Night," the terrifying, eleven-minute "The End"). *Strange Days*, also from 1967, has the blues-vamping, sexually suggestive "Love Me Two Times," the Brechtian "People Are Strange," and another intense, eleven-minute closer, "When the Music's Over" (whose line "We want the world and we want it now" the Ramones borrowed for "We Want the Airwaves"). *Waiting for the Sun* (1968) is slightly more autumnal, but has no shortage of aggressive interludes (the fuzz guitar–singed "Hello, I Love You," and the menacing "Five to One"). Morrison's loungey crooning and the big-production brass of "Touch Me" from 1969's uneven *The Soft Parade* divided fans, but the album has reliably pounding cuts like "Wild Child" and "Shaman's Blues." In 1970, *Morrison Hotel* marked a concerted return to raw hard rock with grinders like "Roadhouse Blues" and and "Maggie M'Gill." The group's final official album, 1971's *L.A. Woman*, is another triumph, and centers on the lengthy title track, a sprawling, speed-building paean to the highways and gutters of the band's hometown. After Morrison died of an apparent drug overdose the surviving Doors cut two forgettable albums. *Legacy: The Best of the Doors* does an excellent job of balancing the chart busters with lesser-heard tracks.

The MC5

"Kick out the jams, motherfuckers!" is the battle cry that begins *Kick Out the Jams*, the MC5's roaring 1969 debut. Once you've had your head smashed by this thunder-clapping album of righteous, revolutionary ramalama, it will come as no surprise that the Ramones were indelibly motivated by the Detroit band. Starting in 1964 as the Motor City Five, the quintet of vocalist Rob Tyner, guitarists Wayne Kramer and Fred "Sonic" Smith, bassist Michael Davis, and drummer Dennis "Machine Gun" Thompson were inspired by the Who, the Yardbirds, and the Rolling Stones, and became the house band at the Grande Ballroom, the city's main underground rock venue. The group's politically radical manager John Sinclair helped broker a deal with Elektra Records (Danny Fields, Elektra's A&R man, also signed the Stooges and later managed the Ramones). *Kick Out the Jams* is the very embodiment of the term "high energy," one of the most powerful albums ever made. Recorded live, it captures the MC5 blasting full-bore, courtesy of the deadly guitars of Kramer and Smith, Tyner's soul-searing voice, and the unyielding force of Davis and Thompson. It's an A-bomb blast, with gate-crashers like "Borderline" and the volatile title track.

The MC5 never quite matched *Kick Out the Jams*, but the two studio LPs that followed are excellent, nonetheless. *Back in the USA* (1970) cooks with a tight, streamlined drive, opening and closing with hot-wired Little Richard and Chuck Berry covers; its rowdy themes of disenfranchised youth burn with the boisterous "Tonight," "Teenage Lust," "High School," "Call Me Animal," and show-stopping "Looking at You." Nineteen seventy-one's swan song *High Time* is more ambitious (horns!) and has some of the band's hardest-hitting songs: "Sister Anne," Smith's roiling guitar workout "Skunk (Sonically Speaking)," and the shuddering "Poison," which of all the MC5's tunes perhaps best encapsulates the band's Molotov cocktail of avant-jazz leanings, radical rhetoric, and super-hard rock. *Big Bang: The Best of the MC5* collates cuts from the above albums and early singles.

The Stooges

Perhaps the greatest and most direct influence on the Ramones was the Stooges. It was the Ramones' shared admiration of the Detroit-area wild men that first united them as friends, and they sometimes described their music as "bubblegum meets the Stooges." Through their music and their unhinged front man, Iggy Pop, the Stooges plugged straight into the primal promise of rock 'n' roll, more than any other act of their time. Their reward for such bravery and commitment? Being reviled by the rock world at large, which saw them as mellow-harshing freaks and ran the other way—or pelted them with rotten eggs and bottles. This made the Stooges outsiders, and actually *liking* them was something only weirdoes did. "There was, like, maybe three people in the whole area [Forest Hills] who liked the Stooges, and everyone else was violently against them," recalls Dee Dee in the film *End of the Century*. "So if you liked the Stooges you had to be friends with each other."

Moved by a love of Chicago blues, British Invasion bands, the Velvet Underground, Jimi Hendrix, and the Doors, Iggy Pop (born James Osterberg, he'd once drummed for garage bands the Iguanas and the Prime Movers) formed the Stooges in 1967 in Ann Arbor, Michigan, with brothers Ron (guitar) and Scott Asheton (drums) and Dave Alexander (bass). While thumping out earsplitting, Cro-Magnon rhythms behind an insanely shrieking Iggy—who often cut himself with glass on stage, dove into the audience, and smeared his shirtless body in blood and peanut butter—the band performed to mainly unreceptive Midwestern audiences.

The band made two musically monumental LPs before imploding in 1970. Produced by the Velvet Underground's John Cale, 1969's *The Stooges* is as primordial as rock 'n' roll would get until *Ramones* appeared, seven years hence. Its primitive performances match the reductive compositions themselves, and the thumping, fuzz- and wah-wah-soaked guitars and adolescent angst of its "1969," "No

Fun," and "I Wanna Be Your Dog" have informed pretty much every punk act. By the time of 1970's *Fun House*, the Stooges had honed their attack to one of precise, devastatingly lethal muscle and acquired the confidence to fully unleash their music's innate power. A strong candidate for the greatest, most unrelenting rock 'n' roll album of all time, *Fun House* commences with the steam-hammer stomp of "Down on the Street," which sets the tone for nearly forty minutes of howling, venom-spewing crushers ("Loose," "T.V. Eye") and screaming skronk ("Fun House," "L.A. Blues"). The Stooges disintegrated not long after its release, but in 1972, at the urging of fan David Bowie, Iggy reassembled the band, with James Williamson on guitar and Ron Asheton taking over bass, as Iggy and the Stooges. With Bowie mixing, they recorded 1973's high-octane flamethrower, *Raw Power*. It crashes wide open with one of rock's foremost scorchers, "Search and Destroy," which is stoked by Williamson's grinding, sheet-metal guitar and Pop's desperate yowl. The payload widens with more impossibly mean, muscular rockers ("Your Pretty Face Is Going to Hell") and moody, threatening pieces ("Gimme Danger," "Penetration"), adding up to a flawless album that, like those before it, sold little and influenced many. After that, the Stooges were toast again until reuniting in 2007 with ex-Minutemen bassist Mike Watt. (Iggy Pop and James Williamson's *Kill City*, a comparatively clean but still rocking set of beefed-up demos, came out in 1976.)

In the late seventies, Iggy, now solo, capitalized on his stature as a punk forefather. While not as aggressive as the Stooges', his first three albums from this period are exemplary. *The Idiot* and *Lust for Life*, 1977 releases produced by Bowie, vividly mirror the cold, Teutonic vibe of postwar Berlin, where they were recorded. *The Idiot* is impressionistic and claustrophobic, its throbbing "Nightclubbing" and "Funtime" hinting at Krautrockers like Kraftwerk. *Lust for Life*'s licentious title track rocks like Bo Diddley on steroids, and the decadent "The Passenger" and adjoining grinders like "Sixteen" round out Pop's best solo set. Williamson produced 1979's strong *New Values*, which includes the hard-riffed genius of "Five Foot One" and "I'm Bored."

The Modern Lovers

Boston's Modern Lovers were started in 1970 by singer/songwriter/ guitarist and Velvet Underground fan Jonathan Richman, future Real Kids (see Chapter Four) guitarist John Felice, and future Cars drummer David Robinson. Felice left early on, but with the 1971 additions of bassist Ernie Brooks and keyboardist Jerry Harrison (later of Talking Heads), things had gelled by the 1972 making of the band's only official album, *The Modern Lovers*, which John Cale produced. Released in 1976, three years after the Lovers had broken up, it decisively influenced the mounting punk movements on both sides of the pond (the Sex Pistols covered the charging "Road Runner"). Other brilliant selections on this certified proto-punk milestone include the snide "Pablo Picasso" and the stark, unsettling anti-drug missive "I'm Straight." Richman revived the Modern Lovers name for other records and has had a fine solo career, but this is the album you need.

The Flamin' Groovies

These guys were the headliners at the Ramones' all-important 1976 London debut, but that's not their only connection. The Flamin' Groovies date back to 1965, when guitarist Cyril Jordan and singer Roy Loney formed the San Francisco band as the Lost and Found, and their exuberant brand of rock 'n' roll, which blends garage, British Invasion, folk rock, and rockabilly, is strongly present in the Ramones' sonic DNA. Their debut EP, 1968's *Sneakers*, moves between jug band-ish, Lovin' Spoonful–style tunes and garagier numbers like "Golden Clouds"; 1969's *Supersnazz* is Stones-ier, but still transitional. With 1970's much rawer *Flamingo*, however, things hop into high gear as the band kicks up a rambunctious house party with rock 'n' roll celebrations like "Comin' After Me" and "Road House." But 1971's *Teenage Head* is the early Groovies' greatest; the snot-blowing title cut and the romping version of Randy Newman's "Have You Seen My Baby?" are two of this punk-paving LP's wall-to-wall winners. Loney left and was replaced by Chris Wilson after *Teenage Head* flopped, and the Groovies signed to Ramones home Sire and remade themselves as heavily British Invasion–influenced power pop pioneers for 1976's *Shake Some Action*, whose title cut is among the greatest rock songs ever waxed (other high-quality tracks include the ballads "You Tore Me Down" and "Yes It's True" and some strong covers). The next two efforts, 1978's *Flamin' Groovies Now* and 1979's *Jumpin' in the Night*, are good, too. *Groovies Greatest Grooves* covers both the Loney and Wilson eras, and has the latter's "Slow Death," a staple for the Dictators (see Chapter Four) and other punks.

The Pink Fairies

The Pink Fairies were the English MC5: radical hard rockers who were always available to play at pot and protest rallies. The band evolved in 1970 out of proto-punkers the Deviants (originally the Social Deviants), who could be called Britain's Fugs (their 1967 debut, *Ptoof!*, is insane). The Fairies initially featured Deviants guitarist Paul Rudolph and bassist Duncan Sanderson and ex-Pretty Things member Twink (John Alder) on drums and lead vocals. Their 1971 debut, *Neverneverland*, kicks with "Do It" and other seditious rockers; Twink was gone by 1972's less focused *What a Bunch of Sweeties*. *Kings of Oblivion* (1973), with new guitarist Larry Wallis, is the band's strongest effort, opening with the forceful "City Kids" (a song Wallis took with him when he cofounded Motörhead with Hawkwind's Lemmy Kilmister). *The Golden Years '69–'71* rounds up ten of their top tracks.

Alice Cooper

Born Vincent Furnier, the faux-sadistic singer Alice Cooper and his accomplices (Michael Bruce and Glen Buxton, guitars; Dennis Dunaway, bass; Neil Smith, drums) were idolized by the embryonic Ramones. The band's stage shows are the stuff of legend, a theatrical riot of monster movie–inspired blood, baby dolls, and boa constrictors years before pitiful imitators like Marilyn Manson. Alice Cooper (the name refers to the band as well as its singer) came to life as early-sixties Arizona garage band the Spiders (née the Earwigs), which became the Nazz (not Todd Rundgren's old band) and then Alice Cooper (supposedly the name of a seventeenth-century witch). The band's first two albums, *Pretties for You* (1969) and *Easy Action* (1970), are psychedelic and peripheral; it's the next five you should check out. The garagey *Love It to Death* (1971) has the worldwide hit and perennial disaffected-teen anthem "I'm Eighteen" (which Johnny Rotten mimed to as his 1975 "audition" for the Sex Pistols), the butt-kicking "Long Way to Go," and the slithering, sleazed-out "Is It My Body." *Killer*, also from 1971, is equally undomesticated and perhaps slightly more macabre, with the roaring "Under My Wheels" and "You Drive Me Nervous" and the ghoulish "Dead Babies." *School's Out* (1972) is famed for its unruly titular hit (to be spun at the end of every academic year to the end of time), and, although more produced, still has its punk touches ("Public Animal #9"). *Billion Dollar Babies* (1973) is an even better balance of rough edges and studio flourish; hear the sweeping, mutinous "Elected" and "Generation Landslide" and the morbid "I Love the Dead." The same year's *Muscle of Love* is the last release by the original band and has a couple of goodies (the title song stands out). *Alice Cooper's Greatest Hits* racks up Alice's pre-solo singles.

The New York Dolls

You might not guess from the photos, but these five dudes dressed like girls were one of the main inspirations for the Ramones and their '77-era counterparts. And as a local phenomenon that hit at exactly the right time, the New York Dolls were a readily accessible influence on our stars. Formed in 1971, the Dolls developed a camp, androgynous image and played unflinchingly amateurish, incredibly fun, ramshackle rock 'n' roll that drew from the Rolling Stones, girl groups, garage rock, and old R&B. Their legendarily shambolic parties/concerts at Manhattan's Mercer Arts Center were regularly attended by each of the original Ramones (Marky even auditioned for the band after the 1972 overdose of their original drummer, Billy Murcia). To them, seeing firsthand how the Dolls could get up there and play without a whiff of technical ability—and totally rock the room—was deeply impressive.

The archetypal New York Dolls lineup was gruff-voiced, showy singer David Johansen, guitarists Johnny Thunders and Sylvain Sylvain, bassist Arthur Kane, and second drummer Jerry Nolan, and it's this edition that made their first two studio albums, both of which you should have. *New York Dolls* (1973) is not just one of the great proto-punk albums, it's one of the best rock albums, period. Loud, rude, and gloriously sloppy, it's as much a celebration of rock 'n' roll as an assault upon it, with Johansen's maniacal screams and Thunders's bent leads that informed a generation of punk guitarists. The rollicking opener "Personality Crisis" is the Dolls' best-known tune, though the snotty "Trash" and "Looking for a Kiss" are deservedly not far behind. *Too Much, Too Soon* (1974) is just a mascara-covered lash or two from the greatness of the Dolls' debut. Overseen by girl group producer Shadow Morton, it snarls with the vicious "Babylon," the joyously careening "Who Are the Mystery Girls?," the scorching, Thunders-sung "Chatterbox," and detonations of various R&B oldies. The band broke up in 1975, with Johansen's solo career and Thunders's Heartbreakers (see Chapter Four) making the biggest post-Dolls splashes; the surviving members reunited in 2004.

GLAM ROCK

Even though a couple of its American exemplars were among the genre's leading acts, glam rock was mainly an English phenomenon. Named for the flamboyant, over-the-top ("glamorous") getups of the early 1970s artists who played it, glam had a gender-bending, sexually ambiguous aesthetic that was simply too challenging for the Middle American market. Broadly speaking, glam was about catchy, crunchy guitar hooks, ostentatious ballads, and flashy visuals that referenced the idealized arcana of old Hollywood, science fiction, 1950s rock 'n' roll, comic books, camp theatre, and Weimar-era cabaret. At the time, in the States the movement was usually referred to as glitter rock, although in the U.K. that label was more commonly applied to poppier, less artistically driven practitioners like Slade, Sweet, Gary Glitter, and Suzi Quatro. But within our context it's all under the same gaudy, sequined umbrella.

In the late eighties the glam name was resurrected by Americans to refer to hair metal bands like Poison and Mötley Crüe, which clearly have their roots in glam but should not be confused with the original artifact; perhaps "neo-glam" is a better descriptor for these garish pretenders.

Much glam was essentially amped-up bubblegum, which is also, as we've noted, how the Ramones initially saw themselves. For their first CBGB gigs in 1974, before they fully adopted their trademark ripped jeans and leather jackets, the Ramones sported glammy satin and lamé. The three-disc *Glam Rock Anthology* is a star-spangled genre intro, with tracks by T. Rex, Roxy Music, the New York Dolls, and several U.K. one-hitters.

T. Rex

Led by preening, pouting, corkscrew-curled singer/guitarist Marc Bolan, Britain's T. Rex is credited with sparking (sparkling?) the glam rock flashpoint in 1971. As acoustic psychedelic-folk duo Tyrannosaurus Rex, the band had released three whimsical hit albums before Bolan electrified the band and shortened its name. If you're new to T. Rex, the albums you want to start with are 1971's *Electric Warrior* and 1972's *The Slider*. *Electric Warrior* defines the classic, head-in-the-stars T. Rex sound: flouncing, sexy, hip-swinging, back-to-basics rock 'n' roll, with widescreen production by Tony Visconti and absurdly silly lyrics about cars, cosmic dancers, and planet queens. Its "Bang a Gong (Get it On)" was the band's biggest U.S. hit, but by no means does this album's top-to-bottom greatness end there; the shuffling "Mambo Sun," rockabilly pastiche "Jeepster," and hard-rocking "Rip Off" are also among its strutting standouts. *The Slider* was T. Rex's biggest-selling record, and its slightly bigger production (strings, backup choruses) gives Bolan's guitar a tougher edge on blazing tracks like "Telegram Sam" and "Buick Mackane," while the sweet "Spaceball Richochet" displays his soft side. The albums that came next, before Bolan died in a 1977 car crash, have only sporadic sparkles. For T. Rex compilations, *20th Century Boy: The Ultimate Collection* shines brightest.

IF YOU LIKE THE RAMONES...

David Bowie

Prior to the Ramones, Joey himself fronted a glam band called Sniper, under the name Jeff Starship. As he was a known David Bowie fan, it's obvious where the inspiration came from: although Bowie has famously reinvented himself several times, it's his early seventies stint as his alter ego Ziggy Stardust, leader of the fictitious rock band the Spiders from Mars, that remains his most electrifying guise. (Bowie, born David Jones, admits the Ziggy Stardust moniker was a reference to Iggy Pop and outsider musician the Legendary Stardust Cowboy). Bowie first hit the charts with the 1969 single "Space Oddity," a pre-Ziggy, psych-folk opus that's less pertinent to our story. His fourth LP, 1970's excellent *The Man Who Sold the World*, is where it really starts. The first album with Bowie's future Spiders foil, guitarist Mick Ronson, is a major reversal from his earlier phase, and pairs his sci-fi lyrics with acid-tinged hard rock (the title cut and "Saviour Machine"). On 1971's *Hunky Dory*, the helium-voiced Bowie beautifully balances his folk-based "Space Oddity" style ("Changes," "Life on Mars?") with the hardness of the preceding album (the Velvet Underground-ish "Queen Bitch"). Next came 1972's colossal *The Rise and Fall of Ziggy Stardust and the Spiders from Mars*, along with Bowie's newly acquired, flame-haired, futuristic persona. The five-star disc made him an international idol and brought a previously unseen level of drama to rock music, along with some of its greatest songs; on "Suffragette City," "Hang onto Yourself," and "Moonage Daydream" Ronson's razor riffs fan the flames for punk. Nineteen seventy-three's *Aladdin Sane* refines the Ziggy Stardust sound and concept with loungey interludes and swaggering crunchers like "Jean Genie" and "Cracked Actor." The same year's *Pin Ups* is an album of inspired covers of mid-sixties British rock hits (Yardbirds, Pretty Things, Kinks). Great, but not for newbies. *Diamond Dogs* (1974) is the last LP from the Ziggy days, as Bowie would next pursue more soul-oriented and experimental (read: less Ramones-relevant) paths. Although he'd ditched Ronson and the Spiders for this album, its rousing title track and "Rebel Rebel" beckon. *Changesonebowie* is the definitive Bowie intro.

Slade

Slade was bellower/guitarist Noddy Holder, bizarrely attired guitarist Dave Hill, and the powerful rhythm section of bassist Jimmy Lea and drummer Don Powell, and was gigantic in glam-time England. From 1971 to 1974 its loud, shouty singles with humorously misspelled titles piled into the U.K. Top Ten, invigorating innumerable prospective punks but never hitting in the U.S. The hip ears of the future Ramones were well tuned to the Anglo action, and they loved the raucous, stomping energy of Slade. Bypass the first two inconsequential 1969 hard-psych albums made under the name Ambrose Slade and 1970's *Play It Loud*, a generic hard rock offering for which the band adopted a skinhead image. The Slade records you want to start with are 1972's in-concert *Slade Alive!*, with the hoarse, emblematically thumping rock 'n' rollers "Get Down and Get With It" and "Keep on Rocking"; the same year's ultra-rowdy *Slayed?*, with the irresistible screamer "Mama Weer All Crazy Now" and the romping "Gudbuy to Jane"; and 1973's *Sladest*, a best-of with hits from the preceding two albums plus blood-pumping singles like the roaring "Cum On Feel the Noize," a totally punk-predicting track (carbon copies of that song and "Mama Weer All Crazy Now" were eighties MTV hits for Quiet Riot).

Sweet

Sweet (initially *the* Sweet) was a classic precursor of the kind of hard-rocking bubblegum approach the Ramones would develop and make much harder. Essentially a vehicle for the tunes of champ songwriters Mike Chapman and Nicky Chinn, the shag-headed Sweet was singer Brian Connolly, bassist/vocalist Steve Priest, drummer/vocalist Mick Tucker, and guitarist Andy Scott, and collectively epitomized the garish, big-sounding teen fun of British glam. The band's first U.S. hit was 1973's "Little Willy," a bouncy, chanting tune built around a crunching, three-chord riff. Its parent album, *The Sweet*, packs comparable punches whose titles betray their attitude: "Hell Raiser," "Blockbuster," "Wig-Wam Bam." Yet it's 1974's *Desolation Boulevard* that's Sweet's most mandatory album.

With suitably tacky and oversized production emphasizing the band's high vocal harmonies, it birthed the mega-smashes "Fox on the Run" and "Ballroom Blitz" (also notable: the proto-speed metal "Set Me Free" and the impudent "No You Don't"). *Give Us a Wink* (1976) has the throbbing "Yesterday's Rain" and the aggressive "Action," but would be the glittery gang's last good album. *Action: The Sweet Anthology* has the big hits and deep cuts.

Roxy Music

If Sweet represented the frivolous, teenage side of glam, Roxy Music was its arty, intellectual big brother. While the 1971-formed group would later move into funk-tinged rock and streamlined, romantic pop, its early albums offer tough, captivating testament to the fruitful tug-of-war between suave, matinee idol crooner Bryan Ferry's pop-soul flair and synthesizer man Brian Eno's Velvet Underground–inspired experimentalism. Dotted with Eno's blipping synths, 1972's *Roxy Music* has the U.K. hit "Virginia Plain," whose driving, Velvets-derived guitar, courtesy of the great Phil Manzanera, is uncannily Ramones-like. *For Your Pleasure* (1973) is Roxy's last LP with Eno (his solo 1974 *Here Come the Warm Jets* and 1975 *Taking Tiger Mountain by Strategy* are fantastic) and among its best. The dynamic opener "Do the Strand," the rocking "Editions of You," and "In Every Dream Home a Heartache," a decadent ode to an inflatable sex doll (?!), feature among the memorable tracks. The same year's darkly melodic *Stranded* is notable for Ferry's trademark trills and Manzanara's soaring on tunes like "Street Life" and "Mother of Pearl," while 1974's *Country Life* dazzles with the churning "The Thrill of It All" and the pounding "Prairie Rose." On 1975's *Siren*, home to the hit "Love Is the Drug," the band mainly embraces soul-rock and moves out of our sphere. The live *Viva!* (1976), though, is a gripping document of the quintet's on-stage powers. *Early Years* compiles remastered cuts from the formative first three albums.

Mott the Hoople

Another big influence on British punks—Ramones followers the

Clash, in particular—Mott the Hoople didn't make an impact in America until the 1972 hit "All the Young Dudes." But by then the group of Ian Hunter (vocals, guitar, keyboards), Mick Ralphs (guitar), Verden Allen (organ), Overend Watts (bass), and Dale "Buffin" Griffin had been plying its mix of hard rock, glam, and Dylan-ish introspection for nearly four years. The great 1969 debut, *Mott the Hoople*, hangs out Mott's heavy shingle with the bone-crushing instrumental version of the Kinks' "You Really Got Me" that opens and the equally heavy groupie elegy "Rock and Roll Queen," and unveils the brusque-voiced Hunter's panache for wounded ballads. Unfortunately, it's the latter aspect that dominates *Mad Shadows*—although the 1970 recording houses two of the band's toughest songs, "Thunderbuck Ram" and "Walkin' with a Mountain." *Wildlife* (1971) is similar in feel, outside of the psychotic reading of Little Richard's "Keep a-Knockin'" that closes it. But things bounce back with that year's *Brain Capers*, among whose venomously rockin' content stands "The Moon Upstairs" and "Death May Be Your Santa Claus." *All the Young Dudes* (1972) is considered the band's best album by many. Its David Bowie–penned title smash and destructive attacks like "Jerkin' Crocus" and "One of the Boys" add up to an overwhelmingly visceral affair. Then again, some peg 1973's *Mott* as the pinnacle for its 1950s-style "All the Way from Memphis," blistering "Drivin' Sister," and appropriately fierce "Violence." Ralphs quit to form Bad Company before 1974's *The Hoople*, which is great anyway, with high points like the raging "Crash Street Kids" and "Born Late '58" and the longing "Roll Away the Stone." Hunter left following 1974's so-so *Live* (taped on tour with new guitarist Ariel Bender), after which the band never recovered. The two-disc *The Ballad of Mott* is the top Mott collection.

Sparks

Sparks is basically Los Angeles brothers Ron (keyboards) and Russell Mael (vocals), who have co-led innumerable lineups of the band since 1970. Subversively quirky and rocking as well, the group's deceptively disturbing, Beach Boys–based pop songs have had minimal commercial impact in the U.S. but have long been exalted in England (sound like anyone you know?). The Todd Rundgren–produced *Sparks* (1971) and 1972's follow-up, *A Woofer in Tweeter's Clothing*, established the Maels' sonic signature: Russell's fluttering falsetto and Ron's corkscrew keyboards against alternately rocking and melodramatic backgrounds. *Kimono My House* (1974) is the band's boilerplate work and the LP you should snag before all others. The Baroque-tinged "This Town Ain't Big Enough for Both of Us" and "Amateur Hour" were U.K. number ones, while the central, descending-riffed "Thank God It's Not Christmas" is noticeably Ramonesy. *Propaganda*, also from '74, is also beguiling, somehow bridging jittery operatic flights with edgy rock (see "At Home, at Work, at Play" and "Don't Leave Me Alone with Her"). Once you've acquired the taste, 1975's *Indiscreet* and 1976's *Big Beat* are recommended. Though Sparks's records get spottier and slicker from there, they usually have a couple of decent tunes: 1982's *Angst in My Pants* actually has some chugging nuggets recalling later Ramones. Ramones fans themselves, the Mael brothers even did da brudders a solid by appearing in the "Something to Believe In" video.

Suzi Quatro

Just like Sparks, this American singer/bassist was virtually unknown in her homeland while she ruled early seventies radio in Britain. Born in Michigan, she played with her sisters in all-girl garage band the Pleasure Seekers before English producer Mickie Most whisked her across the Atlantic to work with Sweet songwriters Mike Chapman and Nickey Chinn (see earlier). The results were three big U.K. hits, "Can the Can," "48 Crash," and "Glycerine Queen," which are found on her blasting 1973 debut, *Suzi Quatro*. Clad in skin-tight black leather and belting out tough, sexuality-oozing ditties, the singer and her band of three greasy, badass, longhaired dudes looked like a fantasy union of the Ramones and Joan Jett (who readily acknowledges her debt to Quatro). Aside from the hot 1974 single "Devil Gate Drive," Quatro didn't do much rockin' for the remainder of the decade, mostly making soft-rock slush like 1979's hit "Stumblin' In." But in 1980 she teamed up again with Chapman and Chinn for the superb, perfectly titled *Rock Hard*. With its battering namesake track, trampling version of the Dave Clark Five's "Glad All Over," and other tarmac-chewers, it approaches the toughness of her grand debut. *The Wild One: Classic Quatro* has twenty hits.

Zolar-X

This way-out early 1970s Los Angeles band was too good to be true: unsigned, super-rocking, antennae-sporting faux-space freaks who communicated in their own alien dialect, on *and* off stage. If they'd been able to hear them, it's a safe bet Joey and company would've loved them. Pick up *Timeless*, a gathering of unheard tracks.

PROTO–POWER POP

Most 1970s pop rock is the stuff of rainbows, feathered hair, and smiley faces, and has little to do with the vital fifties and sixties pop that inspired the Ramones. Still, there are a few instances of early seventies pop that have the lasting guts and well-crafted songwriting that our guys appreciated. Such acts are the forerunners of the movement known as power pop, which we'll cover in Chapter Six. We'll call them proto–power pop bands.

The Bay City Rollers

Scotland's Bay City Rollers were the ultimate boy band of the day, tartan-wearing heartthrobs whose chirpy bubblegum-glam hits had adolescent girls going wild for two years straight. Formed around brothers Derek (drums) and Alan (bass) Longmuir and fronted by singer Les McKeown, the group had eight Top Ten hits in England before reaching number one in the U.S. with 1975's "Saturday Night," which they followed with four straight gold albums. As far as proper albums go, the first two, 1974's *Rollin'* and 1975's *Once Upon a Star*, are the most consistent. After some vain attempts at grown-up rock, McKeown left and was replaced by Duncan Faure. As simply the Rollers, they reinvented themselves as a power pop band and made two surprisingly decent LPs in that vein: 1979's *Elevator* and

1980's *Voxx*. But of course for such a singles-driven sensation the smartest introductory route is via *Greatest Hits* or *Absolute Rollers: The Very Best of the Bay City Rollers*. Dee Dee was a devout fan, and for a time it looked like there'd be a teenybop–blitzkrieg bop crossover as, according to the late bassist, the Rollers intended to record a version of our boys' "I Wanna Be Your Boyfriend." But, alas, it never came to be.

Badfinger

This U.K.-based act came from the same British Invasion tradition that spawned the Ramones. You may know Badfinger's "No Matter What," "Baby Blue," and Paul McCartney-penned "Come and Get It," all proto–power pop classics. The quartet of singer/guitarist Pete Ham, drummer Mike Gibbins, bassist Tom Evans, and singer/guitarist Joey Molland evolved from sixties beat group the Iveys. Badfinger's superb vocal harmonies, ringing guitar chords, and associations with the Fab Four saw the band saddled with the unwieldy mantle of "the new Beatles" throughout its existence. But while the Beatles influence is undeniable, the group had its own pop-classicist approach, which is recognizably more modern and not just some slavish mop-top re-creation. After one album as the Iveys on the Beatles' Apple Records, the band changed its name to Badfinger and between stints backing George Harrison and John Lennon recorded 1970's *Magic Christian Music* and *No Dice* and 1971's *Straight Up*; 1974's lost treasure *Wish You Were Here* was under-promoted by Warner Bros. upon its release. *The Very Best of Badfinger* touches on both the Apple and Warners years.

The Raspberries

Touted as America's "new Beatles," the Raspberries hailed from the Cleveland, Ohio, area and sprouted in 1970 from the remains of two locally popular bands, Cyrus Erie and the Choir (the latter's "It's Cold Outside" is a garage classic). The vanguard lineup featured singer/guitarist/keyboardist Eric Carmen, bassist Wally Bryson, guitarist Dave Smalley, and drummer Jim Bonifanti. With the hippie era still in full swing, the Raspberries' matching suits made them stand out—as did their superbly crafted singles, which melded Who-style guitar crunch with skyrocketing vocal harmonies and lyrics recalling the teenaged themes of earlier rock 'n' rollers. The first big one, the hormone-injected "Go All the Way," hit in 1972, and was followed by the likewise soaring "I Wanna Be with You" and the tough rockers "Tonight" and "Overnight Sensation (Hit Record)." The band's four studio albums, *Raspberries*, *Fresh* (both 1972), *Side 3* (1973), and *Starting Over* (1974), are rich in punchy guitars and Merseybeat-inspired hooks, with the occasional heartbreaking ballad thrown in. Capitol/EMI's *Greatest* picks twenty of the Raspberries' juiciest.

Big Star

This truly transcendental group was fronted by singer-songwriter and guitarist Alex Chilton, who'd previously sung for blue-eyed soul greats the Box Tops ("The Letter," "Cry Like a Baby"). One of rock's quintessential cult bands, Big Star drew strongly from the Beatles' songwriting, as well as the Who's heaviness and the Byrds' rich harmonies, and is undyingly revered today for its deeply beautiful ballads and scrappy rockers. Chilton joined not long after the Memphis band was formed in 1971 by singer/guitarist Chris Bell, bassist Andy Hummel, and drummer Jody Stephens. *#1 Record* (1972) is a faultless debut, bearing such riches as the vulnerable "Thirteen" and "The Ballad of El Goodo" and the ornery "Don't Lie to Me." Unfortunately, the title didn't exactly prove commercially prophetic. Bell and Hummel quit during the making of 1974's *Radio City*, a record imbued with weighty tension but no less fantastic than its antecedent; listen to the bounding "Oh My Soul" and "Mod Lang" and the tender "September Gurls," the band's best-known track. *Third/Sister Lovers* was released in 1978, four years after the act broke up, and features great Kinks and Velvet Underground covers. Its pop perfection, however, centers mostly on affecting ballads ("Holocaust," "Jesus Christ") that will tug hardest at your more sensitive side (it's okay, even the Ramones had one). Bell died in an auto accident the year the album appeared, but not before waxing the gorgeous single "I Am the Cosmos." In

1977 Chilton moved to New York, where he played punk venues with a band that included Televison guitarist Richard Lloyd before producing the Cramps and other acts and playing with Panther Burns. And Chilton's solo stuff is generally stellar itself.

PUB ROCK

In the U.S. the term "bar band" is usually a put-down. But pub rock, in its 1970s U.K. usage, didn't refer to those breathing jukeboxes who play oldies in neighborhood bars. It's the name for a movement of street-level bands that happened in England just prior to the arrival of punk rock. These groups reacted against the overblown stadium rock of the early to mid-seventies by playing raw, unpretentious, rootsy music, mostly drawn from early rhythm and blues and sixties beat bands, in packed, sweaty pubs. Besides developing the infrastructure of venues that would host early punk gigs, the scene nurtured many first-wave punks: the Clash's Joe Strummer came from the 101ers; Ian Dury came from Kilburn and the High Roads; Nick Lowe came from Brinsley Schwarz; Eddie and the Hot Rods emerged fully formed; and both Elvis Costello and Graham Parker cut their teeth on the pub rock circuit.

The leading pub rock band was the ferocious Dr. Feelgood. In their shorter hair and dodgy suits, the Feelgoods looked like East End mobsters—and played like it. Tall, harp-blowing front man Lee Brilleaux cast a menacing presence, and the hot-wired Wilko Johnson remains one of the greatest and most unique guitarists ever to strap on a Telecaster, his percussive, minimal style becoming a reference point for ranks of aspiring players. The Ramones opened for Dr. Feelgood's May 1976 show at New York's Bottom Line. Oh, what a night that must've been. The gang's first four albums, *Down at the Jetty* (1975), *Malpractice* (1975), the live *Stupidity* (1976), and *Sneakin' Suspicion* (1977), are brilliant; *Singles: The UA Years* is the best anthology.

Also excellent was Ducks Deluxe, which injected Chuck Berry licks with MC5-inspired heaviness and whose members ended up in the Motors and Graham Parker and the Rumour. The first two LPs, *Ducks*

Deluxe (1974) and *Taxi to the Terminal Zone* (1975), are rockin'. The Pirates had been the backing band for U.K. rock 'n' roll pioneer Johnny Kidd, and featured another amazing guitarist, Mick Green. They split up when Kidd died in a 1966 car crash but returned during the pub rock epoch. The vigorous *Out of Their Skulls* (1977) and *Skull Wars* (1978) will crack *your* skull. *Pub Rock: Paving the Way for Punk* and *Goodbye Nashville Hello Camden Town* offer broader insight.

Gutter poetics: Along with the Ramones, the Patti Smith Group was one of the main bands on the early New York punk scene. (Photofest/© Arista Records)

4

BLITZKRIEG BOP:
THE RAMONES LEAD THE PUNK REVOLUTION

While punk had its audible precedents in the retroactively labeled proto-punk acts covered in the last chapter, it was the Ramones who really fired the shot heard 'round the world. They were the first *true* punk rock band, the first act to pointedly seize on the underlying sounds and ideas that united the disparate proto-punk pioneers, distilling them down even further and putting a revolutionary new spin on rock 'n' roll. And while the New York scene they helped begin contained other acts that began around the same time—Patti Smith, Television, the Dictators, Talking Heads—it was the Ramones who became the figureheads, their visceral, aggressive, fun, bare-bones approach going down as the blueprint for just about every punk that picked up an instrument in their wake.

Why the Ramones? Simple: simplicity! More than any band before or since, they showed kids that music could be something that's easy to play, something those kids could be doing immediately—no experience necessary. It was a gospel the Ramones spread on the road; wherever they played on their early tours, they left behind audiences of kids who went home and formed the *next* wave of punk bands. Just before the Ramones' 1976 London debut, an aspiring young bassist named Paul Simonon met Johnny Ramone and told him his just-formed band, the Clash, wasn't good enough to perform yet. "Wait 'til you see us," offered Johnny. "We stink, we're lousy, we can't play. Just get out there and do it."

In punk's early days, before it became codified by angry, leather-jacketed Ramones imitators, the bands that played it didn't have a specific sound or aesthetic. What mostly united the Ramones and their groundbreaking peers was the common desire to do something *different* from the turgid, mediocre stuff that blighted the mainstream, to do it passionately, and to have a blast at the same time. And punk's upheaval was by no means confined to music: There were artists working in film, literature, theatre, the visual arts, and other media who were inspired by the movement to shake up their own disciplines. But of course this chapter is focused on the music, which initially had far more variety than casual listeners may realize. While groups like the Sex Pistols and the Dead Boys are sonically close to the Ramones, early punk also encompasses the poetic garage rock of the Patti Smith Group, the dark minimalism of Suicide, the beer-soaked R&B of the Heartbreakers, the Dadaist synth rock of Devo, the jazz-like flights of Television, the neo-mod attack of the Jam, the art-school quirkiness of Talking Heads, the rockabilly raunch of the Cramps, the girl group pop of Blondie, the sinister sneer of the Stranglers, and dozens of other permutations.

The most visible centers of early punk activity were New York and London. But at the same time as those scenes were on the rise, similar developments were taking place away from the media spotlight in Boston, northeastern Ohio, and parts of Australia. Soon the fire spread to Los Angeles, San Francisco, Paris, and pretty much every decent-sized city with a college and an arts community—from Oslo to Tokyo (and sometimes in the least expected backwaters: Chickasha, Oklahoma, proto-punk trio Debris' unveiled 1976's freakish *Static Disposal* months before *Ramones* appeared). For a brief period after punk began the term "new wave" was used interchangeably with "punk rock," but eventually the former label became a marketing phrase used to push newer, less edgy acts to timid radio programmers. Things later morphed into post-punk, a wildly ill-defined genre that built on punk's uncompromising stance by broadening its basic sound with more diverse influences and experimentation. This chapter, however, is about the amazing bands that blasted forth during the first waves of punk, some of whom are still at it today. Rhino's *No Thanks!* makes a pretty solid punk primer, although its omission of the Ramones' biggest rivals, the Sex Pistols, is glaring. After you've gorged on that four-CD box set, there are stacks of reissues covering obscure punk from the farthest-flung corners of the globe to devour.

NEW YORK PUNK

New York is considered the birthplace of the 1970s punk rock movement, which isn't very surprising. The cultural hub of the Western world for over a century, Gotham has also long been the first-stop magnet of extreme and eccentric artists from the rest of America and around the globe—a tradition that stretches from Walt Whitman through the Harlem Renaissance, jazz's beboppers, the Beat poets, Andy Warhol, and hip-hop. The city was home to three live music spots that served as punk rock's cradles: the Mercer Arts Center, where the New York Dolls, Suicide, and other bands performed; Max's Kansas City, a nightclub/restaurant and notorious artists' hangout; and CBGB, a urine-stained biker bar that became the music's best-known venue and launched the careers of the Ramones, Patti Smith, Talking Heads, Blondie, and hundreds more. *New York Rocks: Original Punk Classics '70s* samples the scene's heavy hitters, as does *The Blank Generation: The New York Scene (1975–78)*, part of the Rhino label's "DIY" series.

The Patti Smith Group

When talk turns to rock's reigning poets, Patti Smith is perhaps second only to her idol, Bob Dylan (some might even say she's surpassed him over the years). Her 1974 single "Hey Joe" / "Piss Factory" is acknowledged as the first punk rock record. Guitarist Lenny Kaye, keyboardist Richard Sohl, guitarist/bassist Ivan Kral, and drummer Jay Dee Daugherty backed Smith for her 1975 John Cale–produced debut, *Horses*, the album that broke the New York punk underground to the outside world. In surrounding her alternately sneering and wounded vocals and evocative wordage with *Nuggets* compiler Kaye's beloved garage rock and Sohl's misty, haunting piano, Smith and her band came up with a compellingly tough style that was rich in the hidden poetics of the Lower East

Side streets and the simple rock 'n' roll of the past. The opening "Gloria: In Excelsis Deo," a revelatory retooling of Them's "Gloria," is one of rock's pivotal moments. The band officially became the Patti Smith Group for 1976's *Radio Ethiopia*, another invigorating classic, with the brawny rockers "Ask the Angels" and "Pumping (My Heart)." *Easter* (1978) is the band's biggest seller thanks to its Top Ten single "Because the Night," a ballad cowritten with Bruce Springsteen, and contains some of the PSG's finest tunes: the storming "Privilege (Set Me Free)," "25th Floor," and "Rock 'n' Roll Nigger," the latter a society-rejecting anthem that turns the n-word on its head by making it an outcast's badge of honor. *Wave* (1979) would be the last of the original group's albums, as Smith waved goodbye to performing in favor of family life with MC5 guitarist Fred "Sonic" Smith. Although it's cleaner and less consistent than the prior releases, there are still some redeeming moments: the poignant "Dancing Barefoot" (famously redone by a gang of Ramones fans called U2) and an inspired cover of the Byrds' "So You Want to Be (A Rock 'n' Roll Star)." Smith re-emerged in the late eighties and again in the nineties. With tracks from her essential first four albums, *Outside Society* is a concise initiation to this American giant.

Television

Without this amazing band, the Ramones—and punk rock—might never have had a home. It was Television singer/guitarist Tom Verlaine (born Thomas Miller) who in 1974 talked CBGB owner Hilly Kristal into letting his band play at the Bowery club, thereby opening its doors to the other early New York punk bands. Prior to Television, Verlaine (who played on Patti Smith's first single) and drummer Billy Ficca had a trio with bassist Richard Hell called the Neon Boys. With the addition of guitarist Richard Lloyd the group became Television, whose lyrical, virtuosic music is far from the simplicity of the Ramones, owing more to jazz and psychedelia, but is as edgy and artistically uncompromising as anything by the other punk-identified acts. Hell left and was replaced by ex-Blondie bassist Fred Smith before the band recorded its 1975 debut single, "Little Johnny Jewel," and 1977's *Marquee Moon*. A crowning release of punk's first wave, its unvaryingly great songs—"See No Evil," "Friction," the epic, labyrinthine title track—burn as Verlaine's and Lloyd's fiery guitars duel and interweave inside garage frameworks. *Adventure* (1978) is less consistent but still pretty great, with smoldering cuts like "Foxhole," "Glory," and "Ain't That Nothin'." The quartet broke up not long after its release but reunited for 1992's *Television*, a shockingly superb set after such a long layoff. *The Best of Tom Verlaine and Television* samples the band and Verlaine's fine solo work, while the raw *The Blow-Up* displays Television's live awesomeness.

Talking Heads

With their twitchy, angular, and arty sound, Talking Heads might seem like an odd opener for the Ramones' early CBGB bills and tours. But even the musically narrow Johnny Ramone, as he stated in later years, saw why the combination worked so well at the time: minimalism. Although Talking Heads later widened their sound by adding phalanxes of ancillary players and making big-production records, their sparse 1977 debut single, "Love → Building on Fire" (engineered by Tommy Ramone), gives a good snapshot of their early bare-bones sound—a cool complement to that of the Ramones.

Former Rhode Island School of Design students singer/guitarist David Byrne, bassist Tina Weymouth, and drummer Chris Frantz came together in 1974, moved to a loft near the Bowery, and started gigging at CBGB soon after. Ex–Modern Lovers (see Chapter Three) keyboardist Jerry Harrison joined just prior to the recording of 1977's *Talking Heads: 77*. Its mix of quirky, sharp-edged Cubist funk, juxtaposed against Bryne's nervous falsetto and surreal lyrics, is like little else of its time. The ominously throbbing "Psycho Killer" remains the band's greatest tune, and "Happy Day" and "No Compassion" typify the album's edgy fare. Brian Eno produced 1978's *More Songs About Buildings and Food*, which puts the rhythm section in front of Byrne's staccato guitar and Harrison's keys, but without sacrificing the group's unique sound. Its pulsating version of soul man Al Green's "Take Me to the River" is hypnotic, and "Thank You for Sending Me an Angel" and "Artists Only" are dizzying swirls of avant-garage. Eno returned to the board for the Heads' next two efforts, 1979's *Fear of Music* (with the psycho-babbling funker "Life During Wartime") and 1980's electro-heavy *Remain in Light*, whose increased moves toward polyrhythmic Afro-pop and electronics show the band leaving our rock-centric Ramones radar. The live *The Name of This Band Is Talking Heads* (1982) has vital 1977–1979 performances.

Blondie

When Blondie first started playing CBGB in 1975, the unfocused, amateurish band was considered a joke by its competitors. But just three years later the joke was on everybody else, as Blondie became the most commercially successful act of the entire late-seventies punk movement. After the demise of their previous ensemble, the Stillettos, guitarist Chris Stein and singer Deborah Harry formed Blondie in 1974 with drummer Clem Burke and bassist Fred Smith; keyboardist Jimmy Destri signed on next. Smith soon left to join Television (see earlier) and was replaced by Gary Valentine, and the group got to working on 1976's *Blondie*. Its fresh, vibrant, and fun mix of garage rock, Brill Building pop, and girl group sounds was overseen by veteran producer Richard Gottehrer (the Angels' "My Boyfriend's Back") and has the sniping "Rip Her to Shreds" and the coolly campy "X Offender." Gottehrer (who soon cofounded Sire Records) also supervised 1977's almost-as-good *Plastic Letters*, which bore the splashy U.K. hits "I'm Always Touched by Your Presence, Dear" and "Denis." In 1978, *Parallel Lines* saw Valentine replaced by Nigel Harrison and guitarist Frank Infante added to the mix, and, thanks to its disco smash "Heart of Glass," made the group superstars. But forget that karaoke fodder and dig into the grinding "I Know but I Don't Know," the leering "One Way or Another," and the desperate "Hanging on the Telephone" (see the Nerves, Chapter Seven). *Parallel Lines* was Blondie's biggest-selling album, but to many 1979's *Eat to the Beat* is its best. On the powerful opener, "Dreaming," Harry's voice soars like a goddess's as Burke pulls out all his Keith Moon-ish moves (in 1987, as Elvis

Ramone, Burke briefly occupied the Ramones drum stool). Things slicken up after that, making these the four Blondie albums to get. *Blondie Singles Collection: 1977–1982* is the best of the comps, as it concentrates on this essential period.

The Heartbreakers

The only early New York band to momentarily give the Ramones a run for their money, the Heartbreakers (not to be confused with Tom Petty's group) spent most of their own money on heroin. As is usually the case, this wasn't the best career move. But whatever their rock 'n' roll lifestyles may have been, the Heartbreakers' music kicks major ass and will rock the world of anyone who digs the hard stuff—musically speaking, that is. Formed in 1975 by ex–New York Dolls Johnny Thunders (vocals, guitar) and Jerry Nolan (drums) and former Television member Richard Hell (bass), the band also included Walter Lure (guitar; he later played on several Ramones albums). Firmly rooted in the trashy R&B the Dolls had mined, the Heartbreakers dragged the music deeper into the gutter and roughed it up even more. Their secret weapons were Thunders's sloppy, sidewinder guitar and nasal whine, which sneered out songs about getting laid and getting high; the band's signature junkie anthem, "Chinese Rocks," was cowritten by Dee Dee Ramone (or entirely written by him, as he maintained) and later recorded by the Ramones, as "Chinese Rock," for *End of the Century*. Hell didn't stay long, leaving to form the Voidoids (see later). With new bassist Billy Rath, the band played England with the Sex Pistols, the Clash, and the Damned on the 1976 Anarchy Tour. The Heartbreakers' lone studio album, 1977's *L.A.M.F.* (for "Like a Mother Fucker") is one of New York punk's critical records, bristling with hopped-up Chuck Berry licks and streetwise swagger on cuts like "Born to Lose" and "Pirate Love." The *Live at Max's Kansas City* (1979) and *D.T.K. Live at the Speakeasy* (1982) capture the band's legendarily unruly stage action, but Thunders's first solo album, *So Alone* (1978), is more necessary. With guests like Sex Pistols Steve Jones and Paul Cook, the Small Faces' Steve Marriott, and Thin Lizzy's Phil Lynott, it's thick with scuzzy rockers and has the gut-wrenching ballad "You Can't Put Your Arms Around a Memory."

Richard Hell and the Voidoids

Born Richard Meyers, Richard Hell, as you may have gathered from the above, is one of punk's pioneers. A founding member of Television and the Heartbreakers and an esteemed writer of prose (seriously), he's credited with crystallizing the spiky-haired, ripped-up, safety-pinned look that was sported by the Sex Pistols and so many others (Pistols manager Malcolm McLaren even tried to get him in the band before Johnny Rotten came along). The singer/bassist put together the Voidoids—guitarists Robert Quine and Ivan Julian and drummer Marc Bell (the future Marky Ramone)—after becoming frustrated by not being able to play more of his own songs in his previous bands. One such ditty, "Blank Generation," which he'd first performed in Television, was recorded in 1976 as the new group's first single. Branded with a recurring, descending bass line and existentialist lyrics, the song stands as punk's defining manifesto of self-reinvention. It's also the title track of the Voidoids' 1977 debut on the Ramones' Sire label, *Blank Generation*, another elemental punk rock album. On top of Hell's expressive bleat and poetic verbiage, the band had an extremely unique sound, thanks much to Quine, whose fractured, avant-jazz leads bring wiry tension to "New Pleasure," "Betrayal Takes Two," and the evocatively named "Love Comes in Spurts." The outfit split up not long after its release but regrouped, with Hell and Quine the only charter members, for 1982's *Destiny Street*. Somehow looser than the first LP, yet nearly as strong, it opens with one of Hell's best tunes, the crazed "The Kid with the Replaceable Head."

Wayne County

Before he was a Voidoid or a Ramone, Marky drummed for Wayne County and the Backstreet Boys, a band best known for the rollicking "Max's Kansas City," an homage to the New York nightclub. The taboo-assaulting, transgender County (born Wayne Rogers) escaped to Manhattan from her native Georgia in 1968, becoming associated with Andy Warhol's milieu, acting in avant-garde plays (including Warhol's seminal "Pork"), and forming the glam/proto-punk Queen Elizabeth, followed by the Backstreet Boys. Next came Wayne County and the Electric Chairs, which, when punk began revving in earnest, moved to London and became a hit on that city's punk scene via highly entertaining sets and lewd, blatantly offensive records—including, well, *Blatantly Offensive*. They're not for prudes, but the Electric Chairs' crude, rude, and very garagey tunes—"Man Enough to Be a Woman," "Toilet Love," "(If You Don't Wanna Fuck Me) Fuck Off"—will make you snort and give you an idea of why County (now known as Jayne County) was one of New York punk's most fabulous attractions. *Rock 'n' Roll Cleopatra* has the above chestnuts and more.

Suicide

Talk about less is more. As austere as the music of the Ramones and Talking Heads is, the dead-simple setup of this groundbreaking, integral New York act challenges even those two minimalist combos for barely-there-ness. Suicide's sole members, singer Alan Vega and synthesizer/electronics manipulator Martin Rev, began playing together in 1970, billing their early shows as "punk music" years before things started happening at CBGB. When the Ramones began playing the Bowery bar, Vega was their very first fan, telling Johnny after their opening set, "You guys are what I've been waiting for!" A confrontational, Stooges-schooled front man, Vega took no prisoners live, picking fights, swinging chains, and alternately screaming like a man on fire or crooning like the ghost of Elvis while Rev generated cold, pulsing tones on his primitive gear. Although Suicide hit many like some nightmarish two-headed thing from outer space, the band's music is rock 'n' roll at its core, with glimpses of rockabilly, blues, and Doors-y garage psychedelia. While insipid eighties synth-pop bands co-opted Suicide's concepts, the original artifact still sounds like nothing else. *Suicide*, the 1977 debut album (with the band name in blood-dripping letters on the cover), is the group's most essential, encompassing the harrowing "Ghost Rider" and "Rocket U.S.A." and the lengthy, terrifying

"Frankie Teardrop." But the twosome was also capable of sweet, achingly beautiful pop; see "Cheree" or "Dream Baby Dream." Nineteen eighty's sophomore outing, also called *Suicide* (reissued as *Second Album*), is cleaner, but the song quality still pokes through.

Tuff Darts

Next to being fellow early CBGB and Max's mainstays and Sire recording artists, these guys have another Ramones connection: guitarist Jeff Salen had previously played with Tommy Ramone and Ramones road manager Monte Melnick in hard rock outfit Butch and with Marky Ramone in Wayne County and the Back Street Boys (see later). With original vocalist Robert Gordon, Tuff Darts made their wax debut with three cuts that include the audacious "All for the Love of Rock 'n' Roll" on the 1976 compilation *Live at CBGB*, a double LP that also stars club regulars Mink DeVille, the Shirts, the Laughing Dogs, and a few lesser-knowns. Gordon left soon after to pursue his rockabilly solo career, and new singer Tommy Frenzy stepped in for 1978's *Tuff Darts*, the quintet's only contemporaneous album. With catchy hooks, funny lyrics, and glammy touches that betray the band's origins as New York Dolls openers, it's an overlooked New York punk staple that features the rude 'n' rockin' "Rats," the poppy, perverted "Phone Booth Man," and the hilariously sick "Your Love Is Like Nuclear Waste."

The Dead Boys

The most archetypically sneery, ugly punk rock band next to the Sex Pistols were these five transplanted Ohio hooligans—who also happen to have been one of the world's most powerful rock bands, an act whose brutal sound readily lived up to its nihilistic, tough-guy image. Originally called Frankenstein, the Dead Boys were formed in Cleveland in 1976 when vocalist Stiv Bators, guitarist Jimmy Zero, and bassist Jeff Magnum joined with two refugees from proto-punk band Rocket from the Tombs, guitarist Cheetah Chrome and drummer Johnny Blitz. After the Ramones played Ohio and the two bands became friends, the Dead Boys moved to

New York, where they quickly made a name for themselves thanks to their wild sets and Bators's Stooge-style antics. With CBGB owner Hilly Kristal as their new manager, the group scored a deal with Sire and made 1977's *Young Loud and Snotty*, an album no punker should be without. With some of the heaviest, densest wall-of-guitar sounds ever put to record, it holds the oft-covered "Sonic Reducer," "Ain't Nothin' to Do," and "What Love Is," and will grind to dust whatever you leave sitting in front of your stereo (be careful!). *We Have Come for Your Children* (1978) is somewhat neutered by Mountain (see Chapter Three) bassist Felix Pappalardi's tamed-down production, but nevertheless has some great songs ("Flamethrower Love," the bleak punk blues "Ain't It Fun") and features Joey and Dee Dee Ramone on background vocals. The album tanked, the group split up, and Bators formed punk all-stars Lords of the New Church. Sadly, he became a real dead boy in 1990 after being struck by a car.

The Cramps

Another expatriate Cleveland crew, the Cramps single-handedly concocted the punk subgenre now called psychobilly: a primitive, sleazy, sex-fueled mix of rockabilly, sixties garage punk, and imagery swiped from old monster movies, hot rod culture, and trashy paperbacks. Sharing many of the same interests, the Ramones were Cramps supporters early on and often tapped them as openers. An unsurpassed live act, the Cramps were formed in 1976 by frenzied front man Lux Interior (Eric Purkhiser) and ice-cool guitarist Ivy Rorschach (Kristy Wallace); guitarist Bryan Gregory (Greg Beckerleg) was next added and the group worked with a couple of drummers before locking into its classic lineup with Nick Knox (Nick Stephanoff). The bass-less band's 1979 debut EP, *Gravest Hits*, stitched together from early singles, has the sinister "Human Fly" and demented, reverb-marinated rockabilly and garage covers (the version of the Trashmen's "Surfin' Bird" is neck-and-neck with the Ramones'). *Songs the Lord Taught Us* (1980) is the Cramps' numero uno release. Produced by Big Star's Alex Chilton (see Chapter Three), it shudders with hiccup-dripping, voodoo-bitten rockers like "Garbageman" and "I Was a Teenage Werewolf." Gregory was replaced by Kid Congo Powers (Brian Tristan) for 1981's similarly swampy and untamed *Psychedelic Jungle*, which oozes and shakes as the band amplifies (metaphorically and aurally) the primal lust and stomp of obscure fifties and sixties nuggets like "Primitive," "Rockin' Bones," and "Goo Goo Muck." Nineteen eighty-three's live *Smell of Female* is off-the-chain crazy; 1986's *A Date with Elvis* is the band's last great studio LP, its "Can Your Pussy Do the Dog?" a standout. When it comes to Cramps comps, the current best is *File Under Sacred Music: Early Singles 1978–1981*.

CLEVELAND/AKRON PUNK

Although no other city is arguably as decadent and happening as New York—especially back in the 1970s—in retrospect, the Dead Boys and the Cramps left a surprisingly active musical region behind when they split their rusty Ohio home for the rotten Big Apple. Thanks to frequent visits by the Velvet Underground and the trailblazing work of local proto-punkers the Electric Eels, Rocket from the Tombs, Mirrors, and the Styrenes, the Cleveland/Akron area invented punk rock concurrently with New York—albeit in a hostile, narrow-minded environment far removed from the encouragement of slumming Manhattan debutantes and their fifteen-minutes-of-fame flashbulbs. In 1975, while the Ramones were starting to turn heads on the Bowery, in Cleveland Rocket from the Tombs was also performing and would soon splinter into the Dead Boys and Pere Ubu (the latter one of America's greatest rock bands, although much more experimental than the Ramones). Neighboring Akron, the home of future Pretenders leader Chrissie Hynde, had Devo, the Bizarros, Tin Huey, and others; nearby Kent had Human Switchboard. Rocket from the Tombs reunited for a tour and new recordings in 2003; *The Day the Earth Met Rocket from the Tombs* is an ear-burning set of early material by these lost pioneers. *Those Were Different Times: Cleveland 1972–1976* has ahead-of-their-time tracks by the Electric Eels, the Styrenes, and Mirrors.

Devo

Although Devo is seen by many as a novelty act thanks to its humorously absurd aesthetic, early on the five Ohio spuds were one of American punk's greatest bands—one that rocked hard amid its trademark hilarity. Formed in 1972 at Kent State University by Mark Mothersbaugh (vocals, synthesizer, guitar) and Jerry Casale (vocals, bass), the band took its name from the concept of "de-evolution," which posits that humankind is devolving rather than evolving. Devo's 1978 debut, *Q: Are We Not Men? A: We Are Devo!*, was shaped by Brian Eno, whose innovative use of synthesizers in Roxy Music (see Chapter Three) made him the perfect producer. But despite the band's fascination with electronics, the album is a guitar-heavy outing, shredding ears with the tension-racked "Uncontrollable Urge" and herky-jerky deconstruction of the Rolling Stones' "(I Can't Get No) Satisfaction"; its pumping "Jocko Homo" and "Mongoloid" echo the Ramones' obsessions with freaks and geeks. *Duty Now for the Future* (1979) brings the synths to the fore, but is recommended for the wacky "Clockout," the wired version of Johnny Rivers's "Secret Agent Man," and the deranged medley "Smart Patrol / Mr. DNA." The Top Forty hit "Whip It" propelled the success of 1980's sleeker *Freedom of Choice*, which also has "Girl U Want," one of the band's quirky best, and the surprisingly stirring, Who-like, "Gates of Steel." But the punk guitars were left well behind, along with most of the interesting song ideas, soon after. *The Essentials* packs twelve of the band's best and best-known.

The Pagans

Criminally overlooked, the Pagans are responsible for some of the grimiest, nastiest, toughest punk rock ever belched forth. Commencing in 1976, this fetid Cleveland crew, steered by the charred throat of front man Mike Hudson and the machine-gun guitar of Mike Metoff, coughed up a string of stupefyingly great singles whose titles spell it all out: "Dead End America," "Street Where Nobody Lives," "What's This Shit Called Love?" Find 'em all on the collection *Shit Street*.

The Rubber City Rebels

These Rustbelt rockers also started in 1976 and were co-led by Iggy-ish singer Rod Firestone and guitarist Buzz Clic, who together ran Akron venue the Crypt, said to be the first punk club in the Midwest. The band put out a split LP with the Bizarros before heading for the even smoggier climes of L.A., where it made one 1980 album for Capitol. The Rubber City Rebels' delightfully thuggish ways are preserved on *The Akron Years (1977)* and *The Hollywood Years (1979–1984)*.

BRITISH PUNK

The Ramones and a few other bands were the sore-thumb exceptions, but the early New York punk scene was largely identified with art and literature. The Cleveland/Akron scene had a collegiate-meets-blue-collar vibe. The emergent British punk community, however, was rooted in glam and pub rock. It started coalescing around the London clothing shop Sex, where the first true U.K. punk band, the Sex Pistols, formed in 1975. Almost as soon as they began playing out, the Pistols set off a revolution with their crude, powerful music and provocative demeanor. In America, early punk was mainly a reaction against boredom and the lame music on the radio. In England it was that as well a full-blown social phenomenon fueled by the Pistols' public irreverence and scathing attacks on the arcane British class system—the more the authorities tried to suppress punk as being dangerous to the social order, the more attractive it became to restless kids. Rhino's "DIY" series has two fine volumes mapping the British scene: *Anarchy in the UK: UK Punk I (1976–77)* and *The Modern World: UK Punk II (1977–78)*.

The Clash

Hyped by its label as "the only band that matters," for a while the Clash actually lived up to the claim. The biggest British act to rival the Sex Pistols (see sidebar), and, eventually, the Ramones, the Clash is fervently recalled as not only one of punk rock's leading bands, but as one of rock's greatest-ever. The group started in

1976: guitarist and main singer Joe Strummer (born John Mellor) came from pub rockers the 101ers, and guitarist/singer Mick Jones came from unrecorded proto-punk band London SS; bassist Paul Simonon and first drummer Terry Chimes were added next, although Chimes was soon replaced by Nicky "Topper" Headon. In addition to being an impossibly powerful and captivating live unit, the band recorded some absolutely indispensable albums. *The Clash* (1977) is first among them. It shows, already firmly in place, the Clash's incendiary mix of Who/Kinks power chords ("Clash City Rockers"), impassioned, emotional epics ("Complete Control"), hard reggae ("Police and Thieves"), and revolutionary lyrics (the breakneck "White Riot," perhaps the first Ramones rip-off on record). *Give 'Em Enough Rope* (1978) is likewise magnificent, exploding with the overpowering "Safe European Home," "English Civil War," and "Tommy Gun," and harboring Jones's poignant "Stay Free." Nineteen seventy-nine's double album, *London Calling*, is repeatedly hailed as a rock 'n' roll milestone—a point that's difficult to argue, even though it's miles away from the Ramones' linear style. While not as gritty as its precursors, it's marked by a triumphant, newfound adoption of other forms (R&B, ska, jazz, sweet pop, rockabilly, and more reggae) into a punk context, and its hard rockers ("Death or Glory," "Clampdown") are fuller-sounding and more focused. The title track is the pièce de résistance, a haunting, alchemical, avant-pop synthesis of punk rock, dub reggae, and apocalyptic, political lyrics. In descending order, the above titles are the Clash records you really need, although 1980's *Black Market Clash* EP (expanded as *Super Black Market Clash*) pulls together great rarities like "The Prisoner" and "City of the Dead." The only Clash anthology that matters is the two-CD *The Story of the Clash Volume 1*.

The Damned

Plagued by an unstable lineup, the Damned never quite attained the notoriety of its chief early competitors, the Sex Pistols and the Clash. But in some ways the Damned beat all the British bands to the punch by becoming the first U.K. punk act to release a single and an album and to tour the U.S. And the Damned ultimately became the longest-lived of the three, still active at the time of this writing. Known for its slapstick humor, the founding edition of guitarist Brian James, drummer Rat Scabies (Chris Millar), bassist Captain Sensible (Ray Burns), and vampire/vocalist Dave Vanian, evolved from the pre-punk London SS (see earlier) and Masters of the Backside. The band's 1977 garage-blasting debut, *Damned Damned Damned*, shares the Stooges / MC5 / New York Dolls / Alice Cooper influences of the Ramones. Besides reprising the group's flaming first single, 1976's "New Rose" (whose spoken intro swipes from Ramones inspirations the Shangri-Las' "Leader of the Pack"), its trashy bashers like "Neat Neat Neat" and "Born to Kill" make it another perfect punk platter. *Music for Pleasure* (1977), lambasted for its lack of focus and muddy production, has some good rockers anyway ("Problem Child," "Stretcher Case"). James left before 1979's *Machine Gun Etiquette*, which is at least the equal of the first album. With ex-Saints man Algy Ward on bass and Sensible now on fiery, Hendrixian guitar, its many amazing moments include the rubbery thrash of "Love Song" and the emblematic flag-waver "Smash It Up." Nineteen eighty's ambitious *The Black Album* finds the group developing the psychedelic-punk fusion hinted at on *Machine Gun Etiquette*; the dramatic "Wait for the Blackout" recalls the Who circa *Who's Next*. After 1982's *Strawberries*, Sensible departed (to return for live reunions) and the Damned's studio work turned toward moody goth-psych. But *Strawberries* is excellent, with the runaway "Ignite" and the pop-punk masterpiece "Dozen Girls" (one guesses Republican Johnny Ramone didn't dig the Reagan-baiting "Bad Time for Bonzo"). *The Best of the Damned* picks from the first four years.

The Buzzcocks

The first major Brit-punk band from outside London, the Buzzcocks hail from Manchester. With original singer Howard Devoto and mainstay guitarists Pete Shelley and Steve Diggle, the band was inspired to form in 1976 by the Sex Pistols. After one self-released EP, Devoto left to form the artier Magazine, and Shelley took over lead vocals for a run of now-classic singles—"Orgasm Addict," "What Do I Get?," and "Promises"—that play like a streamlined, high-speed mix of the Ramones and early Beatles. These and later forty-fives are collected on the 1979 compilation *Singles Going Steady*, which remains the definitive starting point for anyone new to the band. *Another Music in a Different Kitchen* (1978) is a fantastic first LP, thanks not only to the brisk cuts ("Fast Cars," "I Don't Mind"), but also to the captivating, more cerebral departures that hint at the direction the band would further explore later ("Autonomy," "Fiction Romance"). The same year's equally stupendous *Love Bites* is more weighted toward driving pop-punkers like "Ever Fallen in Love," "Love You More," and "Noise Annoys." *A Different Kind of Tension* (1979) is a resounding display of diversity: Alongside the pop bliss of "You Say You Don't Love Me" and the hard, Diggle-sung "Mad Mad Judy" and "Sitting Round at Home," it has the staggering closer "I Believe," a seven-minute, ever-shifting social critique that serves as the perfect coda to this last effort by the definitive lineup.

The Jam

The Jam launched the British mod revival and bore the unmistakable influence of Ramones favorites the Who and the Kinks, along with fellow sixties icons the Small Faces. Sparked into action by the Sex Pistols and the beginnings of London punk, singer/guitarist Paul Weller, bassist Bruce Foxton, and drummer Rick Buckler formed the group in 1975 in suburban Woking. The threesome's furious 1977 debut, *In the City*, quickly established it as a savage musical unit. Its title track, the Jam's first single, bursts with slashing guitar, as do its electrified R&B-based ravers like "Art School" and "I've Changed My Address" (the band even rips through the "Batman Theme"). Released later in 1977, *This Is the Modern World* is less even but has one of the trio's many great reflective numbers, "Life from a Window," and the righteous, rallying title single. In 1978, *All Mod Cons* cemented Weller's reputation as a fine songwriter with a distinct lyrical voice focusing on youth frustrations and British life. Considered the band's pinnacle by many, it straddles Beatles-y acoustic ballads ("English Rose") and tough, harmony-laced tracks ("Billy Hunt," "A Bomb in Wardour Street"). *Setting Sons* (1979) is a little too produced in some spots (strings), but actually has more rockers than its immediate predecessor (see "Private Hell," "Saturday's Kids," and "Eton Rifles"). The band's sixties revisionism reaches its full flower on 1980's *Sound Affects*, whose ambitious, poetic leanings may not move all Ramones lovers. (The same goes for 1982's soul-influenced, final studio LP, *The Gift*.) "Going Underground," perhaps the band's greatest track, is on *The Very Best of the Jam*, which compiles album cuts and singles.

Generation X

While best known as the launch vehicle of eighties MTV staple Billy Idol, Generation X deserves much better—as anyone who hears the band's wonderfully glammy, bubblegum punk will agree. The group of vocalist Idol, bassist Tony James, drummer Mark Laff (all previously in the band Chelsea; see below), and guitarist Bob Andrews opened for the Ramones in London and released a couple of excellent singles in 1977. *Generation X* (1978) is exactly the kind of wall-to-wall chunka-chunk that Ramones fans go gaga for, a claim that its shout-alongs "One Hundred Punks," "Ready Steady Go," and "Your Generation" loudly support. Nineteen seventy-nine's *Valley of the Dolls* (produced by Mott the Hoople's Ian Hunter) isn't quite as raw, but does have some of the band's stronger tunes: "King Rocker," "Running with the Boss Sound," "Night of the Cadillacs." Rechristened Gen X, the band was down to Idol, James, and guests for 1981's glossy bow-out, *Kiss Me Deadly* (with the Ramones-derived crossover hit "Dancing with Myself"). *The Best of Generation X* draws from the first two albums.

The Stranglers

The Stranglers started playing pubs as the Guildford Stranglers in 1974, the same year the Ramones formed, and were on the bill for the Ramones' first London show in 1976. Their *Rattus Norvegicus* (1977) stands well apart from other punk albums, thanks largely to keyboardist Dave Greenfield's creepy lines, which bring the Doors to mind; the band's other strengths include Dee Dee double J. J.

Burnel's dirty bass sound, singer/guitarist Hugh Cornwell's dark voice and lyrics, and ex-jazz drummer Jet Black's steady beats. Cornwell and Burnel trade off on lead snarls for ghostly and grimy grinders like "(Get a) Grip (On Yourself)" and "Hanging Around." But *No More Heroes*, also from 1977, is the Stranglers' belligerent best, with aggressive cuts like "Something Better Change" and the title track. *Black and White*'s production (1978) is barely less abrasive, but kicks arse with songs like "Tank" and "Hey! (Rise of the Robots)" and has the naughty "Nice 'n' Sleazy." Released in 1979, *The Raven* is the band's point of departure into a more psychedelic pop vein, but its "Dead Loss Angeles" and "Nuclear Device" still rank among the Stranglers' punkest tunes. *The Collection 1977–1982* and *Greatest Hits 1977–1990* are pragmatic introductions.

The Vibrators

Another set of pubbers-turned-punks, the original Vibrators were singer/guitarist Ian "Knox" Carnachan, guitarist John Ellis, bassist Pat Collier, and drummer John "Eddie" Edwards. The foursome waxed 1977's *Pure Mania*, a clobbering, must-have album guaranteed to get you pogoing. Its surfeit of energetic tracks includes "Yeah Yeah Yeah," "Petrol," and "Whips and Furs"; "Baby, Baby," the Vibes' best-known song, is a sweet punk ballad not dissimilar to the Ramones' "I Wanna Be Your Boyfriend." Nineteen seventy-eight's *V2* and 1984's *Alaska 127* are also worthwhile.

The Undertones

Some call these guys "the Irish Ramones." And that's not far off the mark, although Feargal Sharkey's tremulous quaver distinguishes the Undertones from other bruddas-influenced bands. Also important to their sound were guitarists and brothers Damian and John O'Neill, the latter of whom penned the band's 1978 debut single, "Teenage Kicks," named as the greatest pop song of all time by top U.K. DJ John Peel. That timeless example of wide-eyed teen punk appears next to similarly joyous gems like "Get Over You" and "Jimmy, Jimmy" on *The Undertones*, the quintet's flawless 1979 debut. The following year's *Hypnotised* doesn't quite match the first LP, but you'll love it as well: the name of its opener, "More Songs About Chocolate and Girls," betrays the group's continued exuberance and Ramones-simpatico outlook. The final two albums by the founding lineup, however, are smoother new wave and pop soul.

The Rezillos

If the Undertones were the Emerald Isle's Ramones, then the Rezillos were Scotland's—albeit with a campy, Day-Glo image and female vocals. The Rezillos were formed in Edinburgh in 1976 around singers Eugene Reynolds and Fay Fife. The success of a 1977 indie single led to a deal with Sire Records and a tour with—ta-da!—the Ramones, circa *Rocket to Russia*. The band's 1978 debut, *Can't Stand the Rezillos*, is class-A punk pop all the way, full of bubblegum guitar crunch and sci-fi/comic-book lyrics. Its single "Top of the Pops" landed the band on the TV show of the same name, and the cover of the rockabilly-ish Fleetwood Mac curio "Somebody's Gonna Get Their Head Kicked In Tonight" inspired further punk versions. The Rezillos split up soon afterward (1979's live *Mission Accomplished... But the Beat Goes On* appeared posthumously), but Fife and Reynolds revamped the band as the Revillos, which sounded much the same and released 1980's ebullient *Rev Up*. As per its title, *Can't Stand the Rezillos: The (Almost) Complete Rezillos* has pretty much everything by the band's first iteration.

Eddie and the Hot Rods

Admired by Dee Dee Ramone, Eddie and the Hot Rods, formed in 1975, bridged the gap between pub rock and punk with their boozy, Stonesy garage R&B (the Sex Pistols played one of their first London dates as a Hot Rods opener). The band's typically frantic gigs are legend, and lead singer Barrie Masters was high energy incarnate ("Eddie" was a stuffed dummy the band kicked around on stage at early shows). After a couple of rampant singles, the band debuted with 1976's *Teenage Depression*, an unstoppably boisterous record with bracing originals like "Double Checkin' Woman" and "On the Run" and spirited romps through the Who's "The Kids Are Alright" and Sam Cooke's "Shake." *Life on the Line* has the Rods' biggest hit, the elevating "Do Anything You Wanna Do," and came out in 1977, the year they toured the U.S. with the Ramones. *Do Anything You Wanna Do: The Best of Eddie and the Hot Rods* covers the peak years.

X-Ray Spex

London's X-Ray Spex was led by the huge-voiced, braces-mouthed Poly Styrene. Although the original group only managed a few singles and an album, its influence far outweighs its scant output. The Spex's screaming, saxophone-smeared 1977 debut single "Oh Bondage Up Yours!" is one of early punk's most arresting tracks, an anti-consumerism, proto–riot grrrl screed that still sounds unique. *Germ-Free Adolescence* (1978) is easily among the top ten British punk LP's, a totally riveting album whose incredible songs—"The Day the World Turned Day-Glo," "Identity," "Art-I-Ficial"—are shot through with underrated guitarist Jak Airport's granite-hard riffs and Styrene's clever, personally political lyrics.

Cool Britannia!

By now you have the idea. The English punk rock upheaval produced enough great bands to fill several books, and has: see this one's appendix of recommended reads. Here are few more U.K. punk acts whose way with a four-four beat will pique the ears of Ramones fans.

Sham 69

All working-class stance and football-chant choruses, Sham 69 was briefly on the same label as the Ramones. The shouty quartet's bruddas-aping "Borstal Breakout" appears in live form on the excellent *Tell Us the Truth*. Also get *If the Kids Are United: The Best of Sham 69*.

The Adverts

Ah, serial killers. A subject dear to the Ramones' hearts. This London quartet's crude, darkly humorous style is best remembered via "Gary Gilmore's Eyes," wherein the song's narrator receives a transplant of the namesake murderer's eyeballs. Get *Crossing the Red Sea with the Adverts*.

The Only Ones

The Only Ones' "Another Girl, Another Planet," penned by their poetically tortured singer/guitarist Peter Perrett, is one of the best singles of any age, its sweetly sad lyric married to a roaring, soaring power pop backing. Kinda like a more sensitive Ramones. Get *Special View*.

Wire

Formed in 1976, these amazing art school punks' songs can be either monochromatically cool and atmospheric ("Lowdown") or like a compact, Piet Mondrian–inspired Ramones ("12XU"). Get *Pink Flag* and *Chairs Missing*.

Slaughter and the Dogs

Manchester ruffians who kicked out one album of Slade/Sweet-based machine-gun punk before their defining lineup collapsed. Their version of the bubblegum hit "Quick Joey Small" is something to behold. Get *Do It Dog Style*.

The Boys

A cross between the New York Dolls and the early Beatles, these guys toured with the Ramones and blasted out tight, tough punk pop. Get *The Boys* and *Alternative Chartbusters*,

Stiff Little Fingers

Noticeably Clash-inspired, this much-loved Irish band cut the classic killers "Alternative Ulster" and "Suspect Device." Get *Inflammable Material*.

Chelsea

Led by the rough-voiced Gene October, Chelsea was a mainstay of "Year Zero" London punk and barked out the crucial '77 single "Right to Work." Get *No Escape*.

999

The long-rocking London quartet's menacing "Homicide" is an early fusion of punk and vintage hard rock. Get *Separates* and *The Biggest Prize in Sport*.

U.K. Subs

Fronted by the unstoppable Charlie Harper—still performing in 2012 at almost seventy—this institution formed in 1976 but didn't make an album until 1979's sturdy *Another Kind of Blues*. Also get *Before You Were Punk: The Very Best of the U.K. Subs*.

The Lurkers

Among the earliest Ramones clones, as evidenced by their pounding debut single, "Shadow." Get *Fulham Fallout*.

Stiff Records

Besides releasing the Damned's "New Rose," the U.K.'s first punk record (see earlier), the Stiff Records label documented other important punk-associated acts like Nick Lowe, Devo, Motörhead, Ian Dury, Wreckless Eric, and Elvis Costello (the latter's early records are much more punk than many listeners might expect). Get *Born Stiff: The Stiff Records Collection*.

Australian Punk

Broadly speaking, early Australian punk has less in common with the literary and artistic sides of the New York and London scenes and shares more of their aggressive, hard-rocking elements—perhaps reflective of the convict-colonized continent's roughneck European settlers. (Notable exception: intellectuals the Boys Next Door, who initially covered the Ramones and eventually morphed into the Birthday Party and, much later, Nick Cave and the Bad Seeds.) Australia's twin punk pioneers were the Saints and Radio Birdman, who, like the Ramones and the Sex Pistols, were markedly influenced by the Stooges, the MC5, and the New York Dolls. On the heels of the Saints and Birdman came ranks of bands that rocked the notoriously hostile barrooms of the land down under: the Psycho Surgeons, Johnny Dole and the Scabs, the Cheap Nasties (featuring future Scientists leader Kim Salmon), the Victims (with Dave Faulkner of the Hoodoo Gurus), the Thought Criminals, News, the Leftovers, Razar, the Survivors, JAB, the Fun Things, X (not to be confused with the identically named American band), and La Femme. The compilations *Do the Pop!* and *Tales from the Australian Underground* (two volumes) act as ass-kicking tutorials on antipodean punk.

The Saints

Starting out on the other side of the world in 1973—a year before the Ramones—the Saints came up with a sound that was uncannily similar to that of their Queens counterparts. The Brisbane-born quartet featuring hollering vocalist Chris Bailey and jet-engine guitarist Ed Kuepper released the scorching 1976 D.I.Y. single "(I'm) Stranded." The first punk record released outside the U.S., it beat the initial singles by the Damned and the Sex Pistols to the bins and drew vociferous praise from the British press and a U.S. deal with Ramones label Sire. The Saints' 1977 debut, *(I'm) Stranded*, had many assuming the band was copying the Ramones' first album—but during its inception the Aussie group had no knowledge of the developing New York and London punk scenes. All hoarse vocals; grinding, sheet-metal guitar; and breakneck bass and drums, the disc is one of punk's most volatile debuts, and deserves a place on your shelf alongside those by the Clash, the Sex Pistols, the Dead Boys, and, yep, the Ramones. From the roaring, opening title track and its fellow face-shredding rockers ("Erotic Neurotic," "Demolition Girl") and tough, bluesy ballads ("Messin' with the Kid," "Story of Love"), it's about as perfect as punk rock gets. Bassist Kym Bradshaw was replaced with Algy Ward (later of the Damned) prior to 1978's *Eternally Yours*, an album that's more sonically diverse than *(I'm) Stranded* but still rocks plenty hard. Besides a growth in songwriting, its most striking development is the addition of the sixties-soul horns heard on the single "Know Your Product." Moody mid-tempo numbers like "Memories Are Made of This" reveal a deeper side, but the punk killers remain in abundance. Later that year the Saints released the winningly deeper *Prehistoric Sounds*, the final LP with the original lineup. *Know Your Product: The Best of the Saints* has twenty-two flaming cuts from the Saints' first three LPs.

THE SEX PISTOLS

Although they only released a few singles and one real album and were together for barely three years (the first time around), the Sex Pistols are one of the most influential acts in music history. The band began when bassist Glen Matlock, who worked at the Kings Road boutique Sex, was enlisted by two shop regulars, guitarist Steve Jones and drummer Paul Cook, for their Roxy Music–inspired outfit, the Strand (a.k.a. the Swankers). Sex's owner, Malcom McLaren, who'd briefly chaperoned the New York Dolls and recently returned from an eye-opening visit to CBGB, became the group's manager. After trying out a few uninteresting lead vocalists, the band recruited green-haired, nineteen-year-old John Lydon, renamed Johnny Rotten for his bad teeth. The singer had no prior experience but would nevertheless turn out to be the consummate front man, a confrontational, charismatic performer-lyricist with an impassioned snarl that matched the band's commanding sound.

The Sex Pistols' first single, November 1976's acerbic "Anarchy in the U.K.," created a furor that saw the band dropped from its label, EMI. A&M stepped in, but after more outrage following a profanity-strewn TV talk show appearance, another caustic single, "God Save the Queen"—which went to number one despite its being banned—and a cancellation-plagued tour, the act was once again label-less. By the time they were picked up by Virgin Records, the Pistols had replaced Matlock with Sid Vicious, whose violent behavior and defining look fit their image to a T. Unfortunately, Vicious had little musical talent, so it was Jones and a temporarily rehired Matlock who played bass on most of the group's 1977 debut, *Never Mind the Bollocks, Here's the Sex Pistols*.

After growing disillusioned with his dysfunctional band mates and McLaren's manipulations, Rotten left the group at the end of its 1978 U.S.

tour, going on to form the decidedly avant Public Image Ltd. McLaren tried to keep the ball rolling with work on *The Great Rock 'n' Roll Swindle*, a half-baked concept film about the Sex Pistols' rise, but the band soon broke up. Jones and Cook started the Professionals, while Vicious attempted a solo career before dying of a heroin overdose in February 1979. In 1996 the original lineup reunited for the Filthy Lucre Tour, which was followed by more performances.

Superlatives fall short when it comes to *Never Mind the Bollocks, Here's the Sex Pistols*. One of the greatest albums—of any genre—ever recorded, it inspired countless bands around the world and continues to do so. Atop its roaring guitars and driving drums, Rotten's rabid vocals deliver venom-packed social tirades with a transcendently addictive momentum. "Pretty Vacant," "Anarchy in the U.K.," and "God Save the Queen" have a near-Wagnerian sweep, while the seething "No Feelings," "Liar," and "EMI," the latter a nose-thumbing kiss-off to the band's first label, bristle with life-affirming fury. Together with *Ramones*, *Never Mind the Bollocks* equals Punk Rock 101, the music's boilerplate. *The Great Rock 'n' Roll Swindle* soundtrack (1979) is worth hearing for its inclusion of early rehearsals and outtakes and couple of decent sans-Rotten tracks, but way too much of it is given over to novelty material cooked up by McLaren. There are releases marketed as "the best of the Sex Pistols," but for a band that only made one studio album—and a flawless album, at that—such a concept is wholly redundant. So never mind the best-ofs, *Never Mind the Bollocks* is all you really need.

Radio Birdman

When Michigan-born guitarist Deniz Tek immigrated to Australia in 1972 to study medicine, he brought along his Stooges and MC5 albums to spread the Motor City gospel down under. In 1974, after leaving a band called TV Jones, he hooked up with ex-Rats singer Rob Younger, guitarist Chris Masuak, keyboardist Pip Hoyle, drummer Ron Keeley, and bassist Warwick Gilbert (another ex-Rat) to form Radio Birdman, whose name comes from a misheard lyric in the Stooges' "1970." The Sydney group's 1977 debut, *Radios*

Appear, appeared on Sire Records in America around the same time the label launched *Rocket to Russia*, and fits neatly alongside that punk landmark. While the album's Detroit influences are unmistakable, songs like "New Race," "What Gives," and "Murder City Nights" have a ringing, glassy guitar sound and tighter, more compact feel that's unique to this quintet, and longer workouts like "Man with Golden Helmet" and "Descent into the Maelstrom" are Doors-like. *Living Eyes* (1978), recorded in England while the band was on tour with the Flamin' Groovies (see Chapter Three), pairs Ramones-ish surf ("More Fun") with uncut scorch ("Hanging On"). Birdman broke up soon after, with Tek, Younger, and Gilbert joining Stooges guitarist Ron Asheton and MC5 drummer Dennis Thompson in the short-lived New Race. The 2006 reunion *Zeno Beach* sees the band still burning brightly after taking nearly thirty years off. *The Essential Radio Birdman: 1974–1978* collates twenty-two Birdman bangers.

CALIFORNIA PUNK

Thanks to its leading presence with the hardcore, ska-punk, and pop-punk movements during the 1980s and 1990s, California is today considered a punk bastion. But when the original punk waves were taking off in New York, London, and Australia, the Golden State's scene was still germinating. By 1977, though, punk had firmly taken hold in Los Angeles and San Francisco and was well up to speed. L.A.'s Rodney Bingenheimer was one of the first American DJs to spin punk on the air, and early visits by the Ramones (in 1976) and the Damned (1977) further energized the scenes in both towns. Prior to that, though, L.A. had hosted galvanizing appearances by the Stooges and the New York Dolls, both of whom enjoyed a second home in the glam rock milieu surrounding Rodney's English Disco, a club and rock star/groupie hangout operated by Bingenheimer. As had been the case in London, in L.A. the early punk scene was largely made up of disaffected ex-glam kids, while in San Francisco it stemmed more from the Bay Area's tradition of political activism and beatnik/hippie dissent. Both cities produced legendary bands that went on to influence successive punk outfits around the world. *Black Hole: Californian Punk 1977–1980* provides a thorough peek at the state's northern and southern scenes.

The Runaways

Managed by the notorious Svengali Kim Fowley, the all-female Runaways' glittery sound and image hewed more closely to glam and hard rock than to the Stoogey styles of the Ramones or the Sex Pistols. Still, the tough approach of the band—singer Cherie Currie, guitarists Joan Jett and Lita Ford, bassist Jackie Fox, and drummer Sandy West—was enough at odds with the prevailing soft rock that it fit in well with the emerging punk trend (the group even opened for the Ramones on a 1978 U.S. tour). The Runaways began in 1975 and signed a much-hyped deal with Mercury. Ahead of the times, the five hard-partying, hard-rocking, sexually aggressive teenage girls were dismissed by critics as a novelty act. But 1976's *The Runaways* nevertheless brims with brutish gems; its belligerent "Cherry Bomb" is an anthem of adolescent angst, while the other slammers ("American Nights," "You Drive Me Wild") keep the bad-girl energy burning. The title cut on *Queens of Noise* (1977) is another defiant signature tune, and its companion image-fostering tracks like "Hollywood" and "Neon Angels on the Road to Ruin" are likewise recommended (interestingly, the Ramones' *Road to Ruin* appeared soon after). Prior to 1977's *Waitin' for the Night*, Fox was replaced by Vickie Blue and Currie also left, leaving Jett to step in as the main vocalist. Musically the group didn't miss a beat, as "School Days" and other raw-throated cuts vociferously attest. The twelve-track *Neon Angels* is the best of the Runaways' best-ofs. Jett of course became a major star with her backing band, the Blackhearts, and her *Bad Reputation* (1980), *I Love Rock 'n' Roll* (1981), *Album* (1983), *Up Your Alley* (1988), and *Pure and Simple* (1994) will also appeal.

The Germs

Jett produced 1979's *(G.I.)*, the only official album by L.A.'s most infamous punks, the Germs. Fronted by Darby Crash (a.k.a. Bobby

Pyn, born Paul Beahm), one of rock's leading live-fast-die-young-sters (he overdosed at twenty-two), the Germs were rounded out by drummer Don Bolles, bassist Lorna Doom, and guitarist Pat Smear (later of Nirvana and the Foo Fighters). Ignited by the Stooges, David Bowie, the Sex Pistols, and the Ramones, the four-some quickly made a name with its grandly shambolic sets, which had the snarling, inebriated Crash prowling the stage and abusing himself and the crowd. But judging from *(G.I.)* you'd never believe the band was such a mess live. A tightly delivered blast of white heat, it easily blows away other West Coast punk albums, thanks largely to Smear's razor-edged playing and Crash's bile-spewing delivery and cryptic lyrics. It's a chore picking faves from this com-pulsory album, but, since you ask, the venomously shredding "Let's Pretend," "Communist Eyes," and "Media Blitz" are three. *(MIA): The Complete Anthology* has everything these durable delinquents did in the studio.

The Dickies

Fast, furious, and funny, the Dickies were the court jesters of L.A. punk. Founded by helium-voiced front man Leonard Graves Phillips and guitarist Stan Lee, these goofy greats shared the Ramones' interests in trashy pop culture, cartoons, and clever covers, making them band favorites and natural tour mates. Their first album, 1979's *The Incredible Shrinking Dickies*, is hyperactive fun that never lets up, from its frenetic originals like "Poodle Party" and "You Drive Me Ape (You Big Gorilla)" to its insane versions of well-known tunes like Black Sabbath's "Paranoid"—which is twice the tempo of the original, making it fun to play for disbelieving metalheads back in the day. (The CD reissue adds the band's manic romp through the theme to TV kiddie show "The Banana Splits.") Later in 1979 came *Dawn of the Dickies*, which is no less uproarious or blistering. Besides more great Dickies compositions ("Fan Mail," "Manny, Moe and Jack"), it keeps up the crazy-covers quotient with a wild reinterpretation of the Moody Blues' "Nights in White Satin" (seriously). The tradition continues with a speeded-up version of Led Zeppelin's "Communication Breakdown" on

1983's *Stukas Over Disneyland*, a set further enhanced by the piston-popping "Rosemary" and side-splitting "She's a Hunchback." *Second Coming* (1989) and *Idjit Savant* (1995) show the Dickies capably continuing the high-octane hilarity almost twenty years after their 1977 formation. *Great Dictations: The Definitive Dickies Collection* will delight the unenlightened.

The Weirdos

Speaking of the Dickies, before he joined the band their erstwhile eighties drummer Nickey Beat had played with this explosive quintet. Formed in 1976 by brothers John (vocals) and Dix Denny (guitar), the Weirdos whacked out two of American punk's greatest singles, 1977's "Destroy All Music" and "We Got the Neutron Bomb." With their bizarre art-school-assemblage look and total wall-of-guitar performances, the band was a top L.A. punk attraction and recorded a pair of excellent EPs during their late-seventies incarnations. *Weird World, Vol. 1* spans 1977 to 1981 and has such obliterating must-hears as "Solitary Confinement" and "Life of Crime."

X

The best-known band of the original Los Angeles punk wave, X was formed in 1977 by singer/bassist John Doe, singer Exene Cervenka, and guitarist Billy Zoom, a tenured rockabilly player who'd been sold on punk after hearing the Ramones (he later became a close friend of Johnny Ramone). The three eventually netted drummer D. J. Bonebrake and developed a singular blend of gutter poetics, skewed country vocal harmonies, roots-punk riffs, and urgent rhythms. Doors keyboardist Ray Manzarek produced X's 1980 debut, *Los Angeles*, and would do the same for the band's next three albums. A paragon album of West Coast punk, *Los Angeles* brims with songs topped by Doe and Cervenka's lyrics of rocky romance (mostly their own, it seems) and dissections of L.A. existence: the revved-up "Your Phone's Off the Hook, But You're Not," the tramping "Nausea," the scathing title track (Manzarek even plays on a kicking version of his old band's "Soul Kitchen").

For greatness, 1981's *Wild Gift* isn't far behind the first disc, with the slithering "White Girl," the rockabilly-fired "Beyond and Back," and re-recordings of "We're Desperate" and "Adult Books" from the group's 1978 single on the Dangerhouse label. *Under the Big Black Sun* (1982), X's major label debut, is less raw, but the playing and writing is as bold as anything from its predecessors. It harbors the menacing "The Hungry Wolf" and the lashing "Blue Spark," among other band standouts. *More Fun in the New World* (1983) is X's last recommendable album, opening with the catchy disillusionment rant "The New World," and following up with reliable X rockers like "I See Red" and "Devil Doll." If you're not hip to X, *The Best: Make the Music Go Bang* is a great way to get there.

The Dils

This politically minded trio was co-led by brothers Chip (vocals, guitar) and Tony Kinman (vocals, bass) and was one of the main bands on the early L.A. scene. The group never made a studio album, although its furious single sides ("Class War," "I Hate the Rich") appear on several California punk compilations. *Class War* has live and studio cuts.

The Zeros

Sometimes called the Mexican Ramones, the Zeros were actually from East L.A., not south of the border. In 1976, singer/guitarist Javier Escovedo, guitarist Robert Lopez, bassist Hector Penalosa, and drummer Baba Chenelle got together while still in their early teens. Another band that never made an album in its heyday, the Zeros only put out a few scarce singles before going dormant in 1980. "Wimp," "Wild Weekend," "Beat Your Heart Out," and other seven-inch sides and rarities are wrapped up on *Don't Push Me Around*.

The Screamers

These lost geniuses easily win the award for Cali-punk's weirdest band. While never releasing a record during their existence, the Screamers were Los Angeles mainstays, notable not just for their impossible-to-ignore, Grand Guignol-esque gigs, but also for their novel instrumentation: manic performance artist Tomata du Plenty (David Harrigan) on lead vocals, Tommy Gear on synthesizer, David Brown on distorted electric piano, and K. K. Barrett on primitive drums. That's right: no guitars (though du Plenty had been inspired to play punk rock in 1977 after seeing the Ramones and other guitar-heavy bands at CBGB). *In a Better World* assembles forty demo and live cuts, while the DVD *Live in San Francisco September 2nd, 1978* conveys the spectacle. That the Screamers never got to make a proper album is a crime.

Crime

Did somebody say Crime? This Northern California act was way too cool: four mean-looking dudes who dressed as cops; played low-down, Stooges-inspired garage punk; and audaciously called themselves "San Francisco's first and only rock 'n' roll band." Crime was formed in 1976 by vocalist/guitarist Johnny Strike and guitarist Frankie Fix. Bassist Ron "the Ripper" Greco (formerly of pre–Flamin' Groovies band the Chosen Few) and drummer Ricky Tractor (later replaced by Hank Rank) joined next, and between gigs at punk clubs and prison yards, the foursome released the trashed-out "Hot Wire My Heart" / "Baby You're So Repulsive," the first of the three singles that make up the band's official output. Hear all three and other archival recordings on *San Francisco's Still Doomed*.

The Avengers

"Doomed" as it may have been, San Francisco gave us another great band you should know about: the Avengers, seen by many as the city's greatest contribution to early punk (the Dead Kennedys came later; see Chapter Seven). With growling and utterly compelling lead vocalist Penelope Houston up front, guitarist Greg Ingraham, bassist James Wilsey, and drummer Danny Furious bring the epically powerful backing on classics like "We Are the One," the band's 1977 debut single, and a 1979 EP produced by Sex Pistols guitarist Steve Jones. Those recordings and other essential examples of this heroic outfit's primal, blowtorch rock are compiled on the double CD *Avengers*.

BOSTON PUNK

Boston punk was greatly shaped by mid-sixties area garage bands like the Remains (see Chapter Two) and their proto-punk heirs, the Modern Lovers (see Chapter Three). Accordingly, Boston was also one of the more receptive spots for the Ramones when they first ventured out of Manhattan (their early shows at The Club, in nearby Cambridge, were key events). While the Modern Lovers' Jonathan Richman is the patriarch of Beantown punk, its second godfather is singer/pianist Willie "Loco" Alexander, who cut his garage teeth in the sixties with the Lost and briefly "replaced" Lou Reed in the declining Velvet Underground. Alexander penned two of the scene's most iconic songs, the wistful "Kerouac" and the Stones-stomping "Mass. Ave.," both recorded with his Boom Boom Band (whose two 1978 LPs are compiled on the CD *Pass the Tabasco*).

Ex–Modern Lovers guitarist and future Ramones roadie John Felice, a superb songwriter with a gravel-gargling voice, started the Real Kids in 1972. The quartet was a mainstay at the Rat (the CBGB of Boston), its classic lineup waxing 1977's *Real Kids*—a record you'd do well to own, as a spin through "All Kindsa Girls," "Do the Boob," and other hooky brawlers attests. The Kids' biggest local rival act was DMZ, a sixties garage–inspired quintet helmed by singer/organist Jeff "Monoman" Connolly. DMZ cut one self-titled album, on the Ramones' label, Sire. Frantic, screaming, and heavy, 1978's *DMZ* bangs with sledgehammer punkers ("Bad Attitude," "Don't Jump Me Mother") and heated garage nuggets by the Wailers, the Troggs, and the Sonics. Connolly next formed eighties garage greats the Lyres.

The Neighborhoods are Boston's equivalents of the Jam or Generation X, modish punk-poppers whose liberating "No Place Like Home" is on the compilation *Mass Ave.: The Boston Scene (1975–83)*, which is also home to tracks by La Peste, the Nervous Eaters, the Outlets, and more.

CANADIAN PUNK

Ah, the Great White North: the land of hockey, Mounties, maple leaves—and great punk rock. Predictably, its main scenes were in its major cities, and Toronto's was the most visible. The Ontario capital's fledgling punk movement revolved around D.I.Y. venue the Crash 'n' Burn and, later, the Horseshoe Tavern. The most notorious of the locals who haunted both spaces were the Viletones, a band of Stooges / Dead Boys-esque miscreants fronted by the sadistic Nazi Dog (a.k.a. Steven Leckie). The group's first single, 1977's raging "Screamin' Fist," ranks among Canadian punk's greatest tracks and features on *A Taste of Honey*, a compendium of the band's snottiest.

Sometimes sharing the bill with Mr. Dog and company were the Diodes, who sound not unlike a Canuck Ramones—in fact, lead singer Paul Robinson's voice is a dead ringer for Joey's on the 1977 single that serves as the title track of *Tired of Waking Up Tired: The Best of the Diodes* (the foursome's self-titled debut album makes an equally fine introduction; both releases include the sardonic "Child Star" and their winning rendition of the Cyrkle's sixties bubblegum hit, "Red Rubber Ball"). Also of note: the Scenics, whose Velvet Underground influences are evident on *Sunshine World: Studio Recordings 1977–1978*. Nearby Hamilton had Teenage Head, formed in 1975. Named for the classic Flamin' Groovies tune and fronted by the ultra-cool Frankie Venom, the four-piece laid out its calling card—rockabilly zip meets Ramones-buzzsaw guitars—on 1979's *Teenage Head*, perhaps early Canadian punk's best long-player. The pumping "Top Down," "Lucy Potato," and "Picture My Face" are chief among its barnstormers celebrating cars, girls, booze, and teenage partying. *Frantic City* (1980) and *Some Kinda Fun* (1981) keep the party going, and in 2008 the band re-recorded some of its best tunes with Marky Ramone on drums—how's that for an endorsement?

Ahead of the entire Canadian curve was Hamilton proto-punk unit Simply Saucer, which began in 1973 and crossed the Stooges and Velvets with early Pink Floyd. *Cyborgs Revisited* has 1974–1975 demos and live cuts. Hamilton's irreverent Forgotten Rebels are worth a peek, too; seek out their 1978 *Tomorrow Belongs to Us*. From London, Ontario, were the Demics, who cut the chugging "New York City," named the greatest Canadian song of all time by the music magazine *Chart*. *New York City* has twenty-seven of that group's rare early and live performances.

Vancouver also had a very strong punk community. The Subhumans (not the later U.K. band) are remembered for the lewd "Fuck You" and "Slave to My Dick." Their 1981 *Incorrect Thoughts* is a treasure. The Pointed Sticks had a poppy, tough sound with sax and keyboards, which is heard on the anthology *Waiting for the Real Thing*. *Vancouver Complication* and *Last Call: Vancouver Independent Music 1977–1988* survey the city's diverse scene. Montreal was a major stop for touring bands, but for years its own were sadly under-documented. The CD/DVD set *MTL Punk: The First Wave* corrects this discrepancy.

FRENCH PUNK

France is finally getting its due as a crucial early hub of punk rock. Always a culture that's known good art when it sees it (look what they've done for jazz and Jerry Lewis), the French were punk boosters from the music's first grumblings. In the early seventies a gang of Lou Reed fans called "Les punks" roamed the Paris streets, and in 1976 the first European Punk Rock Festival, headlined by the Damned, was held in a Mont-de-Marsan bullring (a second one took place in 1977). Paris band Stinky Toys even played 1976's landmark 100 Club Punk Festival in London, along with the Sex Pistols, the Clash, the Buzzcocks, and other giants. While much of France's homegrown punk is, admittedly, overly derivative of U.S. and U.K. bands, the country has nevertheless produced some acts that more than hold their own against their English-singing counterparts. The best and most unique was Metal Urbain, an outfit that crossed grinding guitars with a synthesizer and drum machine—highly innovative and proto-industrial, but still decidedly rock 'n' roll. *Anarchy in Paris!* corrals the group's essential output. The Dogs, from Rouen, began in 1973; their thrashing, sixties pop–rooted rock sounds like the Heartbreakers hanging with the Flamin' Groovies, and 1979's *Different* shows the Dogs' bite was as tough as their bark. Little Bob Story was a heavily R&B-based band born in the pub rock days. Fronted by pint-sized powerhouse Bob Piazza, the quintet would've fared well on a bill between the MC5 and Dr. Feelgood. For French punk compilations, the two-volume *Les Plus Grands Succès du Punk* is the crème de la crème.

THE DICTATORS

In many ways, the Dictators were the Ramones before the Ramones existed—from their clothing (jeans, leather jackets) and their lowbrow infatuations (fast food, trash TV) to their musical influences (garage and British Invasion rock and the Stooges, the MC5, and the New York Dolls). They're considered one of the original New York punk bands—and, by many, the best live act of all them. Yet the Dictators actually spanned the gap between the initial CBGB wave and the above-mentioned, earlier proto-punk bands; frustrated by the apathy that greeted their 1975 debut, *Go Girl Crazy!*, they broke up, but soon reunited to join the fun on the Bowery when they sensed an appreciative new audience. And they were a definite influence on the Ramones, who, prior to forming, regularly caught their thundering, over-the-top sets at area clubs.

The group was cofounded by bassist, singer, and main songwriter Andy "Adny" Shernoff, guitarists Ross "the Boss" Funicello and Scott "Top Ten" Kempner, sometime vocalist and "secret weapon" Handsome Dick Manitoba, and drummer Stu Boy King, who was replaced by Richie Teeter not long after *Go Girl Crazy!*'s release. Highly rocking and just as hilarious, *Go Girl Crazy!* stands tall alongside any of its lauded contemporaneous peers, with its sturdy, punk-and-heavy-metal-fusing sluggers ("Master Race Rock," "Two Tub Man"), gutsy, teen-themed pop ("Teengenerate," "[I Live for] Cars and Girls"), and sarcastic sixties covers (the Rivieras' "California Sun," which inspired the Ramones' version). By 1977's *Manifest Destiny* future Twisted Sister member Mark "the Animal" Mendoza was on bass, Shernoff had moved to keyboards, and Manitoba, though contributing more lead vocals, had yet to take his rightful place as the band's irrepressible front man. Slightly slick and less focused than its predecessor, the album is still worthwhile for possessing two of the Dictators' top tunes, "Science Gone Too Far" and "Young, Fast, and Scientific," and a furious version of the Stooges' "Search and Destroy." Redemption comes loudly with 1978's *Bloodbrothers*, which is all Manitoba's show on the mike, and its opener's title, "Faster, Louder," says everything. The thudding "Minnesota Strip" and super-catchy "Stay with Me" and "Baby, Let's Twist" further epitomize this genius hunk of solid punk, which you must be the owner of. Neck and neck with *Bloodbrothers* is 2001's *D.F.F.D.*, a shockingly great album that shames the best by most younger bands (see its epic and ironic "Who Will Save Rock 'n' Roll?"). Dictators forever, forever Dictators!

Here he comes to save the day: *Mighty Mouse* and other cartoons helped shape the Ramones' aesthetic. (Photofest/© 20th Century Fox)

5

BAD BRAIN: INSIDE THE MINDS OF THE RAMONES

What, besides music, shaped the personas and twisted the ripe, young heads of the Ramones? As teens, while their with-it peers were fawning all over the high-minded stuff that got them laid at fondue parties—yoga, Bergman films, macramé—our four reprobates were busy absorbing the kind of marginalized, "immature," lowbrow effluvia that was beneath the contempt of the big kids. You know, crap like comic books, cartoons, musical TV performance shows, wacky sitcoms, and horror, sci-fi, and monster movies. The fun, kitschy material we now call trash culture—a phenomenon whose elevation to respectability is due in no small part to the Ramones' reminding everyone how innocently and utterly *enjoyable* this stuff is ... "high art" be damned.

CARTOON CORRAL

It stands to reason that the Ramones would dig cartoons. They seemed like cartoon characters themselves, long before they were immortalized on TV as such (see sidebar). Practically since television sets first entered American homes in the late 1940s kids have had their brains bent by animated shorts filled with goofy characters whacking each other over the head with frying pans and blowing each other up with bundles labeled "TNT." And, really, is there a better way to be introduced to this wonderful thing called society? No! Cartoons are a key part of the glorious, innocent brain rot that informed the Ramones' aesthetic. Not all of the cartoons below were actually on the air when the Ramones were wee ones, but hey—who says ya gotta stop watching cartoons once you're a middle-aged punk rocker? And if there's one thing that never gets old, it's dumb, juvenile yuks.

Warner Bros. Cartoons

"Eh ...what's up, Doc?" A subsidiary of Warner Bros. Pictures, Warner Bros. Cartoons studios created the popular Looney Tunes and Merrie Melodies series, which ran from the early 1930s through the late 1960s. Drawn and directed by legends like Chuck Jones, Fritz Freleng, and Tex Avery, these cartoons starred some of the most recognized characters in animation history: Daffy Duck, Porky Pig, Road Runner, Wile E. Coyote, Yosemite Sam, Tweety Bird, Speedy Gonzales, Foghorn Leghorn, and, of course, Bugs Bunny. Voiced with a Brooklyn accent by the great Mel Blanc, the wisecracking, carrot-chomping Bugs is a punk predecessor if ever there was. Originally intended for adults, many of the early Warner's cartoons are impressively subversive, with references to sex, drugs and alcohol, and pop/celebrity culture. Indeed, when comparing Warner's work to the tame, squeaky-clean output of its chief early competitor, Disney Studios, the latter's looks positively, er, Mickey Mouse. (Johnny actually loved the Disney cartoons as well, but come on, you know he thought Bugs was cooler.) Warner Home Video has several multi-DVD volumes in its *Looney Tunes: Golden Collection*.

Woody Woodpecker

Another irreverent Golden Age character is Woody Woodpecker, who, like his screwball rival Bugs Bunny, was once voiced by Mel Blanc. Also like Bugs, in each of his wacky episodes the manically giggling Woody finds himself outwitting and bringing pain to his hapless nemeses. At the behest of party-pooping censors, however, Walter Lantz was forced to tone down the violence when the studio began producing Woody Woodpecker cartoons specifically for television. Lame! Each of the two volumes of *The Woody Woodpecker and Friends Classic Cartoon Collection* has three DVDs of madcap fun.

Mighty Mouse

Mighty Mouse was created by the Terrytunes studio and lasted for eighty theatrical subjects produced from 1942 through 1961 (the character was revived for TV in 1979 and 1987). Unlike the slapstick style of most contemporary cartoons, the serial was largely satirical; initially called Super Mouse and intended as a parody of Superman, the overly heroic rodent lampoons the popular cliffhanger serials and hoity-toity stage operas of the pre–World War II era. Singing, "Here I come to save the day!" in a chest-swelling tenor as he flies into action, Mighty Mouse brings high-impact chin music to his archenemies (usually evil, predatory cats) while simultaneously serving an amusing affront to bland, self-important, white-bread do-gooders everywhere. Several early Mighty Mouse segments are now in the public domain and scattered across various DVD compilations.

The Flintstones

Started by Hanna-Barbera, the team behind prior characters Tom and Jerry, Huckleberry Hound, and Quick Draw McGraw, *The Flintstones* is arguably the first animated sitcom. A stone-age spoof of the 1950s sitcom *The Honeymooners* (we'll get to them later), in its original incarnation the show ran from 1960 to 1966 and is an obvious influence on later animators like Matt Groening and Seth MacFarlane. It focuses on the lives and families of Bedrock resident and working man Fred Flintstone, his wife, Wilma, and their neighbors, Barney and Betty Rubble, satirically juxtaposing late-twentieth-century lifestyles against a dinosaur-filled prehistoric setting. As the rise of rock 'n' roll was in full force during the show's height, "The Flintstones" frequently incorporates music as a central element; one episode has Fred impersonating singer Rock Roll and lip-synching "The Bedrock Twitch"; another stars Beatles-esque group the Way-Outs. *The Flintstones'* 1960s seasons are available as four-DVD sets.

Top Cat

Another Hanna-Barbera effort, *Top Cat* ran from 1961 to 1962 and followed the adventures of a gang of insolent Manhattan alley cats led by the cheeky namesake character. Top Cat and his crew live in a garbage-strewn rat hole called Hoagie's Alley, from which the local beat cop, Officer Dibble, is constantly trying to evict them. Although Top Cat himself clearly recalls Bugs Bunny, the gang as a whole is reminiscent of MGM's live-action Bowery Boys from the 1940s and fifties. The goofs and guffaws gotten up to by Top Cat and his homeys are well worth a gander—and with four DVDs, *Top Cat: The Complete Series* has ganders in abundance.

The Jetsons

The Jetsons are the cosmic counterpart to the Flintstones—but while one clan lives in a dinosaur-powered Stone Age, George and Jane Jetson; kids Judy and Elroy; robot maid Rosie; and Astro, the family dog, dwell in a utopian future, a hundred years from the show's original 1962–63 airing. A stoned Ramone who happened to have sat in front of the TV, watching George jetting around between Orbit City's colorful, bizarrely shaped, futuristic buildings and push-button amenities, must have had quite a time. A revived version of the show ran in the 1980s, but the 1962 and '63 seasons are still out of this world. Each is available as a four-DVD box set.

Alvin and the Chipmunks

Alvin and the Chipmunks were the stars of *The Alvin Show*, a 1961–1962 series drawn up to capitalize on "The Chipmunk Song (Christmas Don't Be Late)," a goofy seasonal novelty record that hit number one in 1958. Ross Bagdasarian Sr. devised the helium-like voices of the three singing Chipmunks—Alvin, Simon, and Theodore—by speeding up recordings of his own voice. (Apparently this was innovative for the time.) For the show Bagdasarian also played the voice of David Seville (a name he'd hit with for 1958's "The Witch Doctor"), the adoptive father and musical supervisor of the chirpy Chipmunks. Each episode finds Alvin leading his brothers into some kind of trouble, only to be bailed out by Seville, who expresses his irritation by yelling, "Alll-vin!" Upon his dad's death, Ross Bagdasarian Jr., took over the family franchise. Junior's first project? A 1979 covers album titled *Chipmunk Punk*, whose front panel depicts Alvin, Simon, and Theodore hangin' tough in front of a back-alley brick wall, à la you know who. Sadly, the LP contains *no* punk songs—unless you consider Queen, Billy Joel, or Linda Ronstadt punk. The misleadingly titled *Alvin and the Chipmunks: The Very First Alvin Show* DVD contains one episode of the original series; the rest are from the inferior revived version. Alll-vin!!

Underdog

"There's no need to fear—Underdog is here!" At the first sign of trouble "humble and lovable" canine Shoeshine Boy dashes into a phone booth to become the crime-fighting lead character of *Underdog*, which debuted in 1964 and, via syndication, aired through 1973. In the series, Underdog, who speaks only in rhyming, heroic-sounding couplets voiced by actor Wally Cox, constantly rescues his girlfriend, newspaper reporter Sweet Polly Purebred, from the clutches of evil scientist Simon Bar Sinister, gangster Riff Raff, and other villains. Underdog was the subject of an eponymous 2007 live-action film, which despite initial box office success is by all reports a steaming dog turd. The nine-DVD box *The Complete Series* has all three seasons of the original *Underdog*, along with the associated shorts *Go Go Gophers*, *Klondike Kat*, and *Commander McBragg*.

Rocky and Bullwinkle

Like *Underdog*, *The Rocky and Bullwinkle Show* (also known as *Rocky and His Friends* and *The Bullwinkle Show*) was produced by General Mills (yep, the cereal folks). Originally airing from 1959 to 1964, it follows the adventures of helmet-wearing flying squirrel Rocky and his friend Bullwinkle, a dull-witted moose. Together the two do battle with Boris Badenov and Natasha Fatale, two spies from Pottsylvania (a Red Scare–era euphemism for Russia), who, under the direction of a menacing character named Fearless Leader, do their best to terrorize Rocky and Bullwinkle's hometown of Frostbite Falls, Minnesota. With a weighty thirteen DVDs, *Rocky and Bullwinkle and Friends: The Complete Series* has it all, plus bonuses and extras. See also *The Complete Tennessee Tuxedo and His Tales*, with *Get Smart* star Don Adams giving voice to the titular penguin.

The Pink Panther

The Pink Panther first appeared as the animated mascot in the opening credits of the popular live-action comedy films *The Pink Panther* (1963) and *A Shot in the Dark* (1964). But the sly, slinky cat was enough of a hit himself that he soon got his own series, *The Pink Panther Show*, which was broadcast on NBC-TV from 1969 to 1978 (*The All-New Pink Panther Show* would air on ABC from 1978 to 1980). Like the Chipmunks, this cool cat tried get with the new wave by releasing a kiddie LP, *Pink Panther Punk*. But, like Alvin and the Chipmunks' "punk" album, it has no actual punk (Blondie's "Call Me"? Maybe. But Pink Floyd? Billy Joel? *The Doobie Brothers?!*). Admittedly, though, the record's between-song skits and idiotic originals ("It's Punk," "Rock and Roll Panther") bring some giggles. *The Pink Panther Classic Cartoon Collection* has five discs of 124 cartoons, plus extras.

Speed Racer

In a somewhat more dramatic vein is *Speed Racer*, an early example of Japanese anime—a cartoon genre the Ramones would become fans of when they toured the Land of the Rising Sun. The show, which first ran as a series on U.S. TV from 1967 to 1968, centers on the adventures of the dashing racing car driver Speed Racer and his gadget-filled vehicle, the Mach V. Supported by a crew that includes Speed's younger brother, Spritle; his father, Pops; his girlfriend, Trixie; his mechanic, Sparky; and his mother, uh, Mom, Speed encounters fast-paced action on and off the track and does battle with the mysterious Racer X (his long-lost brother Rex in disguise). Comic relief comes from the antics of Chim-Chim, the family's pet chimpanzee. *The Complete Classic Series Collection* has all fifty-two original episodes.

Spider-Man

Based on the immortal Marvel Comics superhero (more to come on that), the first animated *Spider-Man* TV series was shown on ABC from 1967 through 1970. True to the premise of the original comic book, the cartoon focuses on the namesake hero, whose secret identity is the bookish Peter Parker. As Spider-Man, Parker uses the superhuman strength and agility he gained from a radioactive spider bite, and the devices he developed that spray indestructible webs, to fight various criminal masterminds. By day Parker is a photographer at the *Daily Bugle* newspaper, whose obnoxious editor-in-chief, J. Jonah Jameson, happens to view Spider-Man as a public menace. (Can you say "ironic plot conflict"?) The Ramones paid tribute to the program by covering its theme song. *The '67 Collection* set sports six web-slinging DVDs.

Ren and Stimpy

The Ren and Stimpy Show, which premiered on U.S. TV in 1991, covers the exploits of a crazed Chihuahua (Ren) and a seriously dumb cat (Stimpy). In addition to being a never-ending cornucopia of bathroom humor, sexual innuendoes, and painfully violent sight gags, the animation (by creator John K., born John Kricfalusi) is best described as Looney Tunes on bad acid. It's safe to assume that at least a couple of the Ramones, who were newly middle-aged at the peak of the show's popularity, were among its mammoth cult following. The made-for-grownups cartoon's decidedly non-PC content, however, did not endear it to those ever-annoying guardians of public decency, and by 1996 Ren and Stimpy were off the air. A spin-off show, *Ren and Stimpy "Adult Party Cartoon,"* ran for exactly three months before it, too, was yanked. *The Ren and Stimpy Show*'s five seasons are spread across three three-DVD sets.

Beavis and Butt-head

When it comes to utterly stoopid, adult-cartoon laffs, *Beavis and Butt-head* might just be the pinnacle—or the nadir, depending on your view. The, uh, brainchild of animator / voice actor Mike Judge, the series evolved from a 1992 short into a smash show broadcast on MTV from 1993 to 1997 (it was revived in 2011). The program's two namesake stars live in the fictitious small American town of Highland (no state given) and are spot-on caricatures of an adolescent breed familiar to many of us: dumb, juvenile-delinquent kids obsessed with heavy metal, sex, and toilet humor who get into trouble at the Ramones' favorite hangouts, fast food restaurants and 7-11s. Several episodes feature Ramones songs. (Also see *King of the Hill, The Goode Family*.) *Beavis and Butt-head: The Mike Judge Collection* exists as three three-DVD volumes.

South Park

Created by "equal opportunity offenders" Trey Parker and Matt Stone, *South Park* takes place in a fictional Colorado town of the same name, and skewers every aspect of society imaginable: celebrities, morality, race, sexuality, politics, the environment, consumerism, pop culture, and whatever else wanders into Parker and Stone's crosshairs. It all dovetails well with the Ramones' mocking outlooks. The show's main characters are four foul-mouthed elementary school students: Stan Marsh, Kyle Broflovski, Eric Cartman, and Kenny McCormick. Actually, it's hard to say if McCormick is foul-mouthed, since his voice is always muffled by his hooded parka. Each of *South Park*'s seasons (fifteen and counting) is out as a three-disc set.

Family Guy

Another brilliant satire of American culture, *Family Guy* looks at the day-to-day realities of another dysfunctional cast in another fictional town: the Griffin family of Quahog, Rhode Island, headed by blue-collar worker Peter Griffin. An episode concerning Peter's obsession with the Trashmen's 1963 frat/garage hit "Surfin' Bird" (a Ramones staple; see Chapter One) led to the original track's revival as a 2008 Top Five U.K. single. *Family Guy*'s seasons are parsed into several four-DVD sets. (See also *American Dad!*, *The Cleveland Show*.)

TRASHY TV

In the days when American television was coming of age, grandmothers across the country all seemed to be asking the same question of their cathode tube—worshipping grandkids: "Why are you watching that *trash*?!" But as aghast as they were at the state of TV in its first two decades, little could they have known what was lurking down the pike in the 2000s: vapid "reality" shows filled with sloppy-drunk Jersey Shore yokels, competitions featuring soulless performances from folks who all sound like they learned to sing in the same high school musical, boring dance contests between down-on-their-luck celebrities, and morons eating bugs for the chance to do something even dumber on the slightest chance that it *might* win them some cash. Uh, you were saying, Grandma?

As theoretically shallow as TV may have been in its early years, it was a hell of a lot cleverer—and more fun—than what passes for network entertainment these days. And it did a number on the creative minds of our young Ramones-in-training, fueling their shared sense of dark, lowbrow humor, absurdist attitude, and fascination with monsters and other cool stuff. Think about it: would a sitcom like *The Munsters* (see later) or a make-it-up-while-we're-on-the-air shambles like *Uncle Floyd* (see sidebar) get made today? Hell, no, and it's the viewers' loss. But in an industry that's increasingly driven by product placement and the ever-quickening buck, that's the way it goes. Still, while we can't all turn the dial back to the glory years of American television, DVDs and the Internet offer a peek at some of the shows that forever bent the brainpans of the Ramones. And many of them are just as much fun to watch now as they were then.

I Love Lucy

One of the earliest situation comedies and the most watched show in America for four of its six seasons, *I Love Lucy* originally ran from 1951 to 1957 and has stuck around via reruns ever since. The first scripted TV program to be shot on 35mm film in front of a live audience, it follows the uproarious travails of Lucy Ricardo (played by Lucille Ball), her husband, Cuban-American bandleader Ricky Ricardo (Desi Arnaz), and the couple's ex-vaudevillian neighbors, Fred (William Frawley) and Ethel Mertz (Vivian Vance). Set in New York, *I Love Lucy* is carried by the physical humor of Ball, one of America's greatest comic geniuses, whose talentless, tone-deaf character constantly tries to bust her way into Ricky's stage show—only to fail hilariously. Small-screen slapstick rarely got better in the decades that followed, and Lucy and Ricky's innocently dysfunctional dynamic laid the path for later TV's more complex "happy families."

I Love Lucy's episodes are available in single-season box sets or as the mammoth, twenty-seven-DVD *The Complete Series*.

The Honeymooners

Another of TV's best-loved early sitcoms, *The Honeymooners* is set in Brooklyn, the hometown of comedian Jackie Gleason, who played lead character Ralph Kramden, a bus driver and everyman whose constant, misguided get-rich-quick schemes provide the grist for gobs of guffaws. Ralph's wife, Alice Kramden (played in the first seven episodes by Pert Kelton and by Audrey Meadows for the remainder), is the rational half of the household, her wry, wisecracking putdowns of Ralph's boneheaded plans irking him to the point of hollowly threatening her with the trademark line "One of these days, Alice. One of these days...*Pow!* Right in the kisser!" (He never does knock her "straight to the moon," instead apologizing at the end of most shows with the admission "Baby, you're the greatest.") Ralph and Alice's nutty neighbors are the dopey but affable Ed Norton (Art Carney), a New York City sewer worker, and his wife, Trixie Norton, Alice's best friend and an ex-burlesque dancer. Although it was most popular before C. J.'s time, as youngsters the other Ramones likely saw something of their own world in *The Honeymooners*' salt-of-the-earth characters and local setting. The *Classic 39 Episodes* five-DVD box comprises the show's 1955–1956 zenith.

Leave It to Beaver

The Cleaver family—naïve young Theodore "the Beaver" (Jerry Mathers), brother Wally (Tony Dow), father Ward (Hugh Beaumont), and mother June (Barbara Billingsley)—qualifies as the ultimate idealized 1950s suburban American clan. A tacky, guilty pleasure of rerun hell, *Leave It to Beaver* was one of the first sitcoms written from a child's point of view (the Beaver's) and lasted from 1957 through 1963. It's a good guess our guys were most drawn to the show's resident juvenile delinquent, Eddie Haskell (Ken Osmond), who seems to always somehow drag the Beaver into trouble. But in the case of Joey, a wide-eyed escapist known for retreating into his own world when he was away from performing, one senses a strong connection to the Beav and his innocent reality-dodging.

The thirty-seven-disc (!) *Complete Series* is the most exhaustive way to test this theory; the double-disc *20 Timeless Classics* is an abridged intro. (See also *The Many Loves of Dobie Gillis*.)

The Twilight Zone

Submitted for your approval: the original *Twilight Zone*, created by suspense master Rod Serling and shown on CBS from 1959 to 1964 (it was revived in the 1980s). An unsettling, genius fusion of science fiction, drama, horror, and fantasy, the series, which changed its cast weekly but retained Serling as its eerily detached narrator, cleverly worked in social and political parables during the height of the Cold War. In addition to Serling, the scriptwriters for the 156 original episodes included greats like Ray Bradbury. Besides its abstract plots and macabre bent, another trademark of *The Twilight Zone* is its penchant for unexpected-twist endings. Deep stuff for the Ramones-in-waiting, perhaps, but the band members were attracted to anything scary. And *The Twilight Zone* is brilliantly so.

The Complete Definitive Collection is just that, with twenty-eight DVDs. (See also *The Outer Limits* and Serling's early seventies series, *Night Gallery*.)

The Addams Family

Back to the hilarity—while keeping the creepiness intact. *The Addams Family* was based on Charles Addams's *New Yorker* magazine cartoons. The patriarch of the family in question, who live in a decaying gothic mansion at 1313 Mockingbird Lane in the town of Mockingbird Heights, is the cigar-puffing Gomez Addams (John

Astin), a mischievous, eccentric multi-billionaire. His wife is the icy, darkly beautiful and aloof Morticia Addams (Carolyn Jones); the couple has two kids, son Pugsley (Ken Weatherwax) and daughter Wednesday (Lisa Loring). The rest of the household includes the loopy Uncle Fester (Jackie Coogan); physically imposing and impossibly deep-voiced butler Lurch (Ted Cassidy); Gomez's witchy mom, Grandmama Addams (Blossom Rock); overly hirsute Cousin Itt (usually Felix Silla); and disembodied hand Thing T. Thing ("Itself," in the credits). The paradoxical gist of the show, which aired from September 1964 through April 1966, is that to the well-meaning and supernatural-empowered Addamses, all things we see as morbid and weird, like Morticia's man-eating African Strangler plant or Uncle Fester's ability to electrify light bulbs with his mouth, are simply normal to them—it's the rest of the world that's puzzling and suspicious. *The Addams Family* is sick, twisted, and funny—much like the Ramones.

The Complete Series box set has the whole run on nine DVDs. (See also *The Beverly Hillbillies*.)

The Munsters

The Addams Family was the Beatles to *The Munsters*' Rolling Stones. Or maybe it's the other way around. Whatever. The two shows, which both focused on the insane, side-splitting exploits of families of good-natured ghouls, aired almost concurrently on network TV. But the characters on *The Munsters*, which lasted a month longer (September 1964 to May 1966), were much more working class than the comparatively cultured Addamses. *The Munsters* satirized classic Hollywood monster movies as well as the typical American sitcom families depicted on shows like *Leave It to Beaver* (above) and *Father Knows Best*. Each member of the Munster family was a send-up of an archetypal Universal Studios movie monster: bumbling, tantrum-throwing dad Herman Munster (Fred Gwynne) was based on Frankenstein; seductively, er, vamping mother Lily Munster (Yvonne De Carlo) is reminiscent of Vampira (a character inspired by, oddly enough, Charles Addams's cartoons of Morticia Addams); the real name of vampire Grandpa (Al Lewis), Lily's dad, is Sam

Dracula, which explains his genesis; and son Eddie Munster (Butch Patrick) resembles the Wolfman. Cousin Marilyn Munster (Beverly Owen, replaced by Pat Priest), however, a stunning blonde à la Marilyn Monroe, is (paradoxically to viewers) considered homely by the rest of the family. As with *The Addams Family*, the fun of *The Munsters* comes when the crazy clan interacts with outsiders. In the episode titled "Far Out Munsters," the family even rents their house to influential garage rockers the Standells (see Chapter Two).

The twelve-DVD *Complete Series* has all seventy episodes. (See also: *I Dream of Jeannie*.)

Hogan's Heroes

Early on, the Ramones had a perverse fascination with World War II–era Nazis, as evidenced in the lyrics of "Today Your Love, Tomorrow the World": "I'm a Nazi schatze / And I'll fight for the fatherland." All part of their black humor, the subject's appeal likely lay in its status as a taboo topic verboten by their elders—Joey was Jewish, after all. Perhaps it also stems from Dee Dee's growing up amid the bombed-out bunkers of postwar Germany, or guitarist Ron Asheton of Ramones heroes the Stooges appearing on stage in the Nazi uniforms he collected. And maybe some of it was inspired by *Hogan's Heroes*, a sitcom set in a prisoner of war camp in World War II Germany. In the show, rakish American Colonel Robert Hogan (Bob Crane) and his crew of Allied prisoners run a special ops unit from within the camp that sabotages the German war effort—right under the noses of the camp's neurotic, oblivious commandant, Colonel Klink (Werner Klemperer, the son of Jewish conductor Otto Klemperer), and the corpulent, inept Sergeant Schultz (Jewish-born John Banner). As improbable and controversial as the program's concept may have been, it was a huge smash and enjoyed a much-loved 1965–1971 stretch.

The Komplete Series: Kommandant's Kollection will detain you with laughs through twenty-eight DVDs.

Batman

Boom! Biff! Pow! As far as comic book heroes coming to life on TV,

Adventures of Superman (1951–1958) was there years before *Batman*. But while *Superman* was hopelessly stiff and seemed like a holdover from its earlier movie-serial iteration, *Batman*, which was shown on ABC-TV from 1966 to 1968, was modern, colorful, sexy, and full of tongue-in-cheek humor. Starring Adam West as the lead crime fighter and Burt Ward as his sidekick, Robin, *Batman* was one of the most popular shows of the 1960s because it appealed to both adults and kids. Its animation-interspersed plots typically begin with a villain like the Joker (Cesar Romero), the Penguin (Burgess Meredith), the Riddler (Frank Gorshin), or Catwoman (originally Julie Newmar, later Eartha Kitt) committing a crime somewhere in Gotham City; Police Commissioner Gordon (Neil Hamilton) then summons the "the dynamic duo," who slide down the Batpole to their secret underground Batcave headquarters, hop in the gizmo-loaded Batmobile, and roar into action, sometimes with the help of the foxy Batgirl (Yvonne Craig). *Batman*'s fast-paced fights and splashy imagery, and the form-fitting costumes of its female characters, make it a pop-culture phenomenon the Ramones would've dug.

The Complete Live Action Series (1966–1968) has all the Bat-excitement on eight Bat-discs.

ROCKIN' THE TUBE

In the 1950s and 1960s American television exploded with musical performance shows that featured the day's top and up-and-coming bands playing their latest singles. Well, "playing" is a bit of a misnomer. On most of these programs, which included local (like New York's *The Clay Cole Show*, a fave in Joey's household) as well as prime-time national shows, the acts usually just lip-synched along to their records. But seeing some cool-looking early rock 'n' roller or longhaired band from England or the States doing their thing on TV, often in front of a screaming female studio audience, was a powerful motivator for the future members of a certain Queens combo. Hence the first verse of "Do You Remember Rock 'n' Roll Radio?": "Do you remember *Hullabaloo*, [Cleveland, Ohio, show] *Upbeat*, *Shindig!*, and *Ed Sullivan*, too?" YouTube is a bottomless goldmine when it comes to moments from these shows, but many are also available on DVD.

The Ed Sullivan Show

One of television's longest-running variety shows, *The Ed Sullivan Show* beamed into American homes every week from 1948 to 1971. Variety was certainly the operative word when it came to the program, which aired Sunday nights on CBS. With the famously stuffy Sullivan as emcee, in addition to featuring musical acts, the show operated in the tradition of earlier vaudeville and music hall revues, presenting everything from stand-up and sketch comedy to jugglers, Broadway performers, ventriloquists, and dancing bears. Although its older host wasn't exactly a fan of rock 'n' roll, the *Sullivan Show* famously spotlighted the new music in its infancy, reluctantly booking a fast-rising young singer named Elvis Presley—to staggering ratings. A six-year-old Johnny Ramone caught the first of Presley's three *Sullivan* appearances (September 9, 1956) and forever after cited it as pivotal. Other early rockers like Buddy Holly and Bo Diddley followed Presley on the show, which in the 1960s was a major harbinger of the British Invasion with key appearances by the Beatles, the Rolling Stones, the Animals, the Dave Clark Five, the Searchers, Herman's Hermits, Gerry and the Pacemakers, and more. It also hosted American Ramones faves like the Beach Boys, the Lovin' Spoonful, the Supremes, and the Doors, who legendarily pissed off Sullivan by refusing to censor the line "Girl, we couldn't get much higher" in their hit "Light My Fire"— a pretty punk move.

The nine-disc *Ed Sullivan's Rock 'n' Roll Classics* box set has appearances by all the above and more. Sorry, though: no dancing bears.

American Bandstand

Inarguably the nation's best-known musical performance show, *American Bandstand* was broadcast in various incarnations from 1952 to 1989 and introduced legions of rock greats and not-so-greats to U.S. teens. The show began as, simply, *Bandstand* on local

Philadelphia TV and was hosted by radio DJ Bob Horn. Horn got the boot after a drunk-driving arrest and allegations of involvement in a prostitution ring (!), and new host Dick Clark took over not long before the show was picked up in 1957 by ABC for national airing and redubbed *American Bandstand*. The format was a simple one: acts hyping their current records were introduced and briefly interviewed by Clark and then lip-synched their songs before an audience of dancing teenagers. But it was wildly successful, as teens tuned in religiously across the country. Another hallmark of the program was its "Rate-a-Record" segment, in which Clark interviewed audience members for their opinions on the new singles played on the show. Across its inescapable, nearly forty-year run *American Bandstand* presented all the stylistic trends that hit the Top Forty, from fiery rock 'n' roll forerunners to pasty teen idols, British Invasion, garage rock, disco, new wave, and early hip-hop; literally from Jerry Lee Lewis to Run-DMC. Although the Ramones never appeared on the show, a few of their hit-making punk classmates did: Talking Heads, Blondie, Devo, the Boomtown Rats, and Public Image Limited, whose front man, John Lydon (a.k.a. ex-Sex Pistols singer Johnny Rotten), gave a memorably uncooperative performance.

Clips of that bizarre occurrence and hundreds of other *American Bandstand* episodes are all over YouTube.

Shindig!

Hipper but much shorter-lived than *American Bandstand* was *Shindig!*, which screened on ABC from 1964 to 1966. Hosted by L.A. DJ Jimmy O'Neill and featuring mod dance troupe the Shin-diggers, house band the Shindogs, and back-up vocal groups the Wellingtons and the Blossoms (with Darlene Love), *Shindig!* reigned throughout the surf, girl group, British Invasion, and garage rock eras. Guests included the Beatles, the Rolling Stones, the Animals, the Beau Brummels, Chuck Berry, the Who, Freddy Cannon, Manfred Mann, the Beach Boys, Jackie DeShannon, the Dave Clark Five, the Spencer Davis Group, the Shangri-Las, Freddie and the Dreamers, the Ronettes, the Kingsmen, the Ventures, the

Yardbirds, the Kinks, Bo Diddley, the Nashville Teens, and many other acts that influenced the Ramones.

In the early 1990s numerous *Shindig!* performances were released on VHS. But currently YouTube is the easiest way to see them, as there's nothing on DVD.

Hullabaloo

Not so with *Shindig!*'s rival show, *Hullabaloo*, which rocked NBC from January 1965 through August 1966 and has been resurrected on DVD. Emceed by a different, admittedly square-ish presenter every week (Sammy Davis Jr., Frankie Avalon, Petula Clark, etc.), the big-budget revue featured routines by the Hullabaloo Dancers and caged go-go girls during its closing "Hullabaloo A-Go-Go" segment. Among the acts that appeared on *Hullabaloo* were the Lovin' Spoonful, the Rolling Stones, the Yardbirds, Sonny and Cher, the Supremes, Herman's Hermits, the Animals, Martha and the Vandellas, Roy Orbison, Paul Revere and the Raiders, Marianne Faithfull, Sam the Sham and the Pharaohs, the Young Rascals, the McCoys, the Hollies, the Byrds, the Everly Brothers, and many more.

Hullabaloo's highlights are compiled on three separate DVDs.

Where the Action Is

Conceived by Dick Clark as an *American Bandstand* spin-off, *Where the Action Is* premiered on ABC in 1965 and ran through 1967. Although its hit theme song, "Action," was sung by Freddy Cannon, the show is arguably better remembered for Paul Revere and the Raiders' (see Chapter Two) stint as its first house band, a role later assumed by Wisconsin quartet the Robbs. Shot in California and narrated by Clark (who didn't appear on camera), *Where the Action Is* included skits, dancing, and pantomimed performances by, among others, the Kinks, Jan and Dean, the Animals, the Music Machine, the Zombies, the Shangri-Las, James Brown, Captain Beefheart, Tommy Roe, the Byrds, the Sir Douglas Quintet, the Turtles, the Castaways, the Strangeloves, the Who, the Outsiders, and the ever-present Paul Revere and the Raiders.

The action is yet to be found on DVD, however, so direct your eyes and ears to YouTube.

Don Kirshner's Rock Concert

Remember the Archies' creator, Don Kirshner, from Chapter Two? In 1972 the Monkees/Archies overlord became the producer of ABC-TV's *In Concert*, which within a year was renamed *Don Kirshner's Rock Concert*. But this show had little to do with its nasal-voiced host's bubblegum past, aiming instead for a more "mature" audience by concentrating on the newly emerging FM radio-driven "progressive" sounds. While this meant a preponderance of pretentious music by yawn-inducers like Kansas, Seals and Croft, and Blood, Sweat and Tears, it also led to network TV appearances by many edgier acts that no doubt had Ramones members glued to their sets. Debuting under its second title with a performance by the Rolling Stones, the program was taped on Long Island at Hofstra University and featured live sets (*no* lip-synching!) by the likes of Black Sabbath, T. Rex, Alice Cooper, the New York Dolls, Slade, Sparks, the Sensational Alex Harvey Band, Aerosmith, Badfinger, Cheap Trick, and others. In the late seventies, the show gave much of America its first glimpses of punk via appearances by the Sex Pistols (on film), Devo, and the Ramones themselves. The series left the air in 1981, but for a generation its weekly late-night broadcasts were a revelatory ritual. (Its later "Don's Disco Dance" segments, however, were interminable.)

Performances by acts that appeared on the show are scattered across single-artist DVDs, but presently no *Don Kirshner's Rock Concert* compendiums exist. Get thee to YouTube!

The Midnight Special

Kirshner's direct competition in the late-light live-rock stakes came from producer Burt Sugarman's *The Midnight Special*. The show, which actually aired *after* midnight Fridays on NBC from 1973 to 1981, had gravel-larynxed DJ Wolfman Jack as its announcer and occasional host; although adult contemporary singer Helen Reddy also hosted at one point (what was Sugarman thinking?), for most of its existence the program was hosted by a different guest musician each week. Acts of interest to Ramones fans that appeared on the show include the New York Dolls, AC/DC, Blondie, David Bowie, Bo Diddley, Roxy Music, Suicide, Cheap Trick, Brownsville Station, Jerry Lee Lewis, T. Rex, and Thin Lizzy. Like *Don Kirshner's Rock Concert*, *The Midnight Special* also featured comedians and clips of pioneering rock 'n' rollers like Bill Haley and His Comets.

Footage from *The Midnight Special* has been sorted into individual DVDs surveying each year of the show and a nine-disc 1973–1980 set. But beware: you'll have to flip through a lot of fluff (Jim Croce, Loggins and Messina, Linda Ronstadt, et al.) to get to the good stuff.

COMIC BOOK CRAZINESS

With the advent of personal electronic gaming devices, modern kids have myriad ways to rot their brains in those rare moments they happen to be *away* from the TV. Back in the time of the Ramones' adolescence, comic books—today marketed toward an older audience as graphic novels—were an essential staple of juvenile fun. Their colorful pages featured superheroes (the late 1930s to the early 1950s was the so-called Golden Age for these characters; the Silver Age was from 1956 to 1970, and the Bronze Age was from 1970 to 1985) and monsters, as well as horror, war, true crime, and science fiction stories; drugs and sex were explored in the countercultural adult "underground comix" of the hippie era. The appeal of comics to a young, bored kid feeling increasingly disillusioned with the world around him is obvious: behind those bold, splashy covers was a world of fantastic escape, one filled with thrilling adventures, grotesque monsters, and heroes with amazing powers they used to kick the asses of the bad guys—just like you dreamed of doing to the school bullies who made your life a living hell. All of which explains how the Ramones came to embrace these iconic characters. The comics scene exploded in the 1980s, when a new generation of independent publishers arose to compete with the bigger names. But during the impressionable years of *our* heroes, the selection was far more limited.

DC Comics

The popularity of comic books in America essentially begins with the introduction of Superman in the June 1938 issue of *Action Comics*, published by National Allied Publications. The firm eventually became DC Comics, after *Detective Comics*, a series that brought more success in 1939 with the first appearance of Batman. Subsequent decades saw the births of ranks of legendary characters with their own titles: Captain Marvel, the Sandman, Wonder Woman, the Flash, Aquaman, Hawkman, Green Lantern, Green Arrow, Swamp Thing, and superhero team the Justice League, to name a few.

Anthologies exist for many of DC's classic titles, but for newcomers the best way to get a feel for the DC universe is the meticulous *DC Comics Encyclopedia*, whose updated and expanded edition has four hundred color-packed pages.

Marvel Comics

For all they'd done to create comic books as we know them today, by the 1960s DC Comics felt a bit too wholesome. Its characters would be remade with more realistic emotional edges in the 1970s, but when the Ramones were kids those once proud heroes had become static, one-dimensional do-gooders whose traits were out of step with the realities of the Cold War, civil rights, drugs, the sexual revolution, and the growing generation gap. But not Marvel Comics, which was founded in 1939 as Timely Comics. Headed by brash editor and writer Stan Lee, Marvel was home to visionary artists like Jack Kirby and Steve Ditko, whose influences can be seen in the rough graphics of punk. In 2009, reflecting on the ascension of Marvel nearly fifty years before, pop culture blogger Geoff Boucher wrote, "Superman and DC Comics instantly seemed like boring old Pat Boone; Marvel felt like the Beatles and the British Invasion." Marvel gave us such recognizable modern folk heroes as Spider-Man, Captain America, the Hulk, Iron Man, Daredevil, Thor, Sub-Mariner, Dr. Strange, Ghost Rider, Conan the Barbarian, the Silver Surfer, super squads the Fantastic Four and the X-Men, and Sgt. Fury and His Howling Commandos (the latter, perhaps, helping inspire the Ramones song "Commando").

The four-hundred-page *Marvel Encyclopedia* is the last word on all things Marvel-ous.

EC Comics

Tales from the Crypt. The Vault of Horror. Shock SuspenStories. Weird Science. Weird Fantasy. Two-Fisted Tales. The Haunt of Fear. In the 1950s, Entertaining Comics, better known as EC Comics, pushed the boundaries of what comic books could get away with. These and other lurid, scandalous EC titles were awash in menacing monsters, graphic violence, and gratuitous gore. No wonder kids loved them! But the edgy publications also provoked a federal investigation and a highly publicized Congressional hearing on juvenile delinquency that blamed comic books for the destruction of the morals of America's youth and saw EC's president, William Gaines, become the scapegoat for this so-called social plague. Although they kowtowed to the dictatorial Comics Code of Authority's censorship for a while, taming their content and doing battle over stories dealing with civil rights and other controversial causes, Gaines and EC's stable of illustrators, which included greats like Basil Wolverton, Frank Frazetta, and Johnny Craig, ceased publishing in 1956, save for one of its newer titles, *Mad* (see later).

The *EC Archives* series chronicles the above and other EC titles. Don't read them at night! (See also *Creepy, Eerie, Vampirella*.)

Mad

Although venerated humor rag *Mad* later took on a more traditional magazine format, it began in 1952 as a comic book published by EC Comics. Primarily the creation of Harvey Kurtzman, who edited the publication for its first few years, *Mad*, which is still kicking today, mercilessly satirizes the hypocrisy, disposability, and fakery of popular culture, politics, and consumerism. With its puckish, iconic mascot Alfred E. Neuman on the cover, *Mad*'s uproarious pages, which since 1955 have featured comics as well as articles,

171

had a field day in the sixties and seventies, undermining censorship while parodying popular music, movies, and TV shows and taking to task everything from the Vietnam War to youth fads, sports, the sexual revolution, drugs, the energy crisis, Watergate, and whatever else society had to offer. *Mad* was a subversive godsend for alienated American kids of the Ramones' generation, who'd given up on trying to make sense of the inanity around them and decided the best way to deal with such a sick world was to make fun of it—a lesson the band's music took to heart.

Totally Mad: 60 Years of Humor, Satire, Stupidity and Stupidity has 256 pages of hilarious high points. (See also *Cracked, Sick, Crazy Magazine, National Lampoon.*)

Underground Comix

Underground comix is the name for the movement of independently published, small-run comic books that proliferated from the late 1960s to the mid-1970s in defiance of the Comics Code of Authority's ban on sex acts, drug use, and violence in comics. According to lore, the "x" in comix arose to differentiate these uncensored publications—often "X-rated" and recalling the racy "Tijuana bibles" of the 1930s—from mainstream titles. Strongly influenced by *Mad* and other EC publications, as well as the hot rod art of Ed "Big Daddy" Roth, underground comix were sold primarily through hippie head shops and featured artwork reminiscent of the psychedelic concert posters of the era; indeed, several artists drew both. Many of these titles began as comic strips in radical newspapers like New York's *East Village Other* and the Bay Area's *Berkeley Barb* or as part of multi-story anthologies. Full of satire, crude humor, and references to rock music, these books would've had an irresistibly subversive appeal to our wayward, youthful Ramones. Leading artists included Robert Crumb (*Zap Comix, Fritz the Cat*), Gilbert Shelton (*The Fabulous Furry Freak Brothers, Wonder Wart-Hog;* did the latter inspire the Ramones' "Wart Hog"?), Spain Rodriguez (*Trashman*), and Bill Griffith (see sidebar).

James Mark Eastren's *A History of Underground Comics* is a lavish look at this supremely freaky epoch.

HEY HO LET'S GO (TO THE MOVIES)

Movies were vitally important in shaping the Ramones' creative stance: as a much more immersive, self-contained artistic diversion than either TV series or comic books (and without the side effects of sniffing glue), film offered another evocative escape from an alternately dull and hostile society. As with their tastes in music and the above media, when it came to cinema, anything weird, disturbing, or sick fit the bill—especially the old, black-and-white and low-budget B/exploitation movies everyone else said were junk. "Movies like this intrigued and delighted us," recalls Joey's brother, Mickey Leigh, in the superb autobiography he cowrote with Legs McNeil, *I Slept with Joey Ramone* (Touchstone, 2009). "They were odd and creepy but certainly intelligent. This was the stuff Ramones songs were made of, in the beginning. The members of the band wanted to convey the essence of these movies in their songs, and when they hit the mark, the songs were as classic as the films."

The guys spent hours in local theaters and in front of the tube soaking up their two favorite genres, horror and science fiction. Early rock 'n' roll movies helped fuel their love for the music—and even made them movie stars themselves (see Chapter Six). They sustained their interests in the silver screen throughout their days: both Joey and Johnny collected vintage movie posters, and after the band's breakup, before he passed away in 2004, Johnny had looked forward to directing movies. The film genres that were of interest to the Ramones already have full, genre-specific books devoted to them, and the most sensible way to begin exploring these areas is to grab one of those (see Appendix B) and start watching. But below we'll take a brief look at the key categories and a few of the Ramones-related movies within.

Horror

People have loved the thrill of being entertained by scary stories since the evil spirits and fire-breathing dragons of ancient mythology. So when film arrived at the turn of the last century, it was no wonder that terror and the big screen were such a popular fit. Indeed, several of the horror flicks that the Ramones held as influential faves were among the earliest made.

Freaks (1932)

This bizarre film's cast of real-life circus freaks includes several "pinheads" (victims of microcephaly, a deformation of the head and brain), who take revenge on the "normal" characters who do harm to one of their own. The freaks' unison chant of "We accept her! We accept her! One of us! One of us! Gooble-gobble, gooble-gobble!" directly inspired the Ramones classic "Pinhead."

ZIPPY THE PINHEAD

Warped brains think alike. Zippy the Pinhead debuted to the world at large in 1976, the same year *Ramones* was released. Born from the mind and pen of underground cartoonist Bill Griffith, Zippy was, just like the Ramones' classic "Pinhead," inspired by a viewing of the real-life "pinheads" in Tod Browning's 1932 film *Freaks*; also influential, and the source of his name, was the P.T. Barnum sideshow performer Zip the Pinhead. Although Griffith had first drawn Zippy for the 1971 premier issue of *Real Pulp Comics*, it wasn't until he got his own strip in the *Berkeley Barb*, five years later, that the now syndicated character really began to accumulate the devoted cult following he has today.

Sporting a bright yellow, red polka-dotted muumuu and a bow atop his pointy noggin, Zippy has a nearly constant, happily numb facial expression. In surreal stories that are basically devoid of any cohesive plot, the clownish character endlessly spouts non sequiturs about the world around him, unwittingly parodying popular culture, consumerism, and other aspects of modernity. Zippy's free-associative exploits often include interactions with other characters like the bizarre Mr. Toad, Griffy (a stand-in for Griffiths himself), and his wife Zerbina, son Fuelrod, and daughter Meltdown. Zippy's patented catchphrase, "Are we having fun yet?," has entered the popular lexicon, and his favorite foods are taco sauce and Ding-Dongs, which certainly would've been at home on a Ramones backstage hospitality rider.

Confusing to many? Sure. But so are the Ramones. And like da brudders, for those with a certain, shall we say, heightened sensibility, Zippy is ridiculously hilarious.

One of many Zippy anthologies, *Connect the Polka Dots* is great for newcomers and old fans alike.

King Kong (1933)

The discovery and capture of a mythic giant gorilla leads to a heart-stopping showdown with fighter planes atop the Empire State Building. Ape-abducted actress Fay Wray also appeared in *Mystery of the Wax Museum* (1933), *The Vampire Bat* (1933), and motorcycle / juvenile delinquent gem *Dragstrip Riot* (1958).

The Bride of Frankenstein (1935)

The Universal Monsters films—legendary horror films produced by Universal Studios from 1923 to 1960—include *The Phantom of the Opera*, *Dracula*, *The Mummy*, *The Invisible Man*, and *Creature from the Black Lagoon*. All were viewing staples of our favorite monster-movie-buffs-cum-rockers. This sequel to *Frankenstein* (1931) sees mad scientist Dr. Frankenstein making a mate for his fabled monster.

The Wolf Man (1941)

Another iconic Universal Monsters release, this terrifying tale stars the great Lon Chaney Jr. (his father, Lon Chaney, pioneered classic horror with his roles in 1925's *The Phantom of the Opera* and 1923's *The Hunchback of Notre Dame*) as the titular lupine man-beast.

Nightmare Alley (1947)

Not to be confused with a 2010 film of the same name, this noir-ish nugget stars Tyrone Power as an ambitious carnie fascinated with "the Geek," a character who bites the heads off live chickens in exchange for free booze and a place to crash. Weird it is.

Psycho (1960)

Considered by many to be master director Alfred Hitchcock's crowning work, *Psycho* remains a horror classic today. The film's "shower scene," which finds sexy Marion Crane (Janet Leigh) being brutally stabbed by twisted innkeeper Norman Bates (Anthony Perkins, whose character was based on mass murderer Ed Gein), is one of cinema's most iconic moments.

Night of the Living Dead (1968)

Directed by George Romero—who, bizarrely, had once worked on TV children's show *Mr. Rogers' Neighborhood*—*Night of the Living Dead* in many ways defines the low-budget horror genre. Shot in claustrophobic black and white, the gruesome tale sees a handful of unlucky folks trapped in a farmhouse as they try to fend off swarms of flesh-eating zombies. Romero followed it up with *Dawn of the Dead* (1978) and *Day of the Dead* (1985).

Werewolves on Wheels (1971)

Alas, it was not to be, but Johnny Ramone had hoped to break into movie directing with a remake of this crazed offering, a hybrid of the outlaw biker and horror categories. It's not hard to see why he chose it as a potential first foray into the film world: you can't go wrong with bikers, chicks, motorcycles, satanic monks, and werewolves all in the same movie. Watch it and see if you don't agree.

The Texas Chain Saw Massacre (1974)

One doesn't have to look far for the connection here. "Chainsaw," off *Ramones*, blatantly references this demented slasher classic. Still shocking, this gore-heavy effort has been cited as one the best horror films made, and depicts the grisly fates of a van full of unfortunate young travelers at the chainsaw-wielding hands of the killer known as Leatherface. Not exactly heartwarming family entertainment.

The Evil Dead (1981)

Another twist on the familiar, successful low-budget premise of ill-fated folks besieged by horrific assailants, *The Evil Dead* finds five college students vacationing in an isolated forest cabin. Their trip turns gruesome when they find a tape recording that releases demons that possess each of the group's members, resulting in buckets of bloody mayhem—as well as several segments of dark humor.

See also: *The Cabinet of Dr. Caligari* (1920), *Nosferatu* (1922), *White Zombie* (1932), *The Invisible Man* (1933), *Re-Animator* (1985).

Science Fiction

Science fiction movies would seem more connected to the lofty lyrics of the prog rockers the Ramones were rebelling against. But there are many sci-fi films that delivered the escapist weirdness the quartet craved.

Dr. Cyclops (1940)

In a South American jungle, a mad scientist miniaturizes a group of explorers when they get in the way of his plans to control the rich Peruvian radium supply—and makes them human guinea pigs for his sadistic experiments.

The Day the Earth Stood Still (1951)

One of the most iconic science fiction films ever made, this Red Scare–era classic uses alien Klaatu (Michael Rennie) and his powerful robot Gort (Lock Martin) as metaphorical Russian stand-ins. After landing their flying saucer in Washington, D.C., they attempt to deliver a mysterious message to the people of Earth—bringing humanity to the brink of annihilation.

The Thing from Another World (1951)

A group of scientists at a research station in Antarctica comes across a spaceship frozen beneath the ice, with its alien pilot still inside. When they take the creature back to their base, he's accidentally thawed out and mayhem erupts. John Carpenter's 1982 remake, *The Thing*, is excellent as well.

The War of the Worlds (1953)

Based on the same H. G. Wells novel about a Martian invasion of Earth that terrorized the nation as a 1939 radio play by Orson Welles, this Technicolor epic is, like *The Day the Earth Stood Still*, now recognized as a classic contemporary Cold War allegory. Also see producer George Pal's *When Worlds Collide* (1951).

Invaders from Mars (1953)

More uninvited guests from you know where. These particular hostile visitors from the red planet are about seven feet tall and green, with bulging, bug-like eyes. Controlled by a silent, disembodied alien head inside a transparent bulb, the aliens, in turn, begin controlling the minds of Earthlings. Archetypal stuff.

Them! (1954)

Radiation from atomic bomb testing in New Mexico turns ants into giant, flesh-eating monsters bent on devouring civilization. But just when FBI Agent Robert Graham (*Gunsmoke* star James Arness, who also plays the alien in *The Thing from Another World*) and his crew they think they've wiped out the critters, another colony appears in tunnels beneath Los Angeles.

Forbidden Planet (1956)

When a scientific research colony on a distant planet ceases to communicate with Earth, a team captained by square-jawed Commander J. J. Adams (Leslie Nielsen in his pre–*Naked Gun*, leading-man days) is dispatched to investigate. Sleek rocket ships, a marauding monster, strange electronic music, and the debut appearance of the iconic Robbie the Robot combine to make this one a fifties sci-fi classic.

The Blob (1958)

"It crawls! It creeps! It eats you alive!" went the promotional tagline. With a young Steve McQueen in the lead role, the sticky storyline begins when a meteorite cracks open to release a mysterious alien life form resembling a giant blob of jelly, which begins devouring everything and everyone in its path. A gang of small-town teenagers discovers the creature and tries to warn the world—but is it too late?

Planet of the Apes (1968)

Although it spawned several successful (and not-so-successful) sequels, it's the first installment of the legendary *Planet of the Apes* saga that stands as one of modern film's most brilliant achievements. In the far-off future, a crew of astronauts led by George Taylor (Charlton Heston) crash-lands on a planet dominated by highly evolved, talking apes—who make humans their slaves. Produced during a time of radical upheaval in the real world, the film conveys a strong aura of social commentary behind the monkeying around.

Death Race 2000 (1975)

No wonder the Ramones worked with producer/director Roger Corman on *Rock 'n' Roll High School*. The king of the B movies, he's behind an endless list of amazing lowbrow jewels, like *The Wasp Woman* (1959), *X: The Man with the X-Ray Eyes* (1963), *The Wild Angels* (1966), *The Trip* (1967)—and this dystopian story starring Sylvester Stallone and David Carradine as high-speed car racers who earn points by running down pedestrians. Watch out!

Rock 'n' Roll Flicks

When the movies and rock 'n' roll combined, naturally the young Ramones were watching. Rock 'n' roll movies began not long after the music itself started hitting the popular charts, and were, pure and simple, little more than exploitation films designed to make a buck off the perceived passing youth fad. And as stilted as the scripts, acting, and lip-synching in these early rock movies can be, they nonetheless offered kids the chance to see and hear the heroes they couldn't get enough of in big-screen action. Eventually the innocence of the 1950s cash-ins gave way to the more evolved storylines and concert films of the following decades. And the more worldly Ramones were watching then, too.

Don't Knock the Rock (1956)

Pioneering disc jockey Alan Freed plays himself in this exploito-flick, wherein the DJ tries to prove to stuffy small-town parents that rock 'n' roll won't make their teenagers into juvenile delinquents. (Heh, heh, heh.) Also stars early rockers Bill Haley and His Comets, vocal group the Treniers, and the great Little Richard.

The Girl Can't Help It (1956)

And it's Little Richard who lights up this 1956 comedy named for his raucous single (he also performs "Ready Teddy" in the film). With the support of her gangster boyfriend, blonde bombshell Jayne Mansfield's character aspires to become a hit singer—she can't sing, but with curves like that who cares? Other attractions include Eddie Cochran, Gene Vincent, and Fats Domino.

High School Confidential! (1958)

Another dynamite blonde starlet of the 1950s was Mamie Van Doren, who provides the eye candy in this period slang–filled yarn intended as a warning against the dangers of drugs (sample line: "If you flake around with the weed, you'll end up using the harder stuff.") Naturally, all this just made the lifestyle more attractive to kids. (Oops!) Stars *West Side Story*'s Russ Tamblyn and the fiery Jerry Lee Lewis and his pumping piano.

Jailhouse Rock (1957)

Arguably Elvis Presley's best movie, *Jailhouse Rock* has the King portraying Vince Everett, who while serving a prison sentence learns about the record business from his cellmate, a country singer. Everett decides to become a singer himself once he's released, and is soon swiveling his hips all the way to the top of the charts. Worth watching for the famed title-song dance sequence alone.

The T.A.M.I. Show (1964)

T.A.M.I. stands for "Teenage Award Music International," a live round-up of most of the greatest rock 'n' roll and R&B acts of the time, all of whom deliver incendiary performances: Chuck Berry,

Ike and Tina Turner, James Brown, the Rolling Stones, the Beach Boys, the Barbarians, Jan and Dean, Gerry and the Pacemakers, Marvin Gaye, the Miracles—hell, even Leslie Gore and Billy J. Kramer and the Dakotas shine. Essential.

A Hard Day's Night (1964)

About the only top act that wasn't in *The T.A.M.I. Show* was the biggest one: the Beatles. But they were more than big enough to have their *own* movies. This is the first, and a brilliant one at that. Shot in black and white, it stars the band at the giddy height of Beatlemania and is full of irreverent, cheek-pulling gags—and, naturally, great music.

Help! (1965)

The Fab Four returned to the silver screen the following year with the full-color *Help!*, a comedy whose plot is a send-up of the "international intrigue" of the contemporaneously popular James Bond films. Here, zaniness reigns when one of Ringo's recently acquired rings makes him the unwitting target of a mysterious human-sacrifice cult. Like *A Hard Day's Night*, this one has a killer soundtrack.

Monterey Pop (1968)

Totally captivating concert film documenting the legendary 1967 Monterey International Pop Festival, which launched the stateside careers of Jimi Hendrix and the Who. Lucky for the wide-eyed future Ramones (and the rest of us!) the cameras were there to capture the explosive sets of both. Also appearing: Eric Burdon and the Animals, Janis Joplin, Otis Redding, Canned Heat, the Mamas and the Papas, Simon and Garfunkel, and more. The expanded DVD release has acts not seen in the original film.

Head (1968)

Acid Eaters notwithstanding, the Ramones, as we've already established, weren't especially inclined toward psychedelia. And this singularly surreal masterwork starring the Monkees is certainly one of the most psychedelic movies ever made. But its constant assault of way-out wackiness takes things far beyond any punks-versus-hippies hairsplitting, adding up to an endlessly weird—and very funny—eighty-six minutes. As a cow being led around by Frank Zappa (?!) in one scene remarks, "Monkees is the *craziest* people."

Gimme Shelter (1970)

Another crucial concert film, this disturbing doc follows the Rolling Stones on their 1969 tour and culminates with their infamous performance at California's Altamont Speedway. That was the tragic evening that saw an audience member murdered by one of the supposedly protective Hell's Angels security guards, and directors Albert and David Maysles do a heroic job of conveying both the tense mood and the power of the Stones' music.

THE RAMONES ON *THE SIMPSONS* AND *SPACE GHOST COAST TO COAST*

Since debuting in 1998, *The Simpsons* has become not only American TV's longest-running situation comedy (animated *or* live-action), but also a cultural institution that's won shelves of awards and was named the twentieth century's best television series by *Time* magazine. The images of Homer, Marge, Bart, Lisa, and Maggie Simpson and the Fox network show's other characters are recognized around the world and their catchphrases have entered the popular parlance ("D'oh!"). In light of the show's M.O. of parodying American middle-class family life, culture, and society, it comes as no surprise that its creator, Matt Groening, would be a devout Ramones fan. So naturally it was only a matter of time before the group—*Simpsons* fans themselves, of course—made it into an episode: "Rosebud," which first aired in October 1993. In the segment, our boys say a few lines and perform a rapid-fire "Happy Birthday" at a party for Homer's evil boss, Mr. Burns. Understandably, Marky called the appearance, which can be seen on the four-DVD *Complete Fifth Season* box set, a career highlight.

The back story of the Adult Swim network's *Space Ghost Coast to*

Coast is decidedly surreal. In his original 1966 Hanna Barbera–produced incarnation, Space Ghost was a stoic superhero who battled outer-space supervillians. But in 1994 he was recast as the host of a late-night TV talk show that featured the animated character interviewing live guests by way of intercut footage. The show, whose theme music was performed first by free jazz guitarist Sonny Sharrock and later by surf outfit Man or Astro-man? and featured house band Zorak and the Original Way-Outs, left the airwaves in 1998, but not before having on such as guests as Alice Cooper, Talking Heads' David Byrne, the Modern Lovers' Jonathan Richman, Sonic Youth's Thurston Moore, Metallica's Kirk Hammett and James Hetfield—and, yes, the Ramones, who appeared on an installment with comedian Bobcat Goldthwait. That interlude of bizarre genius is one of many on *Space Ghost Coast to Coast: Volume One.*

CARBONA NOT GLUE

Don't try this at home, kids.

It's a sad, age-old fact: when teenagers are bored they can get into some bad things. Looking to escape the tedious and sometimes oppressive surroundings they're born into, they often turn to intoxicants. Usually this means alcohol or various illicit substances. In the drug-wild 1960s and seventies, when the Ramones were growing up, they and their peers certainly sampled their share of consciousness-altering contraband. Dee Dee's longtime heroin addiction finally took him from us in 2002, one of the millions of similarly avoidable tragedies that continue to occur around the world, far too often. It remains unclear what the other Ramones might have messed with, but where did Johnny, Joey, and Dee Dee get their mind-altering thrills when they couldn't access booze or certain nefarious goods? Often they found them in the neighborhood hobby store or right under Mom's kitchen sink—and, being the Ramones and thereby fascinated with sick, real-life stuff that people just didn't sing about, what did they do? They wrote songs about the stuff.

It's been pointed out repeatedly by band members that, following numbers like "I Don't Wanna Go Down to the Basement," "I Don't Wanna Walk Around with You," and "I Don't Wanna Get Involved with You," the first *positive* song the Ramones wrote was "Now I Wanna Sniff Some Glue." A bit black humor, a bit tell-it-like-it-is adolescent reality. The particular adhesive our heroic delinquents sniffed was commonly called model airplane glue, used to assemble the plastic model kits parents bought their kids. At some point the little buggers discovered that inhaling the vapors of this toxic mucilage resulted in feelings of exhilaration and euphoria, dizziness, loss of coordination and muscular movement, slurring of speech, mental deterioration, hallucinations, and finally drowsiness. Unfortunately, it can also lead to coma, respiratory failure, and doing stupid stuff like trying to fly off high rooftops. After abuse among teens had become epidemic, many popular glue makers like Testors removed the offending ingredients from their formulas.

Carbona is short for Carbona Cleaning Fluid, a popular, non-flammable stain-removal product developed as an alternative to the volatile solutions used in the 1880s. It once contained carbon tetrachloride, a chemical used in pesticides, refrigerants, fire extinguishers, and, perhaps ironically, lava lamps. Imbibing this stuff affects the central nervous system and produces dissociative, hallucinogenic affects—as well as damaging your liver and kidneys and very possibly inducing a coma and/or leading to cancer. The Ramones referenced their encounters with the product in "Carbona Not Glue," a track on the initial release of *Leave Home*. After objections from the Carbona Products Company, Sire replaced the song on later pressings, first with the B side "Babysitter" and later with "Sheena Is a Punk Rocker"—making the first issue of the LP a collector's item.

ANDY WARHOL

A ndy Warhol's contributions to contemporary art are almost beyond estimation. The leading light of the movement known as pop art, Warhol utilized a widely diverse array of media (drawing, painting, printmaking, photography, silk screening, sculpture, theater, film, literature, music, performance art, fashion) to explore and comment on modern consumer society and how we see ourselves, each other, and the very idea of artistic expression within that society. The Ramones' similar obsessions with and celebration of the seemingly mundane—7-11, cartoon icons, Burger King, soda machines—were at least encouraged, if not inspired, by what they picked up from Warhol, the arbiter of underground cool in late-sixties New York.

Avant-garde films such as Warhol's *Batman Dracula* (1964), *Vinyl* (1965), *Chelsea Girls* (1966), and his even earlier, more experimental works would seem to have been among the outsider movies that leached into the Ramones' congealing young brains. Actor Joe Dallesandro was the star of Warhol's *Lonesome Cowboys* and *Flesh* (both 1968), *Trash* (1970), and *Heat* (1972), the latter three produced by Paul Morrissey with Warhol's backing. Johnny cited Dallesandro as a direct influence on his pre-Ramones look: tie-dyed headband, jean jacket, no shirt. Hard to picture, huh?

Every bit as important as the actual art he made was the social scene Warhol created. He gravitated toward, attracted, and vocally supported other artists and people he saw as having something unique to say, individuals who led interesting lives and did interesting things. The Factory, his fabled studio, originally located in midtown Manhattan and later downtown, on Union Square, was the site of drug-fueled parties and Fellini-esque happenings peopled with artists and social freaks of all stripes. Part artistic laboratory, part think tank, it housed the glittery, sexually defiant drag queens and kings, transgendered individuals, and other radicals who set the stage for glam rock, as well as stark, hard-edged urban minimalists like the Warhol-produced Velvet Underground (see Chapter Three), who cast the dark die for the Ramones and punk.

Fun, fun: A hilarious send-up of late '50s and early '60s teen exploitation films, *Rock 'n' Roll High School* remains one of the most beloved rock movies ever made. (New World/Photofest)

6

IT'S ALIVE:
THE RAMONES AND PUNK ON FILM

Theoretically, at least, at its core punk rock is chiefly about the music itself. But from the get-go its practitioners have also had a keen sense of visual image, to further set themselves apart from the mainstream acts they've reacted against—even if their stance has been to defy the show-biz machine by having a nerdy image (see Television and early Talking Heads). And early punk's combination of sounds and aesthetics added up to a slam-dunk subject for the big and small screens. In this chapter we'll turn the lens on several of the better movies that document punk and punk-related topics, as well as a few scripted films that involve punk. Let's start with the ones that focus directly on our Converse-clad conquerors.

RAMONES MOVIES

As the cartoonish but complex flagship act of punk rock, the Ramones were a phenomenon ready-made for the movies. Indeed, they're the stars of one of the most iconic rock movies ever made, *Rock 'n' Roll High School*. But the saga of the Ramones as a band and their individual stories, their music, and of course their live performances have also provided rich matter for a brace of other films.

Rock 'n' Roll High School (1979)

It ain't *Casablanca*. But as far as punksploitation movies go it's the pinnacle. Produced by B-movie master Roger Corman (see Chapter Five), *Rock 'n' Roll High School* is both a sarcastic send-up of the late fifties and early sixties teen / rock 'n' roll exploitation films and a fun, entertaining, straight-up teen comedy. Much like the early Beatles movies the Ramones so loved (see Chapter Five), it relies on high-speed antics and cheap sight gags. The story concerns the bouncy, Barbie-esque Riff Randell (P. J. Soles), a student at the oppressive Vince Lombardi High School, whose tyrannical principal, Miss Togar (Andy Warhol associate Mary Wornov), has declared war on rock 'n' roll. The Ramones are playing in town, and Riff is dying to see her favorite band and present them with a song she's written—but Togar has other plans. Things come to an explosive climax, but not before the Ramones make a few absurdly funny appearances to lip-synch some tunes and burp out a few lines of minimal dialogue. (Dee Dee: "Pizza? I'll take some!") Mandatory viewing, naturally.

End of the Century (2003)

Even *more* mandatory for Ramoniacs, however, is *End of the Century*, Jim Fields and Michael Gramaglia's award-winning, rips-and-all documentary on the band. Few documentaries match it for not only getting the story straight, but also expressing it in a way that speaks even to the uninitiated. The directors provide poignant and revealing glimpses into the complicated and, in some cases, famously guarded personalities of the members. And they succeed spectacularly in conveying the perfect contextual storm that gave birth to the band, as well as the movement it sparked and flourished creatively within. Besides deeply insightful interviews with all the players, we hear from others who were there: childhood friends, family members, CBGB owner Hilly Kristal, manager Danny Fields, Richard Hell, the Clash's Joe Strummer, road manager Monte Melnick, lighting designer / graphic artist Arturo Vega, *Punk* magazine's Legs McNeil and John Holstrom, Blondie's Deborah Harry and Chris Stein, producer Ed Stasium, Sire Records chief Seymour Stein, and legions more. The live footage is great, of course, and overall the film is a powerful reaffirmation of the genius of the music. But what's more startling is the revelation of just how emotionally messed up the core Ramones were as human beings.

You come away shaking your head at how utterly dysfunctional the group you thought you knew actually was—which gives you a whole new appreciation for its odds-defying, twenty-two-year lifespan. As Johnny remarked about the film, "It's accurate. It left me disturbed."

Hey Is Dee Dee Home (2003)

In candid, self-deprecating, and unapologetic terms, bassist Dee Dee holds forth to filmmaker Lech Kowalski (*D.O.A.*, *Story of a Junkie*) about his crazy life and career. (Re-released in 2006 as *History on My Arms*.)

Ramones Raw (2004)

Rough home video tour footage shot by Marky and first released on VHS in 1998 as *Ramones Around the World*. This DVD edition adds a full 1980 Italian concert, clips from *Uncle Floyd Show* and *Howard Stern Show* appearances, and commentary from Marky and Johnny.

THE UNCLE FLOYD SHOW

From the mid-1970s through the early 1980s, *The Uncle Floyd Show* was just about the coolest and craziest program on TV in the New York metropolitan area. And it was a favorite of the Ramones, who showed their love for it by regularly sporting *Uncle Floyd Show* T-shirts and buttons and name-checking it in the lyrics of *Pleasant Dreams*'s "It's Not My Place (In the Nine to Five World)." Hosted by the quick-quipping Uncle Floyd (a.k.a. Floyd Vivino, the brother of musicians Jimmy and Jerry Vivino), the show was a loosely scripted (at best), largely improvised slapstick train wreck taped in an East Orange, New Jersey, basement in its early years for airing on UHF television every weekday afternoon. Depending on a viewer's perspective, it was either a children's show or a show that *parodied* children's shows, much like TV's earlier *Lunch with Soupy Sales* or later *Pee Wee Herman Show*. The vaudeville-inspired broadcasts featured the host interviewing guests à la *The Joe Franklin Show* (another New York–area institution that had the Ramones on as guests and was a lifelong favorite of both the band and Uncle Floyd), and included wacky comedic skits; interludes of Floyd trading barbs with his puppet sidekicks, Oogie and Bones Boy; off-camera catcalls and other anarchic behavior by the demented cast and crew; and rollicking ragtime and stride piano music by the emcee. In addition to the Ramones, other fans of *The Uncle Floyd Show* included the New York Dolls, John Lennon, and David Bowie, who paid tribute to it in 2002 with the song "Slip Away."

Music was always a big part of *The Uncle Floyd Show*, which presented appearances by dozens of New York–area punk and new wave bands, as well as bigger-name performers. Besides the Ramones and Dee Dee's later band the Spiky Tops, some other notable acts that appeared on *Uncle Floyd* were the Troggs, Madonna, Squeeze, the Misfits, Pussy Galore, Peter Tork of the Monkees, Chubby Checker, Bon Jovi (!), and Cyndi Lauper's early group Blue Angel (sadly, the show's cash-strapped creators erased nearly all of the musical clips to save on tape costs, although some exist on YouTube). In 1982 the program briefly moved to a weekly national slot on NBC, before getting busted down to cable.

The DVD *The Best of the Uncle Floyd Show* has 120 insane minutes from this wild program's peak years.

Lifestyles of the Ramones (1991)

Early group-authorized compilation of promo videos interspersed with interviews with the band and members of Blondie, Talking Heads, and Anthrax; producer Daniel Rey; New York Yankees player Dave Righetti (!); and others. Reissued on DVD in the 2005 box set *Weird Tales of the Ramones*.

We're Outta Here (1997)

Hour-long document of the band's final concert, which took place on August 6, 1996, at L.A.'s Palace Theater. Rushed and overly festooned with guest cameos (Motörhead's Lemmy, plus members of Pearl Jam, Rancid, and Soundgarden), it makes you wish the boys had just gone it alone this one last time. But it is what it is.

It's Alive: 1974–1996 (2007)

Now *this* is more like it. Besides the earliest known live Ramones footage (raw, revelatory black-and-white video shot at CBGB in 1974), this superlative two-disc set follows the band's whole career and includes concerts from the peak years, spots on U.K. TV's *Old Grey Whistle Test* and *Top of the Pops*, rare promo clips, interviews, and photos. Essential.

Music Milestones: Pleasant Dreams (2005/2012)

U.K.-produced doc about the band's first five albums that culminates with an examination of the making of the sixth, 1981's *Pleasant Dreams*. The TV performance footage, offset here by commentary from unfamiliar rock critics, is found on other Ramones DVDs.

The Ramones Videobiography (2007)

End of the Century pretty much renders this seventy-two-minute effort redundant. Nevertheless, the interviews with Tommy, C. J., Arturo Vega, Monte Melnick, and others do have the occasional insightful nugget that hard-core fans won't mind hearing. Sets on *Don Kirshner's Rock Concert* and Germany's *Musikladen* are sampled, although the latter appearance is well served via its own release (see later).

Impact! Songs that Changed the World: I Wanna Be Sedated, The Ramones (2007)

This one's definitely for avowed pinheads only. In thirty-six minutes, it offers a treatise on the genesis and influence of one song, "I Wanna Be Sedated," while dashing through the basic backstory of the band. Quick-hit interviews with Marky, Legs McNeil, Joey's brother Mickey Leigh, and others.

Too Tough to Die (2008)

Concert film of the 2004 Johnny Ramone tribute show that took place in Los Angeles two days before the guitarist passed away. Produced by Mandy Stein, the daughter of Sire Records'

Seymour Stein and band comanager Linda Stein, it stars Rob Zombie, Deborah Harry, Henry Rollins, X, the Dickies, the Red Hot Chili Peppers, and other acts mostly performing Ramones classics.

The Musikladen Recordings: 1978 (2011)

Absolutely imperative document of the quartet's blazing twenty-five-song set for German TV in September of 1978. The shots of the budding Kraut-punkers in the audience are almost as precious as the music. More dubious releases of the show are out there as well, but this high-quality edition supersedes them all. Also includes an audio CD of the program.

Ramones: Punk 'n' Rock 'n' Roll (2012)

Fairly workmanlike band bio built around some rare live French TV footage from the 1980 tour for the *End of the Century* album. Includes band interviews and photo gallery.

Rockaway (2012)

A whopping forty-eight songs recorded live, circa 1978–88 in Finland, France, and the U.S. Quality varies throughout.

RAMONES-RELATED FILMS

There's a handful of movies less directly associated with the Ramones that may be of interest, due to key use of their music and cameos by a couple of members.

Over the Edge (1979)

One of Matt Dillon's earliest films, this winningly trashy exploitation effort about a gang of destructive, rebellious suburban kids is a guilty pleasure. The rockin' soundtrack includes "Teenage Lobotomy."

Pet Sematary (1989)

Besides being the most famous horror writer of our day, Stephen King is clearly a man of musical taste—he's a huge Ramones fan, after all. Thus, the boys were commissioned to record the theme for this frightful modern classic about a family that moves in next to a mysterious wooded cemetery. The song "Pet Sematary" went on to become one of the band's best-known. "Sheena Is a Punk Rocker" also appears on the soundtrack. (For the soundtrack of 1992's *Pet Sematary II*, the Ramones returned with another chestnut, "Poison Heart.")

What About Me (1993)

Dee Dee plays a character called Dougie in this indie yarn about a woman (played by filmmaker Rachel Amodeo) who ends up living on the New York streets. Also stars New York Dolls / Heartbreakers Johnny Thunders and Jerry Nolan, Richard Hell, ex–Sid Vicious bodyguard Rockets Redglare, and others.

Bikini Bandits (2002)

Dee Dee crops up again as the Pope (!) in this comedic hunk of B-movie trash about, you got it, a team of bikini-clad, machine gun-toting bandits. Acting alongside him are Dead Kennedys vocalist Jello Biafra, child star Corey Feldman (*The Goonies, Lost Boys*), and *Howard Stern Show* regular Hank the Angry Drunken Dwarf. (Also released as *Bikini Bandits Experience*.)

The Brooklyn Boys (2002)

Marky stars as a character named Tommy (intentionally ironic?) in this violent drama about a Brooklyn mafia family.

Marky Ramone and Tequila Baby: Live (2006)

The drummer sits in for a concert by Brazilian band Tequila Baby. Many a Ramones song is played.

Marky Ramone: Punk Rock Drumming His Way for Beginners (2010)

Learn to play punk rock drums from the man himself! As a narrator Marky's not exactly Mr. Personality, but this one-hour lesson will appeal to beginners and pros alike.

IF YOU LIKE THE RAMONES...

PUNK ROCK DOCS

In addition to those devoted exclusively to the Ramones, there's a raft of other fine documentaries and concert films concerning punk rock in general, the group's fellow punk acts, and cool bands that came before and after. So warm up your remote control and check these out.

Punk: Attitude (2005)

For a history of punk rock, start here. The Ramones are rightfully prominent in this ninety-minute doc by director Don Letts, which covers most of the major players, from proto-punks (the Velvet Underground, the Stooges, the New York Dolls) through the early U.S. (the Dictators, Patti Smith, Suicide) and U.K. bands (the Sex Pistols, the Clash, the Damned), 1980s hardcore and noise (Black Flag, Bad Brains, Sonic Youth), and nineties grunge and pop-punk (Nirvana, Green Day). Australia's influential contributors (the Saints, Radio Birdman, Birthday Party) are, frustratingly, omitted—a film on that scene is needed—but this epic opus nevertheless remains the best first stop when it comes to an account of the music. (The 2011 reissue includes a full disc of extras.)

The History of Rock and Roll (1995)

Like it says in the title, more history awaits in this ten-part miniseries that originally aired on PBS. Our guys appear in the "Punk" installment, which is excellent and focuses on the music's genesis in New York and London. But the rest of it is also well worth your time.

The Tomorrow Show: Punk and New Wave (2005)

Hosted by Tom Snyder, *The Tomorrow Show* was a late-night staple on U.S. TV in the mid-1970s and early 1980s that gave many American viewers their fist glimpses of punk. In addition to those by the Ramones, this double disc has interviews and performances by the Jam, Iggy Pop, Elvis Costello, Patti Smith, John Lydon, Joan Jett, the Plasmatics, and more.

The Blank Generation (1976)

Not to be confused with the punksploitation flick *Blank Generation* (see later), this grainy, black-and-white document of the nascent CBGB scene captures several early New York bands—the Ramones, Blondie, Patti Smith, Talking Heads, the Heartbreakers, Wayne County, others—at home in their primal element. Filmmaker Amos Poe shot the acts with no sound, dubbing in their music (from studio demos) afterward. Annoying viewing, but a vital artifact nevertheless.

The Punk Rock Movie from England (1978)

Also released as, simply, *The Punk Rock Movie*, this raw, Super 8 effort by Don Letts covering the U.K. scene includes rockin' footage of the Clash, the Sex Pistols, the Slits, Siouxsie and the Banshees, Eater, Slaughter and the Dogs, and visiting Yanks Wayne County and the Electric Chairs, most of it shot at London's Roxy club, where Letts was the DJ.

D.O.A. (1980)

Another Lech Kowalski doc, this one intercuts film footage of the Sex Pistols' ill-fated 1978 U.S. tour with performances by the Dead Boys, Generation X, Sham 69, the Clash, X-Ray Spex, ex-Pistol Glen Matlock's Rich Kids, and others. Morbidly memorable are the interviews with a strung-out Sid Vicious and his girlfriend Nancy Spungen, both of whom would be dead within months of filming.

The Filth and the Fury (2000)

The definitive Sex Pistols film, however, is this one. Produced by *Great Rock 'n' Roll Swindle* (see later) director Julien Temple, it deftly dishes up the whole gloriously dirty story, from the group's 1975 formation through its controversial rise and messy 1978 demise. Unmissable.

The Clash: Westway to the World (2000)

While it's tempting to call *The Filth and the Fury* the British counterpart to *End of the Century*, one could say the same about this superb Don

Letts–produced bio of the Clash. Using recent interviews and powerful live footage, it follows the influential band's storied career.

Joe Strummer: The Future Is Unwritten (2007)

In which the Clash's late front man gets his own bio treatment by Julien Temple. Inspiring and poignant, it covers the singer's unique personality and his life before, during, after the band.

New York Doll (2005)

Arguably even more inspiring and poignant is this 2005 look at New York Dolls bassist Arthur Kane, who in his shortened life went from being poised for stardom to the depths of alcoholism, a conversion to the Mormon faith, and performing again with his reunited, legendary band.

Lookin' Fine on Television (2011)

Kane and the New York Dolls are the focus of this compilation of early video of the group's mid-seventies New York and West Coast shows and offstage moments captured by photographer Bob Gruen. (Portions were previously released as *All Dolled Up*.)

The Last Pogo (1978)

Student-made short on what was touted as the final punk concert at Toronto's Horseshoe Tavern. Wild performances by local legends the Viletones, Teenage Head, the Scenics, the Ugly, and more.

Burning Down the House: The Story of CBGB (2009)

Made by Mandy Stein, this ninety-minute feature tells the story of CBGB and the doomed fight to save it. Interviews with Joey, Tommy, and various celebrity supporters and vintage performances by Patti Smith, Talking Heads, Television, Bad Brains, and, yes, the Ramones.

Blondie: One Way or Another (2006)

Speaking of CBGB, there's this BBC bio on its biggest-selling graduate act. Performance clips from throughout Blondie's career;

non-band-member interviewees include Tommy, Iggy Pop, and Talking Heads' Tina Weymouth and Chris Frantz.

Talking Heads: Chronology Deluxe (2011)

Talking Heads were regular early Ramones openers, and are thus worth investigating. But skip Jonathan Demme's overwrought 1984 concert film *Stop Making Sense*. Instead, grab this compendium of mostly scarce early clips packed in a hardcover book complete with a rare Lester Bangs essay.

Dream of Life (2007)

Director Steven Sebring's engrossing portrait of poet and punk icon Patti Smith charts her rise from Max's Kansas City and CBGB, retirement from music to start a family, and ongoing re-emergence since the late 1980s.

The House of the Rising Punk (2008)

Yet another doc on the embryonic New York punk scene, this one done for German TV in 1998. Besides the Ramones, there's the New York Dolls, Patti Smith, Television, the Stooges, Blondie, and Suicide; interviews with Lenny Kaye, Patti Smith, Tom Verlaine, Richard Hell, and Jim Jarmusch.

Punk: Early Years (1978)

Great street-level document of early London punk. Interviews and performances by the Adverts, Eddie and the Hot Rods, X-Ray Spex, the Sex Pistols, the Slits, Generation X, Siouxsie and the Banshees, Alternative TV, even T. Rex's Marc Bolan.

Punk in London / Punk in England (both 2009)

Two separate releases shot by a visiting German filmmaker during and after the U.K. punk explosion. *Punk in London* has storming live footage of the Clash, X-Ray Spex, the Adverts, the Jam, and the Lurkers, plus a Chelsea rehearsal and the Boomtown Rats on TV. *Punk in England* is the sequel, with more Clash, Jam, and Adverts, plus Ian Dury and others.

Urgh! A Music War (1982)

Live performances from 1980 by an avalanche of high-profile punk and new wave acts. No Ramones, alas, but the nearly forty bands include Magazine, the Go-Go's, the Fleshtones, Joan Jett and the Blackhearts, XTC, Devo, Dead Kennedys, Pere Ubu, the Surf Punks, 999, Gang of Four, the Alley Cats, the Members, and the pre-arena Police. But to these eyes it's the Cramps who burn brightest, with an unhinged version of "Tear It Up."

The Cramps: Live at Napa State Mental Hospital (1981)

And the Cramps have free reign in this surreal black-and-white chronicle of the band's 1978 appearance at, you got it, a California mental hospital. Gives new meaning to the phrase "the lunatics have taken over the asylum."

Oil City Confidential (2010)

"Prequel" to *The Filth and the Fury* and *The Future Is Unwritten*, in which Julien Temple trains his capable camera on pub rock outfit Dr. Feelgood. Makes the case for the quartet's influence on punk, which stretches far beyond its tough, blue-collar roots.

The Ballad of Mott the Hoople (2012)

The story of another act that left its mark on the punk generation, glam rock powerhouse Mott the Hoople (see Chapter Three). Invigorating.

1991: The Year Punk Broke (1992)

Grunge-era travelogue of a 1991 Sonic Youth / Nirvana tour. Includes live performances by the Ramones, Dinosaur Jr., Mudhoney, Babes in Toyland, and others.

Born to Lose: The Last Rock and Roll Movie (1999)

Dee Dee offers commentary in this Lech Kowalski–produced bio-doc about his troubled pal Johnny Thunders. Also features Wayne Kramer (MC5), Willy DeVille (Mink DeVille), and Sylvain Sylvain

(New York Dolls). Not to be confused with a similarly named indie drama about a fictional L.A. punk band released the same year.

X: The Unheard Music (1986)

Documentary on Los Angeles punk band X. Performances and band interviews plus testimonials from the Doors' Ray Manzarek, the Dead Kennedys' Jello Biafra, and others.

The Decline of Western Civilization, Part 1 (1981)

X also appears in this, Penelope Spheeris's acclaimed snapshot of the L.A. scene as it transitions from first-wave punk to hardcore. Band and audience interviews and fiery footage of Black Flag, the Germs, the Circle Jerks, Fear, and more.

Another State of Mind (1982)

More L.A. punk is on offer in this saga of a problem-plagued tour by the bands Social Distortion and Youth Brigade. Before it all collapses, the two bands visit Washington, D.C., where a rehearsal by legendary hardcore unit Minor Threat is filmed.

American Hardcore (2006)

Minor Threat figures in this doc on the thriving 1980s U.S. hardcore scene. Among the other big names are Black Flag, Bad Brains, the Circle Jerks, MDC, Negative Approach, Flipper, SSD, Die Kreuzen, Gang Green, and the Adolescents.

D.O.A.: Smash the State (2011)

Although D.O.A. hails from Canada, the band was a staple on the U.S. hardcore circuit and also appears in *American Hardcore*. But here the long-running, politically charged group gets the spotlight, with live video from the vital early years, 1978 to 1983.

Bad Brains Live at CBGB 1982 (2006)

Shot over two nights at the storied club, right here is the explosive evidence that the Bad Brains were one of the greatest live bands ever. Your jaw will drop.

Bad Brains: A Band in D.C. (2012)

The tumultuous career of the trailblazing Washington, D.C., hardcore/reggae quartet goes under the lens of Mandy Stein in this award-winning examination.

We Jam Econo (2005)

The tale of California trio the Minutemen, whose inventive, angular punk stood far apart from the eighties hardcore pack.

You Weren't There: A History of Chicago Punk, 1977–1984 (2009)

Fine overview of Windy City punk, from its formative days around DJ nights at gay bar La Mere Vipere through the hardcore of the Effigies, Naked Raygun, and Articles of Faith.

Hype (1996)

Covers the pivotal Northwest U.S. grunge/punk scene with live and interview clips of Nirvana, TAD, Mudhoney, Soundgarden, the Gits, the Melvins, the Mono Men, the Supersuckers, Pearl Jam, the Fastbacks, and others.

Hated (1998)

Blood-and-feces-smeared chronicle of notoriously extreme performer G. G. Allin. Dee Dee, who auditioned for Allin's band the Murder Junkies but didn't take the gig, appears briefly.

Lemmy (2010)

The colorful biography of Motörhead front man and founder (and dedicated Ramones fan) Lemmy Kilmister. Marky Ramone is among the many who are interviewed.

PUNK FICTION

As is the case with other modern cultural movements, punk has motivated many screenwriters and filmmakers to pick up their pens and cameras to pay homage to the music and the scene—with varying degrees of artistic and commercial success. Some of these punk-inspired pictures are fictional stories that use punk as a backdrop, while some are based on actual events. Here are a few you'll find peek-worthy.

Jubilee (1978)

In a bleak, dystopian future England, a trio of emotionally detached punk girls amuse themselves with murder. Stars Adam Ant, Wayne County, Chelsea's Gene October, *The Rocky Horror Picture Show*'s Nell Campbell, and Sex Pistols associates Helen Wellington-Lloyd and Jordan. Weird and arty.

Quadrophenia (1979)

Okay, it's not about punk rock per se, but this coming-of-age classic based on the Who's identically named 1973 concept album tapped into the punk explosion that raged while the movie was in production and mirrors its rebellious attitudes. (And of course the Who was a significant influence on the Ramones; see Chapter Three.) Easily one of the best rock movies ever, it helped spark the mod revival in post-punk England.

Rude Boy (1980)

Part fiction, part documentary, this story follows a wide-eyed young punk who becomes a roadie for the Clash. The dramatic parts are occasionally credible, but the real draw is the ferocious concert footage and the studio scenes, the latter showing the band recording *Give 'Em Enough Rope*.

Blank Generation (1980)

No relation to the Amos Poe film mentioned above, this torturously turgid attempt at a "punk love story" stars Richard Hell as the male lead. Recommended, however, for the scenes of Hell and the Voidoids live at CBGB and the DVD extras interview.

Smithereens (1982)

Mr. Hell returns in this downtown '80s tale of a starry-eyed chick who runs away to the East Village and becomes hopelessly smitten with his character, punk singer Eric. Great soundtrack featuring Hell and the Feelies.

The Great Rock 'n' Roll Swindle (1980)

With 2000's *The Filth and the Fury*, Julien Temple redeemed himself for this infamously convoluted Sex Pistols "documentary" driven by the band's estranged manager, Malcolm McLaren. Selling points: great live Pistols footage, fiendish animated segments, and Sid Vicious's disturbingly prescient performance of "My Way."

Ladies and Gentlemen, the Fabulous Stains (1980)

Screenwriter Nancy Dowd claims she was inspired by the Ramones when she concocted this hilariously bad yarn about the rise and demise of an all-girl punk band called the Stains. Stars Laura Dern, Diane Lane, the Clash's Paul Simonon, the Sex Pistols' Steve Jones and Paul Cook, and the Tubes' Fee Waybill.

Times Square (1980)

Another hack story about runaway teenage girls who start a punk band. *The Rocky Horror Picture Show*'s Tim Curry plays a benevolent DJ. One memorable scene has the gals dropping TV's from rooftops—a beloved pastime of a certain young Ramones guitarist. Soundtrack has "I Wanna Be Sedated" and cuts by Patti Smith, Talking Heads, and others.

Suburbia (1984)

Real-life punks are the untrained cast of this foray into fiction by *Decline of Western Civilization* director Penelope Spheeris in which a gang of squatter kids deal with life and each other in suburban L.A. Hardcore-heavy soundtrack has the Germs, T.S.O.L., the Vandals, and D.I.

Repo Man (1984)

Insane sci-fi comedy from director Alex Cox. The world of disaffected punk Otto (Emilio Estevez) goes from bleak to hyper-weird when he gets a job repossessing cars with a veteran repo man

(Harry Dean Stanton) and helps hunt for a mysterious Chevy with glowing cargo in its trunk. Truly one of the great punk movies. Soundtrack: Iggy Pop, Black Flag, Fear, L.A. trio the Plugz, and the Circle Jerks, who make a hilarious appearance.

Sid and Nancy (1986)

Cox also called the shots for this smash story of the volatile and doomed lives and relationship of Sex Pistols bassist Sid Vicious (Gary Oldman) and New York groupie Nancy Spungen (Chloe Webb). Hole singer Courtney Love has a minor role. The soundtrack features the Clash's Joe Strummer (who also stars in Cox's *Straight to Hell*), John Cale, X-Ray Spex, the Circle Jerks, Link Wray, and Black Sabbath.

Tapeheads (1988)

Comedic takedown of the music video industry starring John Cusack and Tim Robbins. Dead Kennedys front man Jello Biafra does a cameo. In addition to Biafra's band, the soundtrack boasts Devo, Stiv Bators, Bo Diddley, the Circle Jerks, and music producer David Kahne covering "I Wanna Be Sedated."

Hard Core Logo (1996)

Called "the punk rock *Spinal Tap*," this Canadian cult comedy follows the messy travails of a punk band on a final-fling reunion tour. The Ramones' "Touring" is, appropriately, on the soundtrack, as well as tunes by Teenage Head, the Dead Boys, D.O.A., and more.

SLC Punk! (1998)

Highly enjoyable comedy centering on the lives of the sole two teen punks in conservative Salt Lake City. A winning soundtrack too, with "Cretin Hop" and "She's the One," plus the Stooges, Blondie, Fear, the Velvet Underground, and Minor Threat.

24-Hour Party People (2002)

Blurring the line between fiction and reality, this comedic drama biopic covers the raucous career of impresario Tony Wilson, a key figure in the early Manchester punk scene and head of the seminal Factory Records label. Fast-paced, funny, and recommended. Soundtrack: Sex Pistols, Buzzcocks, Stooges, Clash, Jam, Stranglers, Iggy, more.

The Runaways (2010)

No, not yet another B movie about fugitive teenage girls starting a punk band. This one's a biopic of all-girl group the Runaways (see Chapter Four). Stars *Twilight*'s Kristen Stewart as Joan Jett and Dakota Fanning as Cherie Currie. Not exactly a masterpiece, but they got the look right. And the soundtrack, with the Stooges, David Bowie, Gary Glitter, the Sex Pistols, and the namesake act, totally slays.

Wave of mutilation: The Pixies define what some call college or alternative rock, a genre that owes its very existence to the punk movement sparked by the Ramones. (Photofest/© Elektra Records)

7

WE'RE A HAPPY FAMILY:
THE LEGACY OF THE RAMONES

It's a lot to answer for, but almost all of the music that today falls under the headings of "alternative rock" or "indie rock" can be traced to the Ramones. How's that? Because by acting as the spark that got the punk rock rebellion rolling in the mid-1970s, the Ramones also lit the fuse that detonated an even bigger bang, a far-reaching, endlessly diverse musical explosion whose repercussions are still being felt and will continue to ripple through generations of musicians yet to come. In this chapter we'll concentrate on the musical movements that took their cues from the Ramones and fanned those waves of inspiration out into other directions: power pop, hardcore punk, college rock, thrash metal, grunge, punk pop, and acts that come full circle to duplicate the sound of the originators—not to mention a few projects that feature the members themselves.

POWER POP

What's power pop? It's all there in the name, really: lean, clean, poppy rock 'n' roll with a bit of a bite. What defines power pop is its use of melodic, hook-filled compositions; a guitar sound that alternates between a punky crunch and a ringing chime; and a vocal style often favoring sweet harmonies that would've been dismissed as ornamental fluff by harder-headed '77 punks. It's a sound that unashamedly draws on the concise rock 'n' roll of the mid-1960s: the Beatles, the Byrds, the Kinks, the Who, the Beach Boys, and the Searchers (the latter even took advantage of the power pop wave to make a respectable comeback). Although power poppers had their 1970s antecedents in sixties torch-keepers like the Raspberries, Badfinger, and Big Star (see Chapter Three), many were also energized by the Ramones, who loved the same classic sounds. The style had the most commercial success in America, where a handful of acts enjoyed sizeable hits in the late 1970s and early 1980s. *20 Greats from the Golden Decade of Power Pop* is an ace starter kit.

Cheap Trick

Arguably the loudest, hardest power pop band of all. The crunching quartet of singer/guitarist Robin Zander, guitarist Rick Nielsen, bassist Tom Petersson, and drummer Bun E. Carlos truly puts the "power" in the genre's name. Starting out in Rockford, Illinois, in 1975, Cheap Trick was a gang of British Invasion obsessives, specifically inspired by the Beatles, the Who, and tough mod outfit the Move at a time when rambling prog rock was king. As the band honed its act on the touring circuit it regularly blew the big-name acts it opened for off the stage, thanks to the charismatic Zander's commanding voice, the mugging Nielsen's absurd lyrics and stellar songcraft and guitar chops, and the dazzling prowess of Carlos, whose used car-salesman image belies his skills behind the kit. While its 1977 debut, *Cheap Trick*, shows the band as more musically proficient than its punk peers, the volume and attitude are the same; see the pummeling "He's a Whore" and "Hot Love." The same year's *In Color* is comparatively polished but still rocks hard with slammers like "Hello There," "Come On, Come On," and the divine "Southern Girls." *Heaven Tonight* (1978) is widely considered to be Cheap Trick's best LP, deftly balancing radio-ready poppers like the widescreen "Surrender" with rockers like "Stiff Competition" and the jackhammer cover of the Move's "California Man." The band's breakthrough came with 1979's ecstatic live *At Budokan* and its giant single "I Want You to Want Me"; 1980's *Dream Police* is glossy but great as well. While the group's always been an amazing live act, and its subsequent releases are dotted with fine tracks, those first three studio albums are Cheap

Trick's most essential. Fifteen of their top cuts are on *The Very Best of Cheap Trick*. Mutual musical admirers, the Ramones and Cheap Trick performed together in the eighties, and Carlos contributed backing tracks to Joey's posthumously produced 2012 album … *Ya Know?*.

Shoes

Cheap Trick wasn't alone in Illinois. A power pop hotbed, the Land of Lincoln was also home to several other like-minded acts, such as Pezband, Off Broadway—and Shoes. Formed in 1975 by brothers Jeff (vocals, guitar) and John Murphy (vocals, bass) and Gary Klebe (vocals, guitar), the band, which over the years has had a succession of drummers, recorded its self-released official debut, 1977's sublime *Black Vinyl Shoes*, in Jeff Murphy's living room. The disc got the attention of L.A. punk/garage label Bomp! Records, which released the brilliant single "Tomorrow Night" before the group signed to Elektra for a run of three excellent albums, *Present Tense* (1979), *Tongue Twister* (1981), and *Boomerang* (1982), all of which were critically exalted but barely sold. Since walking away from Elektra, Shoes have continued to kick out albums of fine, Beatles-based pop, and 2012's *Ignition* shows their talents are undimmed. Totaling twenty-one cuts, *35 Years: The Definitive Shoes Collection* is a sole-ful career snapshot.

Milk 'n' Cookies

Well ahead of the curve, Milk 'n' Cookies foreshadowed the power pop sound and also bridged the gap between glam and punk. Indeed, early on the Ramones often shared bills with the Long Island outfit at Max's Kansas City and CBGB. Featuring singer Justin Strauss, keyboardist Ian North, bassist Sal Maida (ex–Roxy Music), and drummer Mike Ruiz, the band played great, catchy tunes but confused audiences and marketing staffers by juxtaposing a wholesome image against brash music. Milk 'n' Cookies cut only one album (produced by studio luminary Muff Winwood) before the group split up, with North going to London and forming short-lived punk act Neo and Maida joining the Kim Fowley–managed

Venus and the Razorblades. Released in 1977, *Milk 'n' Cookies* is a sugar rush of snappy rock 'n' roll that hints at early Who.

The Romantics

Detroit's Romantics are responsible for one of power pop's most massive hits, the storming, British Invasion–styled "What I Like About You." Originally comprised of singer/drummer Mike Marinos, singer/guitarist Wally Palmar, guitarist Mike Skill, and bassist Richie Cole, the band formed in 1977 and, like Shoes, was briefly signed to the Bomp! label before being picked up by a major for their eponymous 1980 debut. Marrying a love of sixties pop with the high energy of punk and the group's Motor City heritage, *The Romantics* is solid power pop through and through, home not only to "What I Like About You," but also likewise frenetic rockers ("First in Line") and sweet beat ballads ("I Tell It to Carrie"). The 1980 follow-up, *National Breakout*, has some decent rockers ("Tomboy," "A Night Like This"), but after that came personnel changes, MTV slickness, and diminishing listenability.

The Dwight Twilley Band

From a less likely rock 'n' roll breeding ground—Tulsa, Oklahoma, to be exact—came the Dwight Twilley Band, which in 1975 scored a huge national hit with the debut single "I'm on Fire." The nucleus of the group, Twilley (vocals, guitar, piano) and Phil Seymour (vocals, bass, drums), legendarily met at a 1967 screening of *A Hard Day's Night* and began writing songs together immediately afterward. The band's first album, 1976's *Sincerely*, is a power pop classic that perfectly reflects its title, blending early Beatles with vocals that recall Sun Records–era rockabilly. *Twilley Don't Mind*, the 1977 follow-up, is another super-solid effort, whose big-hooked songs bring to mind an American T. Rex. The two songwriters went their separate ways after that, with Seymour recording 1980's *Phil Seymour*, a crisp, superlative set topped with the soaring hit "Precious to Me," and Twilley unveiling the solid *Twilley* in 1979. Seymour died in 1993, but Twilley has continued to make fine records.

The Nerves / The Breakaways / Paul Collins' Beat / The Plimsouls

Los Angeles proto-punk / power pop trio the Nerves released only a seven-inch EP during their three-year lifespan, but the group's reputation would be assured when Blondie recorded one of that record's tracks, "Hanging on the Telephone." Founded in 1975 by guitarist/singer Jack Lee, bassist Peter Case, and drummer Paul Collins, the Nerves were one of the first D.I.Y. acts to tour the U.S. *One Way Ticket* has studio, live, and demo cuts. After the Nerves ended in 1978, Case and Collins formed the Breakaways, which after some lineup changes found the two of them on guitars and vocals with a new rhythm section that included ex–Milk 'n' Cookies drummer Mike Ruiz. The Breakaways broke up before releasing anything, but the archival *Walking Out on Love: The Lost Sessions* shows the raw promise. Collins and Ruiz next formed the Beat, which changed its name to Paul Collins' Beat to avoid confusion with ska revival act the English Beat (known as the Beat in the U.K.). Collins and group's 1979 debut, *The Beat*, is home to "Rock 'n' Roll Girl," a recognized power pop staple. Meanwhile, Case had assembled the Plimsouls. One of the Sunset Strip's best live bands, the Plimsouls released a superb EP and album (collected on *The Plimsouls … Plus*) before 1983's stellar *All Over the Place*, which includes their haunting, Byrds-esque signature "A Million Miles Away."

The Knack

You know these guys for the 1979 smash "My Sharona." But that funk-based track isn't representative of the rest of the debut album by the L.A. foursome of Doug Fieger (lead vocals, guitar), Berton Averre (guitar), Prescott Niles (bass), and Bruce Gary (drums). Its merciless hyping at the hands of Capitol Records, as well as the group's own blatant retro-Beatles image, saw the Knack reviled by many ("Knuke the Knack," read the buttons). Nevertheless, that first album, *Get the Knack*, is an exercise in tight, well-delivered rock 'n' roll that stands up to anything else in the power pop canon; see the driving "Let Me Out" or the Fabs-harmonica-fueled "Good Girls Don't." Alas, 1979's inferior, carbon-copy sophomore disc,

But the Little Girls Understand, reveals how early the Knack lost its, er, knack. Get *Get the Knack* and you've got enough.

20/20

Another California quartet worth your time is 20/20, whose "Yellow Pills" is one of the most infectious power pop tracks ever waxed. The trio of singer/guitarist Steve Allen, singer/bassist Ron Flynt, and drummer Mike Gallo cut a single for Bomp! before adding keyboardist Chris Silagyi in time to record its self-titled 1979 debut. A genre benchmark, *20/20* contains the uplifting "Yellow Pills" and the crashingly pleading "Cheri." *Look Out!* (1981) is excellent as well, with the chugging "Nuclear Boy" and other teen anthems.

The Rubinoos

San Francisco's Rubinoos were hooked on bubblegum. Their first and only charting single, from 1977, was a cover of Tommy James and the Shondells' "I Think We're Alone Now," and during a 1974 slot opening for Jefferson Starship they were booed and pelted with garbage for playing the Archies' "Sugar, Sugar." Clearly an act after the Ramones' own hearts. Core members Jon Rubin (vocals, guitar) and Tommy Dunbar (guitar, keyboards, vocals) started the band in high school and eventually signed with hip local label Beserkley Records (also home to Jonathan Richman, whom the Rubinoos sometimes backed). The group's debut, *The Rubinoos*, hailed as "the best pop album of the decade" by *New York Rocker*, is filled mainly with swooning, sunny teen pop, but the ironically named "Rock 'n' Roll Is Dead" is a winning, hard-edged aberration. *Back to the Drawing Board* (1979) is less consistent, but features "I Wanna Be Your Boyfriend"—no, not the Ramones song, but a sparkling classic, nonetheless.

Artful Dodger

This underrated Virginia quintet crossed Beatles tunefulness with Stones and Faces raunch. With the raspy-voiced Bill Paliselli out front, Gary Herrewig and Gary Cox on guitars, Steve Cooper on bass, and Steve Brigida on drums, the band made its 1975 debut with Alice Cooper / Cheap Trick producer Jack Douglas at the board. *Artful Dodger* is a masterful offering marked by a good balance of rockers and ballads and the roaring signature single "Wayside." Nineteen seventy-six's *Honor Among Thieves* is great as well, with fine tracks like the title piece and "Remember." *Babes on Broadway* (1977) has its share of cool moments ("Idi Amin Stomp," a Slade-ish version of Eddie Cochran's "C'mon Everybody"), but Artful Dodger's last album, 1980's *Rave On*, is the hard-rocking high water mark. On that platter's expertly written songs ("Get in Line," "I Don't Wanna See Her"), the band plays like it's going for broke.

The Records

England's leading contribution to power pop, the Records are revered for 1979's shimmering, Byrds-inspired, "Starry Eyes," one of the greatest rock singles of any era. Drummer Will Birch and singer/guitarist John Wicks, both formerly of pub rockers the Kursaal Flyers, added guitarist Huw Gower and bassist Phil Brown to form the Records in 1977. *Shades in Bed* (released in the U.S. as *The Records*) is one of the finest albums of the new wave years and a power pop imperative, worth it alone for "Starry Eyes" and "Teenarama," a pulsing, melodic ode to underage lust. *Crashes* (1980) is stellar, too, and opens with the ringing "Hearts in Her Eyes," a song Birch and Wicks had written for the reunited Searchers. The best-of *Smashes, Crashes and Near Misses* lays out twenty of the Records' most brilliant cuts.

The Smithereens

Power pop was basically left for dead until this durable New Jersey quartet picked up the mantle at the dawn of the 1980s. Besides having one of the finest pop songwriters of the age in singer/guitarist Pat DiNizio, the Smithereens (including fellow charter members drummer Denis Diken and guitarist Jim Babjak—original bassist Mike Mesaros has seen several replacements) are a superb live band that no lover of great rock 'n' roll should miss. Like any power pop crew worth its salt, they're ardent Beatles and

Byrds lovers, but they channel their influences into a much heavier sound than most of their peers; perhaps only Cheap Trick (see earlier) eclipses them for sheer volume. The band first turned heads with the 1983 EP *Beauty and Sadness*, but really arrived with 1986's debut album *Especially for You*. Capped by DiNizio's smoky voice, the record earned fame with the haunting hits "Blood and Roses" and "Behind the Wall of Sleep," and is notable for its Ramones lyrical kinship on Babjak's punked-up "White Castle Blues." *Green Thoughts* (1988) rocks with Who-like muscle on "The World We Know" and "Drown in My Own Tears." The 1989 album *11* has the crunching "A Girl Like You" and the bittersweet "Blue Period," while 1991's *Blow Up* boasts the monster-riffed "Top of the Pops." Since then the band has kept right on touring and recording, even waxing some fun Beatles and Who tribute sets. *Blown to Smithereens* is the definitive anthology.

HARDCORE PUNK

Another genre whose name explains its game, hardcore punk (commonly called, simply, hardcore) is a harder—and much faster—twist on the basic, earlier punk style popularized by the Ramones and their Class of '77 brethren. Although it would eventually spread around the world, hardcore originated in America when a generation of kids who were just a couple of years too young for the initial punk boom started bands, bringing with them a precocious, urgent, and violently thrashing injection of energy. Unlike first-wave punk, hardcore, which was born at the tail end of the 1970s and peaked in the mid 1980s, was primarily a suburban phenomenon: although urban centers like New York; Los Angeles; Washington, D.C.; Boston; and San Francisco provided venues for the bands, most of the younger players lived and rehearsed outside the bigger cities. (In England, a parallel outburst occurred with anarchist/street punk and Oi! bands.) With its emphasis on self-released recordings, promotion via photocopied flyers and fanzines, and independent touring, hardcore gave rise to the underground D.I.Y. culture that continues today.

The Ramones were re-energized by hardcore, seeing themselves as the original article and reclaiming their influence on the style with 1985's *Too Tough to Die*. By the late eighties, hardcore had been taken over by violent, macho ex-jocks and flawed forays into hybrid punk metal, but for a few years it was the most vital rock 'n' roll going. The soundtrack to the 2006 documentary *American Hardcore* (see Chapter Six) samples most of the greats.

Black Flag

Ranked as the sole hardcore outfit in his list of top ten punk bands by the legendarily irascible Johnny Ramone, Black Flag is massively important and perhaps the archetypal L.A. hardcore band. Started by guitarist Greg Ginn in 1977, the constantly touring group successfully wove elements of heavy metal and experimental jazz into its ferocious music and across its nine-year existence had a revolving cast of lead singers. The first was Keith Morris (see later), who appeared on *Nervous Breakdown*, the quartet's pivotal 1978 debut on Ginn's SST label, later the home of acts like Hüsker Dü and influential avant-core trio the Minutemen (see later). Ron Reyes stepped in on vocals before Chavo Pedarest took over for 1980's *Jealous Again* EP. Pedarest was replaced briefly by ripped-throat growler Dez Cadena, who soon switched to second guitar when Henry Rollins at last grabbed the mike for the band's definitive recording, the 1981 album *Damaged*. Simply one of the most visceral, nihilistic, incredibly intense, and hard-as-nails LP's in rock, *Damaged* is a disc you must own, a record that leavens its explosive rage ("Rise Above," "Six Pack," "Thirsty and Miserable") with humor ("TV Party") and claustrophobic crawlers ("Room 13," "Damaged I"). The latter, slower approach would set the tone for most of Black Flag's subsequent releases, which feature Ginn's boldly innovative playing but are less consistent, song-wise.

The Circle Jerks

After leaving Black Flag, singer Keith Morris formed this seminal four-piece in 1979 with guitarist Greg Hetson, formerly of L.A.

hardcore veteran act Redd Kross (see later). Clocking in at just under sixteen minutes, *Group Sex*, the band's fourteen-song 1980 debut, is a high-speed L.A. hardcore classic. But where Black Flag had been dark and bleak, the Circle Jerks brought a bratty, mischievous bent to the proceedings. Across brief, blistering blasts like "Live Fast, Die Young" and "Red Tape," the snot-voiced Morris rants about drugs, teenage boredom, sexual frustration, and politics, and seethes against the idle rich in the slower, menacing "Beverly Hills." The following two sets, *Wild in the Streets* (1982) and *Golden Shower of Hits* (1983), are both rocking and humorous records that are well worth checking out. But for raw, immediate aggression the group never again matched *Group Sex*. In the 2010s Morris resurfaced in the band Off! with Redd Kross bassist Steve McDonald.

The Dead Kennedys

As perhaps the most politically outspoken band in hardcore, it makes perfect sense that the Dead Kennedys were from traditionally radical San Francisco. In addition to the incendiary, sarcasm-filled lyrics and distinctly nasal warble of confrontational front man (and onetime mayoral candidate) Jello Biafra, it was the twangy, swampy surf/rockabilly/ psychedelic licks of guitarist East Bay Ray that made the DKs stand out. The two formed the group in 1978 with bassist Klaus Flouride and drummer Ted (later replaced by Darren H. Peligro) and cut a pair of instant classic singles, "California Über Alles" and "Holiday in Cambodia." Both songs appear on the landmark 1980 debut, *Fresh Fruit for Rotting Vegetables*, a mandatory purchase. *In God We Trust, Inc.* (1981), the first release on Biafra's Alternative Tentacles label, draws inspiration from the breakneck thrash of younger bands like Minor Threat (see later). *Plastic Surgery Disasters* (1982) is nearly as good as *Fresh Fruit...*, with sneering bashers like "Terminal Preppie" and the soaring, anthemic "Moon Over Marin"; the band's final two LPs, *Frankenchrist* (1985) and *Bedtime or Democracy* (1986), have their moments as well. For introductory compilations, try *Give Me Convenience or Give Me Death* or *Milking the Sacred Cow*.

Bad Brains

No other hardcore band could touch Bad Brains for sheer speed or live ferocity—and how can you go wrong with a band named after a *Road to Ruin* song? One of the few all-black punk outfits, the Washington, D.C., group—wailing human tornado vocalist H.R., searing guitarist Dr. Know, raging bassist Daryl Jenifer, and drummer Earl Hudson—mystically mixes earth-shattering, lightening-quick rock 'n' roll with cooled-out reggae. The band began in 1977, releasing the insanely fast single "Pay to Cum" in 1980, which also features on the 1982 debut, *Bad Brains*. One of hardcore's holy grails, *Bad Brains* is seen by many as the genre's all-time best album, and includes further volatile numbers like "Banned in D.C.," "The Big Takeover," and "Sailin' On." Several of that set's songs were reprised for 1983's *Rock for Light*, which was produced by the Cars' Ric Ocasek and is nearly as amazing. But despite the greatness of those releases, for many it's *I Against I* that stands as the band's masterpiece; the 1986 album rattles the walls with thundering hard rock and funk-dub that makes competing punk and metal acts look like toddlers. Since then the band has soldiered on, briefly without Hudson and his brother, the famously unstable H.R. The twenty-three-track *Banned in D.C.: Bad Brains Greatest Riffs* is an unbeatable anthology.

Minor Threat

In 1980 Bad Brains moved to New York, leaving Minor Threat to become the definitive Washington, D.C., hardcore band. Known for the clean-living "straight edge" philosophy espoused by vocalist Ian MacKaye, Minor Threat started after the breakup of MacKaye and drummer Jeff Nelson's previous band, the Teen Idles. To document the D.C. scene the pair launched the seminal label Dischord Records, which in 1981 released their new band's *Minor Threat* and *In My Eyes* EPs. Packed with clattering, careening, anger-filled cuts like "Filler," "Screaming at a Wall," and "In My Eyes," these seven-inchers are among early hardcore's most important releases. For Minor Threat's only full-length, 1983's *Out of Step*, the band delivers tracks that are reliably tough but also demonstrate a newfound mastery of stop-start dynamics and more developed confessional lyrics. The group disbanded in 1983, with MacKaye going on to the seminal Fugazi. *Complete Discography* collects this key band's entire output.

D.O.A.

While L.A. band the Middle Class's 1978 *Out of Vogue* EP is cited as the first example of the hardcore sound, it's *Hardcore 81*, the second album by Canada's D.O.A., that many credit with giving the genre its name. Originally the trio of singer/guitarist Joe Keithley (a.k.a. Joey Shithead), bassist Randy Rampage, and drummer Chuck Biscuits (later of Black Flag and the Circle Jerks, among others), D.O.A. formed in 1978 and comes on like a revved-up version of the Clash: politically charged punk with hard-hitting, hooky melodies. The group's first album, 1980's *Something Better Change*, is full of fine examples: "New Age," "The Enemy," "The Prisoner." The band added guitarist Dave Gregg for the following year's *Hardcore 81*, another killer set highlighted by blitz-speed blasters like "D.O.A." and "Smash the State." With a new lineup that featured drummer Dimwit (Biscuits's older brother) and ex-Subhumans singer Wimpy Roy on bass, the band, by now a touring machine, released its last essential offering, 1982's *War on 45* EP, which includes "Let's Fuck," an uproariously rude rewrite of the Chris Montez / Ramones fave "Let's Dance." Speaking of rudeness, *Greatest Shits* has the Vancouver band's best crap.

Channel 3

This L.A.-area band cofounded by singer/guitarist Mike Magrann and guitarist Kimm Gardener made its 1980 debut playing "Blitzkrieg Bop" at a keg party. Like D.O.A., Channel 3 (or CH3) is strongly suggestive of early, angry Clash. Its first two albums, *Fear of Live* (1982) and *After the Lights Go Out* (1983), are Cal-punk classics. Both are combined on *The Skinhead Years*.

Hüsker Dü

This Minneapolis trio went from being one of the hardcore underground's major bands to being one of college radio's most influential acts. Besides boasting two amazing singer-songwriters in guitarist Bob Mould and drummer Grant Hart (the pair first bonded over a shared love of the Ramones), Hüsker Dü also included bassist Greg Norton and started out in 1979, kicking out a harder, faster spin on the pop-based styles of the Buzzcocks and the Jam. The well-named 1981 debut *Land Speed Record* is a blinding live set marked by Mould's distinctively distorted guitar. *Everything Falls Apart* (1982) and *Metal Circus* (EP, 1983) are transitional works that see the threesome's sound developing with inventive melodic touches. The creative and critical breakthrough is 1984's *Zen Arcade*, a revelatory double album that bent the rules of hardcore by weaving elements of folk, metal, and psychedelia into the group's destructive attack, a method that influenced Nirvana, the Pixies, and countless others. The band made two more excellent indie discs, 1985's *New Day Rising* and *Flip Your Wig*, before signing to Warner Bros. for *Candy Apple Grey*, which includes the well-known "Don't Want to Know If You Are Lonely" and "Sorry Somehow." Hüsker Dü split after the spottier *Warehouse: Songs and Stories*, another double album, with Hart forming the short-lived Nova Mob. Mould went solo before assembling a new trio, Sugar, whose hard-hitting, modern guitar pop also demands your attention via its *Copper Blue* (1992), *Beaster* (1993), and *File Under: Easy Listening* (1994).

The Minutemen

It's impossible to talk about the 1980s hardcore scene and leave out this critical and hugely inventive California band. The Minutemen—singer/guitarist D. Boon, bassist Mike Watt, and drummer George Hurley—were consummate road dogs, rocking rooms around the nation from 1980 to 1985, the year Boon died in a car accident. Their singularly astonishing style is artier and only nominally rooted in the four-four drive of the Ramones, seamlessly crossing punk with elements of jazz, funk, and folk. Albums like 1982's *What Makes a Man Start Fires*, 1983's *Buzz or Howl Under the Influence of Heat*, and 1985's *Three-Way Tie for Last* provide excellent evidence. But for a faster grip on these guys try 1984's influential two-LP masterpiece, *Double Nickels on the Dime*, or the compilation *Introducing the Minutemen*.

Fear

Formed in 1977 and fronted by the potty-mouthed, bluesy-voiced Lee Ving, Fear, along with Black Flag and the Circle Jerks, put L.A. hardcore on the map. The quartet made a memorable showing in *The Decline of Western Civilization, Part 1* (see Chapter Six) and found a fan in "Saturday Night Live" star John Belushi, who talked his producers into booking the band for what became an infamous on-air appearance. Fear only made one good album, 1982's *The Record*, before it broke up and Ving went into acting (although he's resurrected the Fear name since then). With a sound that's as punk as any of their peers ("I Don't Care About You," "I Love Livin' in the City") yet occasionally exhibits odd meters and unexpected musicianly precision ("Let's Have a War," "Camarillo"), *The Record* is roundly recommended.

Angry Samoans

For rocking, blatantly offensive early Los Angeles hardcore, Fear's rival act was the Angry Samoans. Begun as a Dictators cover band in 1978 by vocalist and rock critic "Metal" Mike Saunders, the Samoans recorded only two albums worth noting—but oh, what albums they are. The first, 1980's *Inside My Brain* (produced by Lee Ving, oddly enough), is a garagey, basement blast stuffed with raw, blaring, and very funny tunes like "My Old Man's a Fatso" and "You Stupid Asshole." The second, 1982's *Back from Samoa*, is even better, with enough great, trashy riffs to fill a bathtub. Its snotty, politically incorrect numbers include "Gas Chamber," "You Stupid Jerk," and "They Saved Hitler's Cock"; there's also a blazing version of the Chambers Brothers' "Time Has Come Today," a song the Ramones themselves famously covered.

Articles of Faith / The Effigies / Naked Raygun

Chicago lagged behind other big cities in the early days of punk, but when hardcore hit it was a central hub. Articles of Faith was a politically oriented quartet helmed by impassioned singer/ guitarist Vic Bondi and strongly inspired by the Clash. *Complete, Volume 1: 1981–1983* and *Complete, Volume 2: 1983–1985* are the comprehensive chronicles. Like AOF, the Effigies were influenced by British sounds, mainly Oi! bands and bass-heavy post-punk like Joy Division and Killing Joke. Singer John Kezdy's lyrics could be political, although he tended to focus locally. *Remains Nonviewable* body-bags up the Effigies' defining output. Naked Raygun was the most melodic of Chicago's big three, and its best albums, *Throb Throb* (1985), *All Rise* (1986), and *Jettison* (1988), feature Ramonesy, Buzzcocky singalongs next to more angular fare. *Huge Bigness: Selected Tracks from the Collected Works, 1980–1992* picks the cherries.

Zero Boys

Indianapolis's contribution to hardcore was the Zero Boys: singer Paul Mahern, guitarist Terry Hollywood, drummer Mark Cutsinger, and bassist Dave "Tufty" Clough (later of Toxic Reasons). Like many such acts, the band only issued one album before splitting. But 1982's *Vicious Circle* is a killer, showcasing the quartet's rapid-fire chops on the neck-twisting title track and other high-velocity buzz-burners.

Negative Approach

In the 1960s the harsh Detroit region bred the tough sounds of the MC5 and the Stooges, but in the eighties it gave us the brutal hardcore of Negative Approach. Led by singer John Brannon, the group managed a seven-inch and one album, the punishing *Tied Down* (1983), before calling it quits until a 2000s reunion. An unstoppable wall of cinder-block guitars and pummeling rhythms, *Tied Down* is further notable for Brannon's overpowering, wire-brush wail. His banshee voice later graced two excellent post-hardcore units, the Laughing Hyenas and Easy Action, both of which featured bassist Ron Sakowski of Ohio hardcore kings the Necros.

Agent Orange

This popular California three-piece crossed punk, power pop, and hardcore with sizzling Dick Dale surf rock and served up two of the era's standout tracks: the one-two punch-out "Bloodstains" and the stuttering "Everything Turns Grey." Those evergreens and punked-out readings of several surf standards light up *Living in Darkness*, Agent Orange's indispensable 1981 debut.

The Descendents

Ramones fans need to hear these guys. Another potent Los Angeles band, the Descendents sound like the Ramones having a caffeine/bubblegum overdose. Formed in 1979 as a trio by future Black Flag drummer Bill Stevenson, the band hit its stride after adding vocalist Milo Auckerman in 1981. The foursome's first LP, *Milo Goes to College*, will snap your neck with its pumping, hilarious, sub-two-minute teen-frustration treats like "Suburban Home." *I Don't Want to Grow Up* (1985) is also uniformly brilliant: see its snidely rocking title cut, band theme song "Descendents," and pissed-off rants like "My World." The retrospective *Somery* has tracks from these and later albums. Stevenson later formed Descendents carbon-copy band All.

Redd Kross

L.A. brothers Steve (bass) and Jeff (vocals, guitar) were, consecutively, eleven and fifteen in 1978, when they formed the Tourists with future Circle Jerks / Bad Religion guitarist Greg Hetson and future Black Flag singer Ron Reyes on drums. After Hetson and Reyes left and were replaced, the band became Redd Kross. Like da brudders, the McDonald brothers have a fascination with pop/trash culture—sick movies, cartoons, breakfast cereal, serial killers. The group's first outings, 1980's *Redd Kross* and 1982's *Born Innocent*, are great thrash-punk adorned with Jeff McDonald's endearing whine. The brothers left puberty and hardcore behind with 1984's *Teen Babes from Monsanto*, a big-sounding collection of cool covers (Stooges, Stones, Shangri-Las). Tommy Erdelyi/Ramone himself produced 1987's *Neurotica*, which is thick with hard-rocking, big-hooked, seventies glam-referencing gems.

COLLEGE ROCK

College rock? Did any of the Ramones even *go* to college? Johnny did, for about a week. Noncommercial college radio was where you first heard punk rock in mid-'70s. America. But by the mid-1980s, college rock, also known as alternative or indie rock, had become largely synonymous with mostly less-edgy post-punk acts that enjoyed heavy college radio airplay and in a few rare cases leaped to the mainstream. While some of these bands, like R.E.M. and the Red Hot Chili Peppers, have cited the Ramones and other early punks as formative inspirations, it's generally not audible in their slick music. The box set *Left of the Dial: Dispatches from the '80s Underground* scans college rock's confusingly diverse patchwork, with its hardcore cuts being the most Ramones-relevant. Here's a handful of college rockers whose records should appeal to readers.

The Replacements

They would later be more strongly identified with jangly guitar pop, but at the beginning the Replacements—Paul Westerberg (vocals, guitar), brothers Bob (guitar) and Tommy Stinson (bass), and Chris Mars (drums)—were purely punk (and often purely drunk). Their first album, 1981's *Sorry Ma, Forgot to Take Out the Trash*, is a hot mess of boozy, bluesy, Stones/Faces/Heartbreakers rock 'n' roll. Nineteen eighty-two's great *Stink* EP continues the ramshackle racket, toys with hardcore, and contains the blasting "Kids Don't Follow," the first of the Minneapolis band's trademark anthems. The eclectic *Hootenany* (1983) sees country rock and confessional pop slotted between elevating crunchers like "Color Me Impressed." Nineteen eighty-four's college radio breakthrough *Let It Be* is considered the foursome's masterwork, and for good reason. With the jangling hit "I Will Dare," the wounded "Answering Machine," and the howling rock of "Gary's Got a Boner," this divine disc shows Westerberg's formidable songwriting skills hitting a new level. Nineteen eighty-five's *Tim* has an immediate Ramones connection in that it was produced by Tommy and was the Replacements' first album for the Ramones' original label, Sire. It's slightly slicker than *Let It Be* but still has some great tracks, like the Clash-y "Bastards of Young" and the college radio ode "Left of the Dial." The fiery Bob Stinson was, er, replaced by the tame Slim Dunlop for 1987's polished *Pleased to Meet Me*; two final LPs followed. The career appraisal *Don't You Know Who I Think I Was?* adds reunion cuts.

Sonic Youth

Sonic Youth's artistic correlations to the Ramones are tenuous. While being immeasurably influential on a whole generation of noise-punk bands, this game-changing New York outfit's music generally owes much more to the avant-garde stylings of the Velvet Underground and composers like LaMonte Young than the in-the-pocket punk of the Queens boys. Still, Sonic Youth's members have long been vocal about their debts of inspiration to the Ramones, and the two bands toured together in the early nineties (the former has even been known to cover Ramones tunes).

Sonic Youth was formed in 1981 by guitarists/vocalists Thurston Moore and Lee Ranaldo and bassist/vocalist Kim Gordon; consecutively, the group's drummers have been actor Richard Edson, Bob Bert, Jim Sclavunos, and Steve Shelley. While the best of the band's music has the *attitude* of punk rock, it may occasionally be a bit out-there for some Ramones listeners. Indeed, the earliest efforts in the band's thirty-year discography—its 1982 self-titled debut EP, 1983 *Confusion Is Sex* album and *Kill Yr Idols* EP, and 1985 album *Bad Moon Rising*—are defiantly experimental. Sonic Youth's records released between the late 1980s and the mid-1990s, however, balance the band's avant M.O. within a conscious rock 'n' roll framework, and make fine starters. Try 1986's *EVOL*, 1987's *Sister*, 1988's double set *Daydream Nation* (cited as the band's magnum opus, it has the punky college radio smash "Teen Age Riot"), 1990's *Goo*, 1992's *Dirty*, 1994's *Experimental Jet Set, Trash and No Star*, or 1995's *Washing Machine*. The anthology *Hits Are for Squares* has sixteen tracks selected by peer acts and celebrity fans.

The Jesus and Mary Chain

Screeeeech!!! The band's early use of extreme feedback had many pegging the Jesus and Mary Chain as an amped-up Velvet Underground, but this Scottish quartet, led by brothers Jim (vocals) and William Reid (guitar, vocals), checks the many of the same boxes the Ramones had on their list of influences: the Stooges, the Beach Boys, Phil Spector, and the Shangri-Las—not to mention the Ramones themselves. After starting in 1984, the group, which early on included future Primal Scream front man Bobby Gillespie on drums, quickly became infamous for its noisy, riotous performances. *Psychocandy*, its 1985 debut, is one of the decade's greatest: fourteen cuts of singsong bubblegum pop smothered in piercing white noise. Its primitive, pounding tunes—"Never Understand," "You Trip Me Up," "Just Like Honey"—demonstrate well-learned lessons in Ramones minimalism. *Darklands* (1987) strips away much of the noise, but not to the band's detriment: cleaned-up, beautifully melodic tunes like the single "April Skies" highlight the Chain's classic pop heart. The rarities collection *Barbed Wire Kisses* (1988) pays fuzzed-out homage to the Beach Boys with a cover of "Surfin' USA" and the original "Kill Surf City." The next three outings, *Automatic* (1989), *Honey's Dead* (1992), and *Stoned and Dethroned* (1994), see too many acoustic songs and dance beats—the melodies and hooks are fine, but you miss the noise. *Munki* (1998), however, is a respectable return reflecting all sides of the band. *Upside Down: The Best of the Jesus and Mary Chain* is just as advertised.

Tom Waits

Tom Waits doesn't really belong in this category. But, then again, he doesn't belong in *any* category. What is he? Rock? Jazz? Blues? Singer-songwriter? Beat poet? Shambolic noisemaker? Actor? Sideshow barker at a Surrealist carnival? All of those, and at the same time none of them. He's an alchemical musical maverick, an American outsider—and a friend and favorite of the Ramones, whose version of his "I Don't Wanna Grow Up" on *¡Adios Amigos!* is, arguably, the most effective Tom Waits cover yet recorded. The California-bred icon's first albums for Asylum Records, 1973's *Closing Time* and 1974's *The Heart of Saturday Night*, are strings-laden songwriterly statements; 1975's *Nighthawks at the Diner* and 1976's *Small Change* see a jazzier sound, a stronger focus on story-

IF YOU LIKE THE RAMONES...

based lyrics, and Waits's adoption of a gravelly, Louis Armstrong / Howlin' Wolf–style growl, all characteristics perfected across his remaining LP's for the label. A switch to Island Records brought with it a dramatic musical switch, as Waits introduced elements of cabaret music into his songs and began increasingly morphing into the weird, experimental, and wildly antonal sonic mischief maker we know and love. While his more recent albums for Anti Records—1999's *Mule Variations*, 2004's *Real Gone*, and 2011's *Bad as Me*, in particular—are heartily recommended, it's his four classic Island albums that embody his legend: 1983's *Swordfishtrombones*, 1985's *Rain Dogs*, 1987's *Frank's Wild Years*, and 1992's *Bone Machine*, a clanking, yowling tour de force featuring the original "I Don't Wanna Grow Up." Waits repaid the Ramones for their rendition of the song by covering their "Danny Says" and "The Return of Jackie and Judy" on the best-of/rarities set *Orphans (Brawlers, Bawlers and Bastards)*.

Social Distortion

Joey was a fan of this long-surviving Southern California band led by singer/guitarist Mike Ness. Although the group is best known for the country-punk sound that broke it on college radio at the end of the 1980s, Social Distortion began in 1978 as a straight-up punk band and was a regular name on early Orange County hardcore bills. After the other founding members joined the Adolescents (another key L.A. hardcore group), Ness put together a new lineup and recorded 1983's *Mommy's Little Monster*, which, Clash-derived as it is, the band never surpassed. *Wreckage from the Past* samples the pre-*Mommy's*... years.

Dinosaur Jr.

This trio of singer/guitarist J. Mascis, bassist Lou Barlow, and drummer Murph arose out the mid-eighties Western Massachusetts hardcore scene and inspired many. While the three-piece's deafening sound, marked by Mascis's fuzzy wah-wah licks and mournful vocals, owes more to Hendrix/Cream acid rock and Neil Young's proto-grunge, at the same time Dinosaur Jr. (originally just

Dinosaur; the suffix was added after a lawsuit filed by hippie band the Dinosaurs) has palpable traces of the "twisted bubblegum" sensibilities of our bowl-cutted boys. And there's also a shared debt to the Stooges; in the early 2000s Mascis even performed Stooges songs with Ron and Scott Asheton themselves and future Stooge Mike Watt. Dinosaur Jr.'s eponymous 1986 debut has some cool noisy psychedelic moments, but things don't fully develop until 1987's *You're Living All Over Me*. A college radio sensation, it melds corrosive hard rock with brutal noise, hardcore, and subversive pop melodies on jams like "Little Fury Things." *Bug* (1988) is perhaps the tiniest bit cleaner but powerful still, and opens with the grinding "Freak Scene." After *Bug*, Barlow left to concentrate on his other project, Sebadoh, and Dinosaur Jr. became Mascis's inconsistent vehicle. The original lineup reunited for *Beyond* (2007) and *Farm* (2009), both of which show the trademark sonic, melodic muscle firmly in place. *Ear-Bleeding Country: The Best of Dinosaur Jr.* is a decent oeuvre snapshot.

The Pixies

If there were a Mount Rushmore of college rock, you'd see the Pixies' heads up there. For many the massively influential Boston foursome represents the genre more than any other band. Comprising manic singer/guitarist Black Francis (né Charles Thompson), bassist/singer Kim Deal (later of hit makers the Breeders), guitarist Joey Santiago, and drummer David Lovering, the band distinctively blended classic pop with hard punk, surf guitar, freakish noise, and weird lyrics on songs full of colossal riffs and heart-stopping dynamics. The Pixies debuted with the 1987 EP *Come On Pilgrim*, whose galloping, stop-start punkers and hooky haunters (the Deal-sung "Caribou") were intended as demos. *Surfer Rosa* dominated the collegiate airwaves in 1988 and makes a vital addition to any post-Ramones library. Its flawless riches include the dementedly thrashing "Broken Face," the off-kilter pop "Where Is My Mind?," and the sweeping, appropriately named "Gigantic." *Doolittle* is a more accessible production that balances playful pop ("Here Comes Your Man") with patented Pixies psychosis ("Tame") and deeper widescreen evolution ("Monkey Gone to Heaven"). *Bossanova* (1990) and *Trompe le Monde* (1991) are reliably solid, but the uninitiated should start with *Surfer Rosa, Doolittle,* or *Wave of Mutilation: The Best of the Pixies.*

The Godfathers

Founded by brothers Peter (vocals) and Chris Coyne (bass), this British band of old-school punks was out of place on college radio. Perhaps it was their sharp suits, along with their nihilistic 1988 hit "Birth, School, Work, Death," that gained them entrée into the upper crust of the academic airwaves. Regardless, Ramones aficionados will enjoy any of the underrated quintet's four excellent albums thus far: *Hit by Hit* (1986), *Birth, School, Work, Death* (1988), *More Songs About Love and Hate* (1989), and *Unreal World* (1991), all of which display a penchant for meaty rock 'n' roll driven by simple, pumping, addictive riffs. The 1996 anthology *Birth, School, Work, Death: The Best of the Godfathers* contains all of the similarly named 1988 disc plus selections from the others.

THRASH METAL

One of the planet's most popular musical styles, thrash metal began in the early 1980s when younger and more aggressive metal bands fused the recent sounds of New Wave of British Heavy Metal groups like Judas Priest and Iron Maiden with the speed, energy, and D.I.Y. mindset of hardcore punk. Unlike hardcore, however, thrash metal (or speed metal) emphasizes tight arrangements, musical dexterity, guitar solos, and bombastic theatricality—it's still heavy metal, after all. Although Britain's Motörhead is thrash's undisputed trailblazer act, the genus gained its highest profile via the later U.S. bands Metallica, Megadeth, Anthrax, and Slayer—collectively known as "The Big Four." The compilation *Thrash 'til Death* concentrates on lesser-known thrashers (Overkill, Kreator, Death Angel) and paints an evocative portrait of the scene's hellish panorama.

Motörhead

Although Motörhead is the acknowledged granddaddy thrash/

speed metal band, it was within the early U.K. punk scene that the group first established itself, to which its marriage of punk energy and heavy metal thunderously attests. Far too ugly and raw for the "heavy rock" scene of the time, the trio fit in much better among the punks; its first records were on punk labels Stiff and Chiswick, and early on it shared bills with acts like the Adverts and the Damned, even collaborating with the latter, as MotörDamned, for a 1979 single. Formed by nicotine-throated singer/bassist Lemmy Kilmister in 1975 after he was kicked out of Hawkwind (see Chapter Three), Motörhead cut a rejected debut album for United Artists (later released as *On Parole*) with ex–Pink Fairies guitarist Larry Wallis, who soon stepped aside after guitarist "Fast" Eddie Clarke joined. The lineup of Lemmy, Clarke, and drummer Phil "Philthy Animal" Taylor is the classic Motörhead configuration that produced 1977's garagey debut, *Motörhead*, as well as 1979's excellent *Bomber* and fang-baring *Overkill*, all of which you could well use. But, as even vaguely aware listeners know, it's 1980's *Ace of Spades* that's the milestone. That recording's rebellious, locomotive-speeding title track is one of rock's eternal outlaw anthems, and its neighboring cuts are no less earthshaking. The ripping live *No Sleep 'til Hammersmith* (1981) captures the band at its onstage peak, while 1982's *Iron Fist*, the last release by the Lemmy/Clarke/Taylor incarnation, is killer as well. Lemmy continues to lead and personify Motörhead, grinding out reliably tough albums, one of which, *1916*, from 1991, contains "R.A.M.O.N.E.S.," a tribute to our bruddas. There are more Motörhead compilations available than there are rounds on Lemmy's bullet belt, but the best is *No Remorse*.

Metallica

Since he's known as the purveyor of some of metal's busiest and most intricately shredding guitar leads, it may come as a shock that Metallica's Kirk Hammett cites the Spartan style of his late friend Johnny Ramone as a major influence. But for all his bombast, Hammett knows the basic truth: you can't go all crazy if you don't have the foundation down first. And when it comes to foundations,

Metallica's main members—Hammett, singer/guitarist James Hetfield, and drummer Lars Ulrich—are effusive about the punk and hardcore that, along with early metal, have informed their music. The Los Angeles quartet formed in 1981 and became the most influential metal band of the next two decades and, for a time, the biggest rock band on earth (original bassist Cliff Burton was killed in a 1986 tour bus accident and replaced by Jason Newsted, who was succeeded by Robert Trujillo). The group's opening salvo, 1983's *Kill 'Em All*, has been called the Big Bang of thrash and is the Metallica record to start with. Its vicious, high-velocity, stop-on-a-dime slash 'n' burners—"Whiplash," "Motorbreath," "Metal Militia"—rescued hard rock from hair-metal hell and birthed a generation of imitators. *Ride the Lightning* (1984) is, arguably, Metallica's greatest effort and home to the stomach-punching riffs of "Creeping Death" and "For Whom the Bell Tolls." But it's also the start of the band's moves into longer, multipart arrangements that may put off cut-to-the-chase Ramones fans. Most metalheads consider 1986's *Master of Puppets* the group's recorded apex, though its continuance of . . . *Lightning*'s tolerance-testing concepts may prove troubling. *The $5.98 E.P.: Garage Days Re-Revisited* (1987), a short set of metal and punk covers (Misfits, Killing Joke), was later expanded into the four-CD covers box *Garage, Inc.* Since Metallica hit power-ballad gold in the early nineties, its listenability has been inconsistent.

Megadeth

Snarling front man Dave Mustaine started Megadeth in 1983, after he was booted from Metallica's lead guitar slot and replaced by Kirk Hammett. With his new band, Mustaine made the wise move of using Metallica's pioneering attack as a starting point but lessening that group's sometimes drawn-out song structures. Although the sound of Megadeth's albums has never quite equaled Metallica's for sheer, dense heaviness, the former's comparatively streamlined style, jackhammer riffing, and nihilistic and political lyrics greatly impacted early thrash. The band's 1984 debut, *Killing Is My Business . . . and Business Is Good!*, is the rawest release in its catalog, populated with choppy, high-speed workouts and squealing lead work. *Peace Sells ... but Who's Buying?* (1986) is considered by most to be Megadeth's best album, thanks largely to its better production. Standout tracks like the angry, anvil-pounding, anthemic title cut and the crashing "Wake Up Dead" make it easy to see why headbangers love it. The cheesy *So Far, So Good ... So What?* (1988) is most memorable for its embarrassing cover of the Sex Pistols' "Anarchy in the U.K." The band bounced back with 1990's careening *Rust in Peace*, which has been hailed as its best release since *Peace Sells....* The two-CD *Anthology: Set the World Afire* burns with lighter-lifting highs from Megadeth's thirty-year resume.

Anthrax

This venerable New York unit led the East Coast's thrash wave and was formed in 1981 by guitarist Scott Ian, who in addition to the expected metal influences claims the Ramones as an early inspiration. The 1984 debut *Fistful of Metal*, with original singer Neil Turbin, is more in the mold of pre-thrash British bands like Judas Priest. The 1985 EP *Armed and Dangerous* features both Turbin and his replacement, Joey Belladonna, whose wailing voice is not nearly as overwrought as Turbin's but can still be grating to the unconverted (the EP's rendition of "God Save the Queen" presages other metal versions of Sex Pistols songs; Belladonna was later succeeded by John Bush). The same year's *Spreading the Disease* gained Anthrax international notoriety, but it was 1986's *Among the Living* that cemented the group's legend as gods of thrash. Besides introducing broader lyrical themes ("Efilnikufesin [N.F.L.]" is a lament for fallen comedian John Belushi; the battering "Indians" decries the treatment of Native Americans), this raging classic lays bare the quintet's hardcore punk influences on cuts like the whirlwind "Caught in a Mosh." Anthrax's last great album was 1990's *The Persistence of Time*, which eclipses even the beloved *Among the Living* for clobbering tempos and distorted guitar abuse. While it touches on the band's later, annoying rap-metal efforts, *The Universal Masters Collection* makes a good intro.

Slayer

If anyone ever decides to make *The Texas Chain Saw Massacre* into a musical, they'd do well to give these guys a call. The final fourth of the Big Four, Slayer got started in 1982, a year after Metallica and Anthrax, but more than made up for the lag by becoming thrash metal's fastest and most extreme band. Formed in Huntington Beach, California, by guitarists Kerry King and Jeff Hanneman, bassist/vocalist Tom Araya, and drummer Dave Lombardo, the group made a relatively orthodox debut with 1983's *Show No Mercy*. Their transitional EP *Haunting the Chapel* (1984), however, pointed the way to 1985's *Hell Awaits*, which sees both the band's speed and its ability to churn out terrifying, imagery-filled lyrics (gore, Satan, apocalyptic devastation) greatly accelerate. Yet, as hard and shocking as *Hell Awaits* can be, there's little that can prepare you for 1986's stripped-down *Reign in Blood*. Produced by Rick Rubin (Beastie Boys, Johnny Cash, Public Enemy), *Reign in Blood*'s mercilessly violent, evil-spewing, beyond-blinding tracks approach the avant-garde with their excessively gruesome imagery and aggression, almost transcending the thrash genre. Just when you thought things couldn't possibly get any faster, cuts like "Aggressive Perfector" suddenly double in speed, then accelerate into a tumbling, unrelenting, horrifying blur that threatens to engulf itself—if the band doesn't blow apart first. No group could keep this up for long; thus 1988's *South of Heaven* adds more textural nuances and slows the tempos—but only somewhat, as lashing numbers like "Cleanse the Soul" display. It's all a bit intense, but, filtered through Slayer's love of hardcore, the Ramones' heads-down barre-chord assault is firmly at the root.

GRUNGE

Although during the 1980s hardcore, college rock, and thrash all greatly helped to keep alive the same rock 'n' roll traditions that motivated the Ramones, the acts in these groupings were still on the fringe of popular music. In the mainstream, it was all Phil Collins's "Susudio" and haircut-driven crap like A Flock of

Seagulls and Duran Duran. Until, that is, grunge exploded, and punk and alternative rock at last came roaring overground. Initially evolving in the Pacific Northwest, grunge grew out of the hardcore scene and fused old-school hard rock and heavy metal with punk rock. The Stooges and Black Sabbath were clear grunge reference points, as were vanguard Portland, Oregon, punks the Wipers, a heavily Ramones-obliged trio you should acquaint yourself with, posthaste (their fantastic first three albums, 1980's *Is This Real?*, 1981's *Youth of America*, and 1983's *Over the Edge*, are available as a budget-priced set). While Pearl Jam and Soundgarden are two of the biggest acts associated with grunge—not to mention close friends and vocal boosters of the Ramones—their musical approaches have little to do with the stars of this book. Their music really leans harder to grunge's heavy metal side and plays like punk never happened (indeed, Pearl Jam is more reminiscent of posey arena rockers like Bad Company than anything else). And although the movement will forever be first identified with Nirvana, that world-changing trio is, as you will see, far from the only game in grunge.

Green River

The ground zero of grunge. Seattle's Green River was, arguably, the first grunge band, and is legendary for being the launch pad of three of the music's foremost acts. The group came together in 1984 when Iggy-indebted vocalist Mark Arm and guitarist Steve Turner (both formerly of jokey punk unit Mr. Epp and the Calculations) were joined by bassist Jeff Ament and drummer Alex Vincent; second guitarist Stone Gossard came in soon after. Turner left after the taping of *Come On Down* (1985), the band's debut, and was replaced by Bruce Fairweather for 1987's *Dry as a Bone* and 1988's *Rehab Doll*. All three releases (the latter two since reissued on one CD) ooze hard with Green River's dark mess of grimy, bluesy, Stooges/Zeppelin-reeking rock. After the quintet split up in 1988, Arm reunited with Turner to form Mudhoney (see later) while Gossard and Ament cofounded Mother Love Bone and, eventually, Pearl Jam.

Mudhoney

Green River managed a few short U.S. tours before imploding, but its music didn't catch on much outside of its home city; instead, it was this amazing band that put the so-called Seattle sound on the map. Known for some of the most electrifying live performances of grunge's glory days, Mudhoney, as of 2013, is still kicking out the same winning brand of sneering, unrepentantly primitive, sludge metal–smeared garage punk with which it reawakened indie rock in the late 1980s. Indeed, after nearly thirty years, the throat-grabbing shriek of singer/guitarist Mark Arm and the primordial roar of guitarist Steve Turner, drummer Dan Peters, and bassist Guy Maddison (who replaced original bassist Matt Lukin of the Melvins, a band we'll meet momentarily) is still undimmed. *Superfuzz Bigmuff* (1988) is an imperative hunk of modern punk, and should be the first Mudhoney record—nay, the first *grunge* record—you buy. In addition to the original EP's explosive and menacing songs ("In and Out of Grace," "Mudride") the CD reissue contains the group's debut single, "Touch Me I'm Sick," grunge's reigning anthem. Commencing with its full-length debut, 1989's *Mudhoney*, the group has continued to make reliably rewarding albums saturated with face-burning scuzz guitar, brutish rhythms, and Arm's wild-man wailing. The two-CD *March to Fuzz* has highlights and obscurities from 1989 to 1998.

Nirvana

Timing is, as they say, everything. Over the course of their entire career, the Ramones failed to even dent the American mainstream. And then, fifteen years after their debut, an Aberdeen, Washington, band they inspired came along and conquered the universe. But such was the zeitgeist by the early 1990s: the Ramones inspired the hardcore bands that inspired the members of Nirvana, singer/guitarist Kurt Cobain, bassist Krist Novoselic, and drummer Dave Grohl (who came from hardcore unit Scream and would, post-Nirvana, front the Foo Fighters). Although Nirvana's murky, devastating music is conspicuously beholden to Black Sabbath, it also exudes the Ramones' subversive sense of pop melody.

And, until Cobain's tragic suicide ended everything in 1994, the commercially reluctant trio never wavered in its seditious punk stance. Recorded for six hundred dollars (even less than *Ramones*), Nirvana's 1989 debut, *Bleach*, cut with drummer Chad Channing, is raw, raging rock at its finest ("Blew," "Negative Creep") and has glimpses of the minor-key magnificence the band would develop later ("About a Girl"). *Nevermind*, of course, is the record that revamped the landscape by making alternative rock a true mass-market proposition. Although bigger-sounding and somewhat tidy compared to the bare-bones *Bleach*, it's a rock milestone, thanks not only to its excellent smash singles ("Smells Like Teen Spirit," "Come as You Are") but to its fearsomely blistering punkers ("Breed," "Territorial Pissings"). Tainted with attached significance following Cobain's death, 1993's *In Utero* is awesome as well. The wistful "All Apologies" is its best-known track, but a deeper look yields aggressive gems of harsh, hoarse genius ("Tourette's," the scathing "Radio Friendly Unit Shifter"). *Icon* samples from *Nevermind*, *In Utero*, and the acoustic *MTV Unplugged in New York*.

The Melvins

It's very likely there'd have been no Nirvana without this hairy, grungy, ultra-heavy bunch from Olympia, Washington. Prior to forming Nirvana in 1987, Kurt Cobain and Krist Novoselic bonded as fans of the Melvins, even jamming early on with their drummer, Dale Crover. Formed in 1985, the group—Crover, singer/guitarist Buzz "King Buzzo" Osbourne, original bassist Matt Lukin and his many successors—was the first notable Northwest act to fully embrace and magnify the lurching, painfully slow approach of Black Sabbath within a punk context. But as sonically dark as the Melvins' music is, the band also has a surreal sense of humor, putting weird cartoon animals on their record covers and titling songs "Hung Bunny" and "Magic Pig Detective." *Houdini* (1993) makes for the most representative first dose of the Melvins' monolithcally molten, molasses-paced music, but 1991's *Bullhead* and 1992's *Melvins* will also do. Or try *Melvinmania: The Best of the Atlantic Years 1993–1996*.

Screaming Trees

Screaming Trees' nucleus of singer Mark Lanegan and brothers Van and Gary Lee Conner (bass and guitar, respectively; Mark Pickerel was their first drummer) got together in 1985 and made a sound that combined punk with sixties garage and psychedelia, foregoing grunge's usual punk/metal formula. No doubt Johnny Ramone would've dug the Trees; overall, their crunching style is reminiscent of his faves the Doors, and Lanegan's deep baritone recalls Jim Morrison's. All of the group's albums for SST Records—1986's *Clairvoyance*, 1987's *Even If and Especially When*, 1988's *Invisible Lantern*, and 1989's *Buzz Factory*—as well as the ones they cut for Epic—1991's *Uncle Anesthesia*, 1992's *Sweet Oblivion* (with the MTV hit "Nearly Lost You"), 1996's *Dust*—are cool, punky psych with a contemporary spin. *Anthology: SST Years 1985–1989* covers the best of the early phase, while *Ocean of Confusion: Songs of Screaming Trees 1989–1996* chronicles the latter.

The Fluid

Not grunge per se, this Denver, Colorado, quintet was still part of the scene and was the first non-Seattle act signed to Sub-Pop Records, the local label that documented the era and became a leading indie imprint. Fronted by the growling John Robinson and armed with the one-two punch of guitarists Rick Kulwicki and James Clower, the band shared the Stooges influences of their grunge cohorts but eschewed their muddier, metallic side in favor of the hard blues rock of the MC5 and the New York Dolls. The Fluid's best records are the 1986 debut *Punch 'n' Judy* and the 1990 EP *Glue*.

L7

An all-female punk metal band from L.A.? No, it's not onetime Ramones tour mates the Runaways. L7 started in 1985 with singer/guitarists Donita Sparks and Suzi Gardner, bassist Jennifer Finch, and drummer Dee Plakas. After two rough-rocking independent albums, 1990's *L7* and 1991's *Smell the Magic*, the group rode the grunge wave to the majors for 1992's tighter *Bricks Are Heavy*. The latter birthed the hit single "Pretend That We're Dead" and among its worthy cuts has the driving "Shitlist." *Best of L7: The Slash Years* spotlights the band's time on the Slash label.

Hole

The biggest estrogen-heavy grunge act, though, was Hole, the L.A.-formed four-piece led by Kurt Cobain's screaming, attention-craving widow and sometime actress, Courtney Love (vocals, guitar). Conceived by Love and guitarist Eric Erlandson in 1989, Hole made its supremely raw debut with 1991's *Pretty on the Inside* and its commercial breakthrough with *Live Through This* in 1994. Although some of the latter album hints at the overproduced music to come, its furious, bile-spitting missives ("Violet," "She Walks on Me") are tempered with melodic numbers ("Doll Parts") that may appeal to Ramones fans.

POP PUNK

In the early 1990s, once grunge had peaked, pop punk was the next big thing. As one might derive from the name, the style plays up the more melodic aspects of punk rock. Thus, every pop punk band that has ever hopped on a stage owes every single one of its catchy choruses to the Ramones. (Who's your daddy, Fall Out Boy?) Pop punk bands have the image, speedy tempos, and loud guitars of standard punk bands, but their records generally have a radio-ready polish that has garnered huge hits, and has taken their music into malls, skate parks, high school proms and football games, even the Broadway stage. Quite a long way from the Bowery.

Green Day

The unchallenged rulers of pop punk are singer/guitarist Billie Joe Armstrong, drummer Tré Cool, and bassist Mike Dirnt—known collectively as Green Day. The trio started up in 1987, cutting its Clash/Jam/Buzzcocks/Ramones-stained teeth at seminal Berkeley, California, D.I.Y. venue 924 Gilman Street and releasing two indie albums; the second, 1992's *Kerplunk!*, is the better one, with memorable singalong crunchers like "Welcome to Paradise." *Dookie* (1994), the trio's platinum-snagging, modern power pop breakthrough, features a re-recording of that song, along with hook-slingers like the megahits "Basket Case" and "Longview." *Insomniac* (1995) treads similar ground (the hit medley "Brain Stew / Jaded" spans brooding slow burn and fast hardcore), as does the slicker *Nimrod* (1997). The next couple of albums see the band attempting to broaden its sound with whimsical Kinks and Beatles touches. Green Day's biggest success came ten years after *Dookie* with 2004's *American Idiot.* A politically themed rock opera boasting some of the group's best compositions—the crashing title tune, in particular—it was combined with the 2009 sequel *21st Century Breakdown* (with the storming "Know Your Enemy") as the basis of a smash musical also called *American Idiot.* The band's three-album sequence from 2012, *¡Uno!, ¡Dos!,* and *¡Tré!,* sees a return to the threesome's more compact roots. *International Superhits!* compiles the 1990s singles. See also: Green Day imitators Blink-182 and Sum 41.

Rancid

Green Day's rival in the Bay Area—and, eventually, on MTV—was Rancid. Concocted in 1991 by Tim Armstrong (vocals, guitar) and Matt Freeman (bass), who'd played together in hardcore/ska act Operation Ivy, Rancid plainly aped the Clash, right down to Armstrong's affecting a British accent while singing. But there's no denying the band's blazing passion—or its tuneful way with a punk-pop hook. *Rancid,* its 1993 debut, and 1994's sophomore *Let's Go* are shouty Oi!/hardcore and lack the ska-punk songs that increasingly became a hallmark starting with 1995's...*And Out Come the Wolves,* Rancid's biggest-selling disc (highlight: Armstrong's catchy marble-mouthed Joe Strummer pastiche "Ruby Soho"). At the Ramones' final show, Armstrong and fellow Rancid guitarist Lars Frederikson joined in on "53rd and 3rd."

Bad Religion

Southern California punk institution Bad Religion was established in 1979 by vocalist Greg Graffin and guitarist Brett Gurewitz after the latter had caught the Ramones live. To release the band's first album, the straight hardcore *How Could Hell Be Any Worse?* (1982),

Gurewitz founded the Epitaph label, which became a pop punk powerhouse, releasing records by Green Day, Rancid, and others. A college professor by day, Graffin writes political, impenetrably erudite lyrics; the group's galloping beats, big riffs, and three-part harmonies have legions of diehard fans. The most popular of the band's nearly twenty albums include 1988's *Suffer*, 1989's *No Control*, 1990's *Against the Grain*, and 1993's *Recipe for Hate*. *All Ages* maps Bad Religion's lengthy history.

The Distillers

Also in the Epitaph stable was this outstanding outfit fronted by raspy, Joan Jett-ish screamer Brody Dalle. Dalle, who was once married to Rancid's Tim Armstrong, writes fabulously anthemic punk blasters, which, on their three first-rate albums, *The Distillers* (2000), *Sing Sing Death House* (2002), and *Coral Fang* (2003), the Distillers deliver with thrashing guitars and utterly gripping abandon. Dalle's next band, Spinnerette, is generally more produced, but her skilled songwriting still shines through.

The Lemonheads

Known for hit covers of Suzanne Vega's "Luka" and Simon and Garfunkel's "Mrs. Robinson" and as the vehicle of alt-rock heartthrob Evan Dando, this Boston band began as a scrappy, post–Hüsker Dü outfit. And it's the records from that period, with their buzzsaw guitars and grabby melodies, that will likely appeal most to Ramones enthusiasts: 1987's *Hate Your Friends* and 1988's *Creator* (both combined on *Create Your Friends*) and 1988's *Lick*.

Weezer

Weezer's self-titled 1994 debut (often referred to as *The Blue Album*) was a runaway MTV smash thanks to the hit "Undone (the Sweater Song)" and the cheeky video for "Buddy Holly," and is much adored for its synthesis of crunching guitars and ice-cream vocal melodies. *Pinkerton* (1996) is somewhat darker, which lost the band some fans, but many returned for the band's third album, 2001's *Weezer* (yes, another eponymously titled set, this one commonly called *The Green Album*). Two thousand nine's *Raditude* and 2010's *Hurley* show Weezer still serving up its power pop hooks; confessional, proto-emo lyrics; and nerdy, heart-on-a-sweater-sleeve aesthetic.

The Muffs

Helmed by singer/guitarist Kim Shattuck, one of the loudest screamers to don a dress—not to mention one of the best sixties-rooted, Ramones-informed pop songstresses working today—the Muffs are criminally underrated. *The Muffs*, the group's boisterous 1993 debut, is flat-out essential, blowing out your speakers with the irresistibly contagious "Lucky Guy" and "Everywhere I Go." The Los Angeles band began in 1991 as a quartet but continued as a trio after second guitarist Melanie Vammen (like Shattuck, a veteran of garage rockers the Pandoras) left to join long-running local punks the Leaving Trains. Ex–Redd Kross drummer Roy McDonald joined for 1995's *Blonder and Blonder*, which is almost as great the first album (see the dizzying "Oh Nina"). Nineteen ninety-seven's *Happy Birthday to Me*, 1999's *Alert Today, Alive Tomorrow*, and 2004's *Really, Really Happy* are similarly terrific.

The Fastbacks

Another unheralded, femme-fronted band, Seattle's Fastbacks got started in 1979. With Kim Warnick on lead vocals and bass and Lulu Gargiulo and Kurt Bloch on guitars, the group went through around twenty drummers during its two decades of rocking. All seven of the Fastbacks' studio albums are joyously played mixes of sunny harmonies and buzzing Ramones guitars, the top examples being ... *And His Orchestra* (1987), *Very, Very Powerful Motor* (1990), and *The Day That Didn't Exist* (1999). The 'Backs cover *Leave Home*'s "Swallow My Pride" on the live *Bike-Toy-Clock-Gift*, while *The Question Is No* summarizes their early years and makes a swell intro.

Supergrass

I Should Coco, the 1995 debut by this (at the time) very young British band, is one of the great guitar pop albums of its time, recalling the fizzy energy of the Buzzcocks, the Jam, the early Who and Beatles, and, yes, a wee bit of the Ramones. The thickly sideburned lineup of singer/guitarist Gaz Coombes, bassist Mickey Quinn, and manic, Keith Moon–like drummer Danny Goffey got together in 1993. The next year they released the cracking single "Caught by the Fuzz," which appears on *I Should Coco*, along with the slamming "Sitting Up Straight," the Bowie-ish "Mansize Rooster," and the aberrant, music hall–flavored "Alright." *In It for the Money* (1997) has some similar moments, but Supergrass's other albums are mainly moodier and far from the trio's succinct base.

The Donnas

Also assembled in 1993, the San Francisco–area foursome of Donna A. (vocals), Donna R. (guitar), Donna F. (bass), and Donna C. (drums) blatantly modeled itself on the Ramones' 1970s pals the Runaways, with a bit of the good ol' bruddas thrown in. The quartet cut one album as the Electrocutes, the endearingly amateurish *Steal Yer Lunch Money*, which wasn't released until after they'd hit it big as the Donnas. For the most part, these winkingly jailbait vixens' party-rocking albums are interchangeable; the best is probably 1999's *Skintight*, though 1998's *American Teenage Rock 'n' Roll Machine* and *The Donnas*, 2001's *The Donnas Turn 21*, 2002's *Spend the Night*, and 2004's *Gold Medal* are all fun-filled and trace a trajectory of tighter musicianship and glossier production. (Skip 2007's metal-ish *Bitchin'*.) The jokingly titled retrospective *Greatest Hits Volume 16* may be enough.

Avril Lavigne

Made you laugh, huh? Taking the jailbait angle of the Donnas to more precarious heights is this multiplatinum Canadian teenybopper, who's included to show just how far into the mainstream the Ramones' sound has been absorbed. Her millions-selling 2002 single "Sk8er Boi" was the first taste, while her third album, 2007's *The Best Damn Thing*, is a surreal illustration of the bubblegum co-opting of the Bowery boys' four-four, downstroked template into bouncy cheerleader pop; see the title cut, "Everything

Back to You," or the hit "Girlfriend," which also borrows from the Rubinoos' "I Wanna Be Your Boyfriend" (see earlier). And hey, her middle name is Ramona.

EIGHTIES AND NINETIES RAMONES CLONES

That heading's not meant as a dis. There are record bins full of cool eighties and nineties bands that openly and tastefully reference our beloved blitzkrieg boppers. Here are fifteen of the best.

The Queers

Snotty New Hampshire trio formed in 1977. Get *Don't Back Down* (1996).

The Lazy Cowgirls

Indiana-by-way-of-L.A. bunch fronted by compact fireball Pat Todd. Get *Ragged Soul* (1995).

Chixdiggit!

Canadian quartet that debuted on Seattle's Sub-Pop label. Get *Chixdiggit!* (1996).

New Bomb Turks

Lit-up Ohio lit majors let loose with life-affirming loudness. Get *Destroy-Oh-Boy!* (1993).

The Didjits

The demented Rick Simms led these Illinois terrors through five scorching LPs. Get *Hey Judester* (1988).

Teengenerate

Named for a Dictators song, these Japanese garagers also smack of the Ramones. Get *Get Action!* (1995).

Nine Pound Hammer

Kentucky quartet affectionately dubbed "the redneck Ramones." Get *Hayseed Timebomb* (1995).

The Celibate Rifles

Australians revered for Kent Steedman and Dave Morris's burning guitars and singer Damien Lovelock's literate baritone. Get *Roman Beach Party* (1987).

The Action Swingers

Steered by flame-throated Ned Hayden, this über-raw New York unit opened bills for the Ramones. Get *Quit While You're Ahead* (1994).

Exploding White Mice

This Aussie outfit's name—a reference to *Rock 'n' Roll High School*'s volatile rodents—makes it clear where its members came from musically. Get *In a Nest of Vipers* (1985).

Screeching Weasel / The Riverdales

Chicago groups, both led by singer/guitarist Ben Weasel—and both sounding very much like guess who. Get the former's *My Brain Hurts* (1991) and/or the latter's *Storm the Streets* (1997).

The Mr. T Experience

Shamelessly Ramones-y Berkeley combo predating both Green Day and Rancid in the pop punk continuum. Get *Love Is Dead* (1996).

The Hard-Ons

Another Australian band, once described as a cross between Motörhead and the Beach Boys—but pure Ramones to these ears (same difference, actually). Get *Suck and Swallow: 25 Years* (2009).

Mercyland

Bassist David Barbe's pre-Sugar (see Hüsker Dü, above) Athens, Georgia, project, whose "Black on Black on Black" is one of the best Ramones swipes yet. Get *Spillage* (1994).

IF YOU LIKE THE RAMONES...

RAMONES BRANCHES AND SPIN-OFFS

While being in the Ramones took a lot of energy, the members did get involved in other musical projects during and after the band's breakup, and there are also some Ramones-related acts to mention that didn't directly involve the guys themselves. The two-CD *Ramones Family Tree* brings together twenty-eight of the members' extracurricular efforts. But as a fan you want the fine points, right?

Joey

Although he'd long talked of making solo albums, the two that bear Joey Ramone's name didn't appear until after his passing. *Don't Worry About Me* (2002) was recorded while he was suffering from the lymphoma that took his life, and much of it feels suitably poignant (the chugging cover of Louis Armstrong's "What a Wonderful World," in particular). But at the same time, it recalls the best of the Ramones' later work and carries an air of upbeat defiance (the title cut, "I Got Knocked Down [But I'll Get Up]"). A good one to go out on. Two thousand twelve's... *Ya Know?* consists of home demos that were fleshed out after the fact. A disaster, you think? Wrong. It's great, thanks to guest players like Joan Jett, the Dictators' Andy Shernoff, and Cheap Trick's Bun E. Carlos, and sympathetic producers like Ed Stasium and Joey's brother Mickey Leigh—plus Joey's magnificent voice and catchy anthems ("New York City") and melancholic chestnuts ("Waiting for That Railroad").

Joey was very active outside the Ramones, making guest appearances with numerous artists. Besides singing on Little Steven Van Zandt's 1985 anti-apartheid single "Sun City," Joey recorded some wonderful duets: a 1982 cover of Sonny and Cher's "I Got You Babe" with Holly Beth Vincent; a 1994 soul version of "Rockaway Beach" with Chairmen of the Board singer General Johnson on the compilation *Godchildren of Soul: Anyone Can Join*; *In a Family Way*, a 1994 collaborative EP with Mickey Leigh; and 1999's "Bye Bye Baby" and "You Can't Put Your Arms Around a Memory" with Ronnie Spector on her *She Talks to Rainbows* EP, which he coproduced with Ramones studio maven Daniel Rey. An inveterate music fan, Joey took many younger bands under his wing, managing and producing ska-punks the Independents (1994's *Unholy Living Dead* EP) and making his last recordings as a backup singer for Navajo band Blackfire (2002's *One Nation Under*).

Dee Dee

Dee Dee's most infamous post-Ramones activity was his dalliance in rap, as Dee Dee King, the name under which he recorded 1987's surreally bad *Standing in the Spotlight*. Its hilariously stilted single "Funky Man" is a good indicator of Dee Dee's shortcomings as a rapper, but there's something endearing about the childlike ballad "Baby Doll"; "Emergency," "Poor Little Rich Girl," and "The Crusher" sound like Ramones demos (indeed, the latter was redone on *¡Adios Amigos!*). Following his hip-hop flop Dee Dee returned to rock, attempting an unrealized punk super group with Johnny Thunders and Stiv Bators called the Whores of Babylon before moving to guitar with the unrecorded Sprokkett and Dee Dee Ramone and the Spikey Tops (a live bootleg of the latter exists). His short-lived Chinese Dragons (one 1993 single) were followed by Dee Dee Ramone I.C.L.C. (Inter-Celestial Light Commune), which released the 1994 EP *Chinese Bitch* and album *I Hate Freaks Like You*, the latter featuring "I'm Making Monsters for My Friends" (re-titled "Makin' Monsters for My Friends" for *¡Adios Amigos!*). Under his own name Dee Dee issued 1997's decent *Zonked!* (also released as *Ain't It Fun*), which has guest vocals by Joey ("I Am Seeing U.F.O.'s") and the Cramps' Lux Interior, and 2000's lackluster *Hop Around*. He put together Ramones covers band the Ramainz with his second wife, bassist Barbara Zampini, and Marky on drums; the group, which occasionally also included C. J. Ramone, released one album, 1999's *Live in NYC*. Dee Dee's last studio recordings were with hardcore band Youth Gone Mad for 2002's *Youth Gone Mad Featuring Dee Dee Ramone*.

Marky

In addition to drumming for the Ramainz and, for a spell, the Misfits (see sidebar), Marky has led several of his own bands, all of whom consciously echo the Ramones. But hey, say Ramones-loving audiences around the world, why fuck with the winning formula? The first, Marky Ramone and the Intruders, released 1996's *Marky Ramone and the Intruders* and 1999's *The Answer to Your Problems (Don't Blame Me!* in South America). Marky Ramone and the Speedkings put out *Legends Bleed* (also released as *No If's, And's or But's*) and the live *Alive!* in 2002. Marky Ramone's Blitzkrieg, a Ramones covers band, followed— along with the marketing of the drummer's own pasta sauce.

THE MISFITS AND HORROR PUNK

Be afraid. Be very afraid.

Ah, just kidding. Horror punk is nothing to be afraid of. A fun, narrowly focused outcropping of punk rock, horror punk (sometimes called horror hardcore) refers to a genre of bands that play music that generally adheres to the traditional punk sound—it's just the players themselves who look a little different from your standard jeans-and-leather-jacketed punks. Well, okay, a lot different. Visually obsessed, many horror punk musicians rock a consciously camp, gothic image inspired by monster flicks and older science fiction B movies, bringing the Ramones' love for such films (see Chapter Five) to the next level—a level smeared with white pancake makeup and lots of fake blood. *Mwahaha!*

Horror punk arose from its shallow grave with a vengeance in the 1980s, and can be traced to one band: the Misfits. Founded in 1977 in New Jersey by singer Glenn Danzig and bassist Jerry Only (real name: Jerry Caiafa), the Misfits took their name from Marilyn Monroe's last film and early on were noticeably influenced by the Damned (whose front man Dave Vanian's vampiric look they emulated) and the Doors (at times Danzig's tuneful baritone is, if you will, a dead ringer for Jim Morrison's). With a drummer the pair cut a creepy, keyboard-dominated single before adding the first of several guitarists. By the time the Misfits released their unbeatable 1982 debut, *Walk Among Us*, Only's brother Doyle (Paul Caiafa) was on guitar and their sound had been well established via classic seven-inches like "Horror Business," "Night of the Living Dead," and *Three Hits from Hell*: a hard, raw, extremely catchy style owing much to the

Ramones and filled with spooky, but ironically humorous, lyrics. The group fell in with the early eighties hardcore scene, which influenced the thrashier sound of 1983's *Earth A.D.*, a record featuring ex-Black Flag drummer Robo (Julio Valencia). The Misfits split up soon after its release, with Glenn Danzig next forming Samhain (essentially a slowed-down, unfunny Misfits) before taking the shtick to its logical conclusion with a band he named after himself. The Misfits gained a huge, after-the-fact following when Metallica and Guns N' Roses covered their songs, leading Only and Doyle to resurrect the band's name in 1995. After they burned through a couple of singers, Doyle was replaced by Black Flag's Dez Cadena, and none other than Marky Ramone drummed for a tour. The Misfits have since continued, with Only as the, er, only original member. If you can't spring for the coffin-shaped box set, the single-disc *Misfits* makes the best starting point. Happy Halloween!

Johnny

After the Ramones announced their impending split, Johnny famously said he was retiring because nothing he could do would be better than the Ramones. Fair enough. But, being a fan of the King, Johnny couldn't resist appearing on *A Tribute to Elvis* (2000) by ex–Stray Cat Slim Jim Phantom's Swing Cats.

Tommy

As we've learned elsewhere in this book, Tommy Erdelyi, the Ramones' founding drummer, has mainly made his name as a producer since leaving the band in 1978. But in 2006 he returned to the other side of the mike with the self-titled debut by Uncle Monk, a bluegrass duo in which he sings and plays mandolin alongside his wife, guitarist Claudia Tienen. *Hay* ho, let's go!

C. J.

Prior to replacing Dee Dee, bassist C. J. Ramone (Christopher Joseph Ward) made two albums with speed metal band Guitar Pete's Axe Attack, *Dead Soldier's Revenge* (1985) and *Nightmare* (1986). He played guitar and sang in the quartet Los Gusanos, which began as a Ramones side project in 1992 and put out one album of

IF YOU LIKE THE RAMONES...

metallic punk, 1997's *Los Gusanos*. His next band was Bad Chopper, which included Daniel Rey on guitar and released *Bad Chopper* in 2007. His first solo recording, *Reconquista*, appeared in 2012.

Birdland / The Rattlers / STOP

These bands featured Joey's brother, singer/guitarist Mickey Leigh. Formed in 1977, Birdland was fronted by legendary rock journalist Lester Bangs. *Birdland with Lester Bangs* didn't come out until 1986—four years after Bangs died—and is a trove of garagey, downtown, Beat-punk. The Rattlers were an underrated New York trio (their debut single, 1979's "Livin' Alone" / "On the Beach," with Joey on backup vocals, is a classic). The band's sole 1985 album, *Rattled!*, shakes with similarly tight punk/power pop. Leigh's next documented band, STOP, also made one album, 1996's *Never*, whose songs are both rocking and ambitious.

YOU SHOULD HAVE NEVER OPENED THAT DOOR

As a parting shot, here are a few more recent acts that carry the brat-beating pulse of the Ramones.

The Raveonettes

Danish duo recalling the Ronettes, the Ramones, Suicide, and the Jesus and Mary Chain. Produced by Richard Gottehrer (Angels, Blondie, Richard Hell). Get *Chain Gang of Love* (2003).

The Detroit Cobras

Fun, femme-fronted Motor City garage greats. Get *Mink Rat or Rabbit* (1998).

The Hives

Besuited Swedish hitmeisters who stormed the charts with crashing garage punk. Get *Your New Favorite Band* (2002).

The Strokes

Suspiciously hyped New York quintet trading on a studied cool Television / Velvet Underground hybrid. Get *Is This It* (2001).

The Vivian Girls

Three Brooklyn girls playing hazy, singsong pop. And hey, the singer's name is Cassie Ramone. Get *Vivian Girls* (2008).

Dum Dum Girls

The West Coast Vivian Girls. Fuzzy girl group pop, again produced by Gottehrer. Singer's name is Dee Dee. Get *I Will Be* (2010).

Titus Andronicus

Rowdy, literature- and history-referencing punk from New Jersey. Get *The Airing of Grievances* (2008).

Cheap Time

Tennessee trio that tears it up à la early Who, the Buzzcocks, and a certain gang from Queens. Get *Fantastic Explanations (And Similar Situations)* (2010).

THE RAMONES AND THE AVANT-GARDE

As the first chapter of this book points out, when *Ramones* appeared it hit a lot of people as something completely outside the realm of rock 'n' roll. Of course, those who knew what rock 'n' roll *really* is got it in a big way. But so did many from the world of contemporary avant-garde music, who saw the Ramones' hard, fast, loud, linear, and boldly stark approach as decidedly forward-thinking.

One of them was studied New York post-minimalist composer and multi-instrumentalist Rhys Chatham, whose first-ever rock concert was a May 1976 Ramones gig at CBGB, where he'd ended up during a night out with three other avant-gardists—and confirmed Ramones fans—cellist Arthur Russell, percussionist David Van Tieghem, and saxophonist Peter Gordon. The performance changed Chatham's life. "[The Ramones] had just put their first album out," Chatham recalled in a 2008 interview with Alan Licht for *Bomb* magazine. "I was completely blown away. I had never seen anything like it. I thought their music was a lot more complex than what I was doing; they were playing three chords instead of one! I

felt a relationship between what they were doing and what I was doing."
Focusing on the buzzing overtones of Johnny Ramone's guitar, Chatham
composed his most famous piece, *Guitar Trio*, which he and his ensemble
played at various downtown venues. A 1979 performance at punk hang
Max's Kansas City was revelatory for a young guitarist name Lee Ranaldo,
who would soon work with the composer and form Sonic Youth (see
Chapter Seven) with another Chatham guitarist, Thurston Moore. (The
work appears on the box set *An Angel Moves Too Fast to See: Selected
Works 1971–1989*.)

Playing guitar for Chatham at *Guitar Trio*'s 1978 public debut was
another luminary downtown Manhattan composer, Glenn Branca. A volume-
worshipping, table-saw-sounding guitar terrorist, Branca played with noisy
no wave bands the Static and Theoretical Girls and led his own ensembles,
which at various times included Moore, Ranaldo, and Swans leader Michael
Gira. Branca's trademark compositions use massed, very loud electric
guitars in unusual tunings to deliver immense aural storms of singing over-
and microtones. Punk was pivotal for him as well. "One day I heard a punk
rock concert in New York," Branca told *Junkmedia* in 2002. "It wasn't the
Ramones, as some people say. It was the Dead Boys [see Chapter Four].
They were much cruder and rawer and more violent than the Ramones....
They were very primitive, savage, powerful....I immediately had the idea to
mix some of my classical training with punk rock." The spiky fruit of this mix
is best imbibed via 1981's *Lesson No. 1* and 1982's *The Ascension*.

It might seem far-fetched to tie the crystalline, constantly circling music
of famed New York composer Philip Glass, who is best known for his 1976
opera *Einstein on the Beach* and scores for films like 1982's *Koyaanisqatsi*,
to the roaring rock of the Ramones. But as he was a member of the
same mid-1970s lower Manhattan arts community (and has worked with
Patti Smith, Talking Heads' David Byrne, and Gotham post-punk band
Polyrock), it seems wholly plausible that the steady, underlying pulse
that informs so much of Glass's work carries sympathetic strains of da
bruddas' "One-two-three-four!" DNA. To quote Allmusic.com, "Many
describe [Glass's] music in the minimalist vein as mesmerizing; others hear

it as numbingly repetitive and devoid of variety in its simplicity." Exactly what non-believers say about the Ramones (and phooey to them!). Spin *Best of Phillip Glass* as you ponder it all.

THE RAMONES MUSEUM

Believe it or not, there really is a Ramones Museum. But it's not in New York on Joey Ramone Place, where CBGB once stood. Nor is it around the corner from the Thorneycroft Apartments complex, where the soon-to-be Fast Four loitered as bored adolescents. And it's not in London, Tokyo, or Buenos Aires, the remaining cities where they arguably had their biggest concentrations of fans. Believe it or not, the Ramones Museum is in Berlin, Germany. Which actually kind of makes sense, given the band's Teutonic lyrical obsessions and Dee Dee's childhood roots in the European nation.

After his girlfriend told him to either find another home for his rapidly growing collection of Ramones memorabilia or find one for himself, mega fan Flo Hayler opened the Ramones Museum in a modest space in September 2005. "The idea was to create a place for fans," says the museum's website. "Not just Ramones fans, but music fans. A place where memories could be shared and stories could be told." In 2009 jacked-up rent forced the museum to move to a new location, which also serves as a café, bar, and performance venue presenting live acoustic acts. Amid the head-banging array of Ramones ephemera on display are rare photos, fliers and tour posters, records, tour T-shirts, signed sneakers and drumsticks that belonged to Marky, a bass drum head signed by Johnny, Joey, Marky, and C. J., and much, much more. The facility, which also shows Ramones-related films on its big-screen TV, is open seven days a week for your blitzkrieg-bopping pleasure As Joey sang, it's a long way back to Germany. But the Ramones Museum makes it worth the trip. Check it out at www.ramonesmuseum.com.

APPENDIX A:
SIXTEEN RAMONES TRIBUTE RECORDINGS
YOU MUST HEAR

If you can hold an instrument in your hands, you can almost play a Ramones song. But that doesn't necessarily mean it'll be interesting. Here's a bunch that are: sixteen very cool recordings featuring artists paying loving tribute to the Ramones by performing songs by and about them.

Various Artists—*Gabba Gabba Hey: A Tribute to the Ramones* (1991)
The first Ramones tribute album. Mostly West Coast hardcore and pop-punk bands (D.I., Bad Religion), but Mojo Nixon's cowpunk version of "Rockaway Beach" was a bit of a college radio hit.

The Nutley Brass—*Ramones Songbook as Played by the Nutley Brass* (1999)
Easy-listening takeoffs of "I Wanna Be Sedated," "Chinese Rock," and others. But, wait, there's more! *Beat on the Brass* has, yep, a remake of "Beat on the Brat" and other punk hits; *Fiend Club Lounge* makes Muzak outta the Misfits.

Various Artists—*We're a Happy Family: A Tribute to the Ramones* (2003)
Here's the star power: among others, Metallica doing "53rd and 3rd," the Red Hot Chili Peppers doing "Havana Affair," Kiss doing "Do You Remember Rock 'n' Roll Radio?," and U2 doing a very credible—seriously—"Beat on the Brat."

Amy Rigby—"Dancing with Joey Ramone" (2005)
Acclaimed power-pop singer-songwriter's addictive, sugar-sweet love note to our number-one vocalist. Find the song on her terrific sixth solo album, *Little Fugitive*.

GABBA—*Leave Stockholm* (1999)
It might sound improbable at first, but it's actually a match made in bubblegum heaven: a London-based band performing ABBA songs in the stripped-down mold of the Ramones. They've dubbed it discopunk.

Various Artists—*Leaving Home: A Norwegian Tribute to the Ramones* (2005)
No huge names here, but it's plain rockin' all the same. Pretty much all of the bands turn in fittingly tough performances, rendered just the way the originators woulda wanted.

Tracy Thornton—*Pan for Punks: A Steelpan Tribute to the Ramones* (2005)
Moving from the Nordic chill of the last two titles to the sunny Caribbean, this one has percussionist Thornton playing Ramones favorites on the steelpan drums. "Rockaway Beach" makes an uncanny fit.

Various Artists—*Bossa 'n' Ramones* (2008)
Jetting even farther south, this comp brims with breezy, sun-dappled electro–bossa nova interpretations of our leather-sporting mutants. In addition to some cool South American acts, David Bowie's ex, Angie Bowie, and Runaways singer Cherie Currie appear.

Screeching Weasel—*Ramones* (1992)
End-to-end cover of the whole first album by this besotted Chicago punk quartet. Other bands who've covered entire Ramones LPs include the Vindictives (*Leave Home*), the Beatnik Termites (*Pleasant Dreams*), the Queers (*Rocket to Russia*), the Mr. T Experience (*Road to Ruin*), Boris the Sprinkler (*End of the Century*), and, perhaps boldest of all, the Parasites (*It's Alive*).

Various Artists—*Gabber Gabber Hey!: A Loud and Fast Accelerated Tribute to the Ramones* (2004)

Weird 'n' wired electronica tribute by "glitch" (computer-generated sound) artists. Emulsion vs. Ahab's (?) version of "Warthog" sounds like a swarm of angry robots.

The Eastern Dark—"Johnny and Dee Dee" (1985)

The debut single by this late Australian trio is a sincere, upbeat ode to our cover boys. It appears on 2000's *Where Are All the Single Girls?*, along with "Julie Is a Junkie" and "Julie Loves Johnny."

Shonen Knife—*Osaka Ramones* (2011)

Long-running, all-female Japanese pop-punkers show their love. Great *Road to Ruin* rip-off artwork.

Full Blown Cherry—*The Rockabilly Tribute to the Ramones* (2005)

Just what it says. Hee-haw, let's go!

Ramonetures—*Ramonetures* (2005)

Also on the retro tip, this outfit's first album delivers sharp, Ventures-type instrumental surf versions of Ramones originals. Fuzz-guitar god Davie Allan (see Chapter Two) guests.

Various Artists—*Rockabye Baby!: Lullaby Renditions of the Ramones* (2007)

Like the cover says: Gabba Gabba Goo Goo! But hey, why no "Carbona Not Glue"?

Blowfly—*Blowfly's Punk Rock Party* (2006)

Internationally infamous for his X-rated re-interpretations of popular hits, the man born Clarence Reid here has his way with "I Wanna Be Sedated" (as "I Wanna Be Fellated") and other punk jams. Parents: Don't mix this one up with the *Rockabye Baby!* CD.

APPENDIX B:
TWENTY BOOKS YOU MUST READ

Hey Ho Let's Go: The Story of the Ramones
By Everett True
(OMNIBUS PRESS, 2002)
The most comprehensive Ramones history thus far, by the former assistant editor of British music weekly *Melody Maker* and editor of *VOX* magazine.

Ramones: An American Band
By Jim Bessman
(ST. MARTIN'S PRESS, 1993)
The next best, by band friend Jim Bessman. Of special note is an appendix listing every Ramones gig from March 1974 through January 1993.

I Slept with Joey Ramone
By Mickey Leigh with Legs McNeil
(TOUCHSTONE BOOKS, 2010)
Heartfelt, richly evocative, and moving bio of Joey by his brother, Mickey. Tied with Johnny's autobio for the best Ramones insider book.

Commando: The Autobiography of Johnny Ramone
By Johnny Ramone
(ABRAMS IMAGE, 2012)
Johnny's excellently written first-person life story. Short, sharp, and no-bullshit—just like his playing.

Lobotomy: Surviving the Ramones
By Dee Dee Ramone
(THUNDER'S MOUTH PRESS, 2000)
First published in 1997 as *Poison Heart: Surviving the Ramones*, here's Dee Dee's riotous, glorious train-wreck tale of life before, during, and after the Ramones.

On the Road with the Ramones
By Monte A. Melnick
(BOBCAT BOOKS, 2007)
The band's long-suffering road manager gives his van-driver's-seat perspective. Hugely entertaining.

Poisoned Heart: I Married Dee Dee Ramone
By Vera Ramone King
(PHOENIX BOOKS, 2009)
Bruises-'n'-all tell-all by Dee Dee's ex-wife. "Like *The Honeymooners* on speed," says Lenny Kaye.

Punk Rock Blitzkrieg: My Life as a Ramone
By Marky Ramone
(TOUCHSTONE BOOKS, 2013)
Marky takes his turn on the shelf, frankly discussing his nearly twenty years as a Ramone.

Legend of a Rock Star: The Last Testament of Dee Dee Ramone
By Dee Dee Ramone
(THUNDER'S MOUTH PRESS, 2003)
Ripped from the pages of Dee Dee's diaries, this conversational, eye-rollingly acerbic read recounts the disaster-plagued saga of one of the rocker's last tours.

Chelsea Horror Hotel
By Dee Dee Ramone
(DA CAPO PRESS, 2001)
Divinely surreal fictional work by the bassist based on his drug-addled

residency at New York's infamous Chelsea Hotel. Who woulda pegged Dee Dee as one of punk's greatest and most prolific writers?

When the Wall of Sound Met the New York Underground: The Ramones, Phil Spector and End of the Century
By Frank Meyer
(Rhino Books, 2012)
Brief (forty-four pages) but in-depth, Kindle-only examination of the legendarily crazed making of *End of the Century* with producer Phil Spector. It gets weird in here.

Please Kill Me: The Uncensored Oral History of Punk
By Legs McNeil and Gillian McCain
(Grove Press, 1996)
The best, most movingly engrossing account of early American punk there is, from the mouths of those who made it. Beyond essential.

From the Velvets to the Voidoids: The Birth of American Punk Rock
By Clinton Heylin
(Penguin Books, 1993)
While the vérité *Please Kill Me* reads like a punk Studs Terkel, this likewise mandatory book expertly weaves well-researched narratives through its own first-person anecdotes.

England's Dreaming: Anarchy, Sex Pistols, Punk Rock, and Beyond
By Jon Savage
(St. Martin's Griffin, 1992)
The definitive account of the early years of punk in the U.K. by one of that nation's best rock writers.

The Best of Punk *Magazine*
By John Holstrom
(It Books, 2012)
Lavish coffee-table anthology of the gritty and hilarious organ of

New York punk. Cartoons by cofounder and *Road to Ruin* and *Rocket to Russia* cover artist Holstrom. And, naturally, much Ramones coverage.

All Revved Up and Ready to Go: Music from the Streets of New York: 1927–77
By Tony Fletcher
(W. W. NORTON, 2009)
This colorful, sweeping history takes in fifty years of wild Big Apple sounds, with the Ramones and the city's early punk scene getting justifiably heavy play.

Love Goes to Buildings on Fire: Five Years in New York That Changed Music Forever
By Will Hermes
(FABER AND FABER, 2012)
Overlapping with *All Revved Up…*, this riveting effort covers Gotham's heady music world, circa 1973–1977. Its vivid punk coverage evokes the era contextually by juxtaposing the Ramones against New York's larger contemporary music world.

We Got the Neutron Bomb: The Untold Story of L.A. Punk
By Mark Spitz and Brendan Mullen
(THREE RIVERS PRESS, 2001)
The Runaways. The Germs. X. The Whiskey. The Masque. Oki Dogs. All here. Spitz and Mullen do for the nascent Los Angeles punk scene what *Please Kill Me* does for New York's.

Punk 365
By Holly George-Warren
(HARRY N. ABRAMS, 2007)
Brick-like volume of amazing photos by some of the best shutterbugs to chronicle the highly visual music known as punk rock. Great shots of the Ramones in New York and London.

The Encylopedia of Psychotronic Film
By Michael J. Weldon
(ST. MARTIN'S GRIFFIN, 1983)

This tome and its equally weighty 1996 sequel, *The Psychotronic Video Guide to Film*, were the handy bibles of confessed movie nut Johnny Ramone. Each describes over three thousand of the most bizarre, offbeat, and trashy cult horror, sci-fi, and exploitation B-grade films and TV shows ever made.

INDEX

Electric Prunes, the, 51
End of the Century (album), 17,
    18, 119, 191, 192,
    195, 254, 259
*End of the Century: The Story
    of the Ramones* (film),
    16, 95, 188
Essex, the, 14
Everly Brothers, the, 9, 167
Every Mother's Son, 68
Evil Dead, The (film), 176–
    177
Exploding White Mice, the,
    243

Faithfull, Marianne, 167
Family Guy (television show),
    158
Fantastic Baggys, the, 25
Fastbacks, the, 200, 240
Fear, 199, 203, 220
Fields, Danny, 94, 188
Flamin' Groovies, 90,
    97–98, 139, 144,
    146, 148
Fleshtones, the, 198
Flinstones, The (television
    show), 153
Flipper, 199
Fluid, the, 236
Foo Fighters, the, 141, 234
Forbidden Planet (film), 178
Forgotten Rebels, the,
    146–147
Frankie Lymon and the
    Teenagers, 18

Freaks (film), 174
Freddie and the Dreamers,
    50, 166
Freed, Alan, 180
Freeman, Bobby, 8, 26
Freleng, Fritz, 152
Frijid Pink, 89
Fugazi, 218
Fugs, the 90–91
Fun Things, the, 136

Gang Green, 199
Gang of Four, 198
Gaye, Marvin, 181
Generation X, 130, 195,
    197
Germs, the, 140–141, 198,
    202
Gerry and the Pacemakers,
    50, 181
Gimme Shelter (film), 182
Girl Can't Help It, The (film),
    180
Gits, the, 200
Glass, Philip, 250
Glitter, Gary, 100, 204
Godfathers, the, 228
Go-Go's, the, 198
Gore, Leslie, 181
Graham Parker and the
    Rumour, 110
Grand Funk Railroad, 76,
    84
Grass Roots, the, 60
Green Day, 194, 237–238,
    239, 243

Manfred Mann (band), 50, 166

Marky Ramone's Blitzkrieg, 246

Marky Ramone and the Intruders, 246

Marky Ramone and the Speedkings, 246

Martha and the Vandellas, 20, 167

Marvel Comics, 170–171

Marvelettes, the, 19–20

Max's Kansas City, 115, 196, 209, 250

McCoys, the, 167

MC5, the, 38, 47, 87, 90, 94–95, 128, 135, 138, 139, 148

McNeil, Legs, 173, 188, 191

MDC (band), 199

Meek, Joe, 25

Megadeth, 230–231

Melnick, Monte, 76, 122, 188

Melvins, the, 200, 234, 235

Members, the, 198

Mercer Arts Center, 115

Mercyland, 243

Merrie Melodies, 152

Metallica, 81, 229–230, 247

Metal Urbain, 147

Midnight Special, The (television show), 168–169

Mighty Mouse, 153

Milk 'n' Cookies, 209, 211

Mink DeVille, 122, 198

Minor Threat, 199, 203, 217–218

Minutemen, the, 200, 219–220

Miracles, the, 181

Mirrors, 124

Misfits, the, 230, 246–247

Mitch Ryder and the Detroit Wheels, 66

Modern Lovers, the, 97, 145

Mondo Bizarro (album), 93

Monkees, the, 69–70, 181–182

Monks, the, 65

Mono Men, the, 200

Monterey Pop (film), 181

Montez, Chris, 8, 218

Moody Blues, the, 141

Morrison, Van, 50

Morton, George "Shadow," 18

Mother Love Bone, 233

Mötley Crüe, 101

Motörhead, 85, 190, 200, 228–229, 243

Motors, the, 110

Mott the Hoople, 87, 104–105, 198

Mould, Bob, 219

Mountain, 79, 122

Move, the, 50, 61

Mr. T Experience, the, 243

Sweet, 100, 103–104
Swingin' Medallions, the, 29–30
Swinging Blue Jeans, the, 50

T. Rex, 101, 168, 169, 197
TAD (band), 200
Talking Heads, 114, 115, 117–118, 166, 183, 187, 195, 196, 202, 250
T.A.M.I. Show, The (film), 180–181
Tangerine Puppets, 53
Teen Idles, the, 217
Teengenerate, 242
Teenage Head, 146, 196, 203
Television (band), 60, 110, 113, 114, 166–117, 120, 187, 196, 248
Tequila Baby, 193
Texas Chain Saw Massacre, The (film), 176
Them (band), 50
Them! (film), 178
Thin Lizzy, 119, 169
Thing from Another World, The (film), 177
Third Rail, the, 51
Thought Criminals, the, 136
Thunders, Johnny, 19, 99, 118–119, 193, 198, 245
Tin Huey, 124

Titus Andronicus, 249
Tommy James and the Shondells, 71–72
Too Tough to Die (album), 40, 215
Top Cat, 153–154
Tornados, the, 25
Toxic Reasons, 221
Trashmen, the, 27–28, 123, 158
Tremeloes, the, 50
Treniers, the, 180
Troggs, the, 46–47, 145
T.S.O.L. (band), 202
Tubes, the, 202
Tuff Darts, 122
Turner, Ike and Tina, 181
Turtles, the, 67, 167
Twilight Zone, The (television show), 161
Twisted Sister, 148

U.K. Subs, the, 135
Uncle Floyd Show, The (television show), 159, 189–190
Uncle Monk, 247
Underdog (television show), 155
Undertones, the, 131–132
Upbeat (television show), 154

Vagrants, the, 80
Valens, Ritchie, 9
Vandals, the, 202